Nabokov and his Fiction: New Perspectives

To mark the centenary of Vladimir Nabokov's birth, this volume brings together the work of eleven of the world's foremost Nabokov scholars offering new perspectives on the writer and his fiction. Their essays cover a broad range of topics and approaches, from close readings of major texts, including *Speak, Memory* and *Pale Fire*, to penetrating discussions of the significant relationship between Nabokov's personal beliefs and experiences and his art. Several of the essays attempt to uncover the artistic principles that underlie the author's literary creations, while others seek to place Nabokov's work in a variety of literary and cultural contexts. Among these essays are a first glimpse at a recently published and little-known work, *The Tragedy of Mr. Morn*, as well as a fresh perspective on Nabokov's most famous novel, *Lolita*. The volume as a whole offers valuable insight into the future direction of Nabokov scholarship.

Julian W. Connolly is Professor of Russian Literature at the University of Virginia. He is author of *Ivan Bunin* (1982) and *Nabokov's Early Fiction: Patterns of Self and Other* (1992), and co-editor of *Studies in Russian Literature in Honor of Vsevolod Setchkarev* (1987), and has published numerous essays and reviews in books and journals.

CAMBRIDGE STUDIES IN RUSSIAN LITERATURE

General editor CATRIONA KELLY

Editorial board: ANTHONY CROSS, CARYL EMERSON,
BARBARA HELDT, MALCOLM JONES, DONALD RAYFIELD,
G. S. SMITH, VICTOR TERRAS

Recent titles in this series include

The Last Soviet Avant-Garde: OBERIU – Fact, Fiction, Metafiction
GRAHAM ROBERTS

Literary Journals in Imperial Russia
edited by DEBORAH A. MARTINSEN

Russian Modernism: the Transfiguration of the Everyday
STEPHEN C. HUTCHINGS

Reading Russian Fortunes
Print Culture, Gender and Divination in Russia from 1765
FAITH WIGZELL

English Literature and the Russian Aesthetic Renaissance
RACHEL POLONSKY

Christianity in Bakhtin: God and the Exiled Author
RUTH COATES

The Development of Russian Verse
MICHAEL WACHTEL

A complete list of titles in the series is given at the back of the book

NABOKOV AND HIS FICTION
New Perspectives

EDITED BY
JULIAN W. CONNOLLY

PUBLISHED BY THE PRESS SYNDICATE OF THE UNIVERSITY OF CAMBRIDGE
The Pitt Building, Trumpington Street, Cambridge, United Kingdom

CAMBRIDGE UNIVERSITY PRESS
The Edinburgh Building, Cambridge, CB2 2RU, UK
http://www.cup.cam.ac.uk
40 West 20th Street, New York, NY 10011–4211, USA
http://www.cup.org
10 Stamford Road, Oakleigh, Melbourne 3166, Australia

© Cambridge University Press 1999

This book is in copyright. Subject to statutory exception and to the provisions of relevant collective licensing agreements, no reproduction of any part may take place without the written permission of Cambridge University Press.

First published 1999

Printed in the United Kingdom at the University Press, Cambridge

Typeset in Baskerville 11/12.5pt [CE]

A catalogue record for this book is available from the British Library

Library of Congress Cataloguing in Publication data
Nabokov and his fiction: new perspectives / edited by Julian W. Connolly.
p. cm. – (Cambridge studies in Russian literature)
Includes bibliographical references.
ISBN 0 521 63283 8 (hardback)
1. Nabokov, Vladimir Vladimirovich, 1899–1977 – Criticism and interpretation.
I. Connolly, Julian W. II. Series.
G3476.N3Z776 1999
813′.54 – dc21 98-47176 CIP

ISBN 0 521 63283 8 hardback

Contents

A note on the contributors	page vii
A note on transliteration	x
A note on abbreviations	xi
Acknowledgments	xiv

Introduction: Nabokov at 100   1
Julian W. Connolly

PART I: ARTISTIC STRATEGIES AND THEMES   13

1 Setting his myriad faces in his text: Nabokov's authorial presence revisited   15
Gavriel Shapiro

2 Vladimir Nabokov and the art of autobiography   36
Galya Diment

3 The near-tyranny of the author: *Pale Fire*   54
Maurice Couturier

4 Jewish questions in Nabokov's art and life   73
Maxim D. Shrayer

5 "The dead are good mixers": Nabokov's versions of individualism   92
Leona Toker

6 Nabokov's trinity (On the movement of Nabokov's themes)   109
Gennady Barabtarlo

PART 2: LITERARY AND CULTURAL CONTEXTS   139

7   Nabokov's (re)visions of Dostoevsky   141
    Julian W. Connolly

8   Her monster, his nymphet: Nabokov and Mary Shelley   158
    Ellen Pifer

9   Vladimir Nabokov and Rupert Brooke   177
    D. Barton Johnson

10 Clio laughs last: Nabokov's answer to historicism   197
    Alexander Dolinin

11 Poshlust, culture criticism, Adorno, and Malraux   216
    John Burt Foster, Jr.

Selected bibliography   236
Index   245

A note on the contributors

GENNADY BARABTARLO, Professor of Russian at the University of Missouri, has published two books on Nabokov (*Phantom of Fact* in 1989 and *Aerial View* in 1993), as well as numerous articles, translations, and editions. He has also written on Pushkin, Tiutchev, and Solzhenitsyn.

JULIAN W. CONNOLLY is Professor of Russian Literature at the University of Virginia. He is the author of *Ivan Bunin* (1982) and *Nabokov's Early Fiction: Patterns of Self and Other* (1992), and the editor of *Nabokov's "Invitation to a Beheading": A Course Companion* (1997). He has published numerous articles on nineteenth- and twentieth-century Russian literature.

MAURICE COUTURIER, Senior Professor of English and American Literature at the University of Nice, France, is a specialist on Nabokov and chief editor of the Pléiade edition of Nabokov's novels, as well as a theorist of the modern novel (*Textual Communication*, 1991; *La Figure de l'auteur*, 1993). He is also a translator, of Nabokov and David Lodge in particular.

GALYA DIMENT is an Associate Professor in the Department of Slavic Languages and Literatures at the University of Washington, Seattle. Author of *The Autobiographical Novel of Co-Consciousness: Goncharov, Woolf and Joyce* (1994) and *Pniniad: Vladimir Nabokov and Marc Szeftel* (1997), she has also edited two books and has written extensively on Nabokov.

ALEXANDER DOLININ is Associate Professor of Russian Literature at the University of Wisconsin, Madison, and a Research Fellow at the Pushkin House of the Russian Academy of Sciences in St. Petersburg. He is the author of *History Dressed Up as a Novel* (in Russian), and many works on Nabokov, including *A Great*

Unknown: Vladimir Nabokov as a Russian Writer (forthcoming), as well as notes and introductions to Russian publications of Nabokov's fiction.

JOHN BURT FOSTER, JR. is Professor of English and Cultural Studies at George Mason University and a former president of the International Nabokov Society. He is the author of *Nabokov's Art of Memory and European Modernism*, several articles in the *Garland Companion to Vladimir Nabokov*, and of numerous other publications devoted to nineteenth- and twentieth-century literature and thought.

D. BARTON JOHNSON, Professor Emeritus of Russian at the University of California, Santa Barbara, is the author of *A Transformational Analysis of OT Constructions in Contemporary Standard Russian* and *Worlds in Regression: Some Novels of Vladimir Nabokov*, as well as numerous articles on Nabokov and other Russian modernists. A twice president of the International Vladimir Nabokov Society, he is the founder of the Nabokov Electronic Discussion Forum, NABOKV-L, and the journal *Nabokov Studies*.

ELLEN PIFER is Professor of English and Comparative Literature at the University of Delaware. Her published works include *Nabokov and the Novel*, *Saul Bellow Against the Grain*, *Critical Essays on John Fowles*, and three-dozen articles and chapters on modern and contemporary literature. She has just completed a new book on twentieth-century fiction.

GAVRIEL SHAPIRO, Associate Professor of Russian Literature at Cornell University, is the author of *Delicate Markers: Subtexts in Vladimir Nabokov's "Invitation to a Beheading"* (1998) and numerous articles on Nabokov and other Russian writers. He is also the author of *Nikolai Gogol and the Baroque Cultural Heritage* (1993). He is currently working on a book about Nabokov and visual art.

A Russian-born scholar and poet, MAXIM D. SHRAYER, teaches Russian literature at Boston College. He is the author of *The World of Nabokov's Stories* (1999) as well as three collections of Russian verse, the latest of which is *The New Haven Sonnets* (1998).

LEONA TOKER teaches in the English Department of the Hebrew University of Jerusalem. She is the author of *Nabokov: The Mystery of Literary Structures*, *Eloquent Reticence: Withholding Information in Fictional*

Narrative, and articles on English, American, and Russian literature. She was the editor of *Commitment in Reflection: Essays in Literature and Moral Philosophy* and co-editor of *Rereading Texts / Rethinking Critical Presuppositions: Essays in Honour of H. M. Daleski*.

A note on transliteration

The Library of Congress system of transliteration (without diacritics) has been used throughout the bibliographic references and the main text of the essays, with the following exceptions:

> For personal names in the main text, the letters ю and я are rendered as "yu" and "ya" at the beginning of the name, and the sequence ий and ый is rendered as "y" at the end of the name, for example, "Yakov," "Yury," "Bely".

> The spelling used by Nabokov for names of characters in his works has been retained, for example, "Yasha Chernyshevski" and "Koncheyev".

> We have retained the familiar English spelling of well-known Russian figures, for example, "Tolstoy," "Gogol," and friends of Nabokov, for example, "Yuri Rausch von Traubenberg".

At times, this procedure may have resulted in inconsistencies within individual essays, but, as the editors of *The Cambridge Companion to the Classic Russian Novel* have stated, "this would not mislead anyone who is able to read Russian and would not interest anyone who is not" (*The Cambridge Companion to the Classic Russian Novel*, ed. Malcom V. Jones and Robin Feuer Miller [Cambridge University Press, 1998], xvii).

A note on abbreviations

While there is no standard edition of Vladimir Nabokov's works, the publication of a series of his works in the United States under the Vintage International imprint and in the United Kingdom under the Penguin imprint has made the bulk of his fiction available in readily accessible editions. The following is a list of abbreviations used by several of the contributors to this volume. The abbreviations refer to the Vintage International editions of Nabokov's work as well as to a number of other major English-language works by and about Nabokov. The contributors have used the following format: abbreviation of the title followed by the page number; e.g. (*Def*, 36–37). To assist readers with no access to the Vintage editions, the editor has also included the number of the chapter from which the cited material is taken; e.g. (*Def*, 36–37 [ch. 2]). For reference purposes, the date of first publication of the English-language version of a text is included below. A list of the Penguin editions of Nabokov's work is included in the *Selected bibliography* at the end of this book. All works are by Vladimir Nabokov unless otherwise stated.

Ada	*Ada, or Ardor: A Family Chronicle.* 1969. New York: Vintage International, 1990.
AnL	*The Annotated Lolita.* Ed. with preface, introduction, and notes by Alfred Appel, Jr., 1970. Revised edition: New York: Vintage International, 1991.
BS	*Bend Sinister.* 1947. New York: Vintage International, 1990.
CE	*Conclusive Evidence: A Memoir.* New York: Harper, 1951.
Def	*The Defense.* Trans. Michael Scammell in collaboration with the author. 1964. New York: Vintage International, 1990.
Des	*Despair.* 1966. New York: Vintage International, 1989.

En	*The Enchanter*. Trans. Dmitri Nabokov. 1986. New York: Vintage International, 1991.
EO	*Eugene Onegin. A Novel in Verse by Aleksandr Pushkin*. Translation with commentary by Vladimir Nabokov, 4 vols., Bollingen Series 72. 1964. Revised edition. Princeton University Press, 1975.
Eye	*The Eye*. Trans. Dmitri Nabokov in collaboration with the author. 1965. New York: Vintage International, 1990.
Gift	*The Gift*. Trans. Michael Scammell with the collaboration of the author. 1963. New York: Vintage International, 1991.
Glory	*Glory*. Trans. Dmitri Nabokov in collaboration with the author. 1971. New York: Vintage International, 1991.
IB	*Invitation to a Beheading*. Trans. Dmitri Nabokov in collaboration with the author. 1959. New York: Vintage International, 1989.
KQK	*King, Queen, Knave*. Trans. Dmitri Nabokov in collaboration with the author. 1968. New York: Vintage International, 1989.
LATH	*Look at the Harlequins!* 1974. New York: Vintage International, 1990.
Laugh	*Laughter in the Dark*. 1938. New York: Vintage International, 1989.
LDQ	*Lectures on* Don Quixote. Ed. Fredson Bowers. New York: Harcourt Brace Jovanovich / Bruccoli Clark, 1983.
LL	*Lectures on Literature*. Ed. Fredson Bowers. New York: Harcourt Brace Jovanovich / Bruccoli Clark, 1980.
LRL	*Lectures on Russian Literature*. Ed. Fredson Bowers. New York: Harcourt Brace Jovanovich / Bruccoli Clark, 1981.
Lo	*Lolita*. 1955. New York: Vintage International, 1989.
LoR	*Lolita*. New York: Phaedra, 1967.
LoScreen	*Lolita: A Screenplay*. 1974. New York: Vintage International, 1997.
Mary	*Mary*. Trans. Michael Glenny in collaboration with the author. 1970. New York: Vintage International, 1989.
NWL	*The Nabokov-Wilson Letters, 1940–1971*. Ed., annotated, and with an introductory essay by Simon Karlinsky. New York: Harper Colophon, 1980.

NG	*Nikolai Gogol.* 1944. New York: New Directions, 1961.
PF	*Pale Fire.* 1962. New York: Vintage International, 1989.
Pnin	*Pnin.* 1957. New York: Vintage International, 1989.
PP	*Poems and Problems.* New York. McGraw-Hill, 1970.
RLSK	*The Real Life of Sebastian Knight.* 1941. New York: Vintage International, 1992.
SL	*Selected Letters, 1940–1977.* Ed. Dmitri Nabokov and Matthew J. Bruccoli. New York: Harcourt Brace Jovanovich / Bruccoli Clark Layman, 1989.
SM	*Speak, Memory: An Autobiography Revisted.* 1967. New York: Vintage International, 1989.
SO	*Strong Opinions.* 1973. New York: Vintage International, 1990.
Song	*The Song of Igor's Campaign.* Trans. Vladimir Nabokov. 1960. New York: McGraw-Hill, 1975.
Stories	*The Stories of Vladimir Nabokov.* 1995. New York: Vintage International, 1997.
TT	*Transparent Things.* 1972. New York: Vintage International, 1989.
USSR	*The Man from the USSR and Other Plays.* Introduction and translations by Dmitri Nabokov. New York: Harcourt Brace Jovanovich / Bruccoli Clark, 1984.

Acknowledgments

The difficult task of editing a multi-author volume has been greatly eased through the fine assistance of several individuals. First of all, I would like to thank my fellow contributors for their unflagging spirit of cooperation and collegiality. I would next like to express my gratitude to the editors with whom I worked at Cambridge University Press: Linda Bree, the European Literature editor; and Catriona Kelly, the General Editor for Cambridge Studies in Russian Literature. I owe a special debt of thanks to Rachel Coldicutt for the careful and thorough attention she devoted to the typescript as it was being prepared for publication. Finally, I would like to thank Dmitri Nabokov, who kindly gave his permission for the use of the photograph that appears on the jacket of this volume.

Introduction: Nabokov at 100
Julian W. Connolly

I

In 1966 Vladimir Nabokov responded to an interviewer's comment about his present fame with the remark, "*Lolita* is famous, not I. I am an obscure, doubly obscure, novelist with an unpronounceable name."[1] Since that time, the reputations of both the novel and the man have increased in stature; it would be unlikely that the writer could make the same claim today. A 1998 poll of the editorial board of the Modern Library (a division of Random House) found *Lolita* in fourth place on a list of the greatest English-language novels of the twentieth century; a second Nabokov novel, *Pale Fire*, was placed fifty-third.[2] Numerous contemporary writers, including John Updike, John Barth, Edward Albee, Edmund White, Donald Harington, David Slavitt, W. G. Sebald, Sasha Sokolov, Yury Trifonov, Vasily Aksenov, and Andrei Bitov have paid homage to Nabokov directly or indirectly in their work. The publication of major editions of Nabokov's work is underway in Germany and France, and Nabokov's English-language novels have been included in the "Library of America" series in the United States. In addition, Nabokov's artistic legacy has become the subject of an enormous and vital critical industry. Brian Boyd's monumental two-volume critical biography (1990–91) reflects a degree of popular interest that has few parallels for Russian-born writers. Articles and monographs on his art are appearing across the globe in a multitude of languages, from Croatian to Japanese, and an electronic discussion group, NABOKV-L, recently listed nearly 500 subscribers from over thirty countries.

The distinctiveness of Nabokov's artistic reputation can be gauged by comparing it with the critical attention paid to some other writers who, like Nabokov, were born in Russia during the 1890s. Though several of these writers, from the slightly older Boris Pasternak (1890–1960), Osip Mandelshtam (1891–1938), Mikhail Bulgakov (1891–1940), Marina Tsvetaeva (1892–1941), and Vladimir Mayakovsky (1893–1930), to the coeval Yury Olesha (1899–1960), have been the subject of some fine critical treatments, none of them are favored with the kind of ever-broadening attention that Vladimir Nabokov now enjoys. This is a remarkable achievement for an individual who was born into a world of aristocratic privilege in St. Petersburg, forced into emigration by the Bolshevik Revolution, and faced with near destitution for many years during the second quarter of the century.

The crucial turning point in Nabokov's career was his decision to shift from writing in Russian to writing in English in the late 1930s.[3] This shift, which Nabokov claimed was necessitated by the diminishing audience of potential readers in the Russian emigration (see *SO*, 36–37), had the effect of unleashing the writer's already established penchant for linguistic play and stylistic innovation. As Jane Grayson put it, "The brilliance of Nabokov's later English style owes not a little to his viewpoint as a foreigner. He sees the English language through different eyes. He sees patterns of sound and potential meaning in words which the native speaker, his perception dulled through familiarity, would simply pass over."[4] The ultimate consequence of this shift, of course, was the creation of the novel that would bring Nabokov both lasting fame and financial security, *Lolita*.

The publication of *Lolita* (in Paris in 1955, and in the United States in 1958), followed by the release of *Pale Fire* in 1962, triggered the beginning of a sustained critical interest in Nabokov's work that has led to ever more insightful and probing explorations of the unique world created in his fiction. With few exceptions, the early émigré reviews of his work did not probe very deeply into its structure and substance, and the émigré critics often concerned themselves over such questions as the depth of Nabokov's "Russianness."[5] Vladimir Weidle and Vladislav Khodasevich, however, initiated a productive line of inquiry into Nabokov's work when they pointed to the writer's recurring concern with art and the making of art: "The life of the artist and the life of a device in the consciousness of the artist – this is Sirin's theme, revealing itself to some degree or other in almost every one of his writings"[6] Such an approach, which focuses on the aesthetic and metaliterary dimensions of Nabokov's work, also became the dominant critical perspective among the early English-language critics who went beyond brief reviews and began a serious examination of the fiction in the mid-1960s. The title of the first monograph in English devoted to Nabokov – Page Stegner's *Escape into Aesthetics: The Art of Vladimir Nabokov* (1966) – signals the prevailing critical orientation of the day. Eventually, however, a reaction to this view of Nabokov as cool aesthete began to emerge, and several astute critics, led by Robert Alter, began to focus on the writer's engagement with, and not retreat from, life itself.[7] This investigation of the "ethical" Nabokov was soon followed by a new approach – the discovery that the intricate play of patterns in Nabokov's fiction pointed beyond the text to an otherworldly dimension: thus was born the "metaphysical" Nabokov.[8]

The evolving, protean shape that Nabokov's work has assumed in the eyes of readers during the last thirty years testifies to its unusual richness and depth, and to its resistance to facile definition. Indeed, when one considers Nabokov's profile in relation to the modernist tradition in which he developed, one comes to appreciate how distinctive that profile was. This aura of distinction begins with his birth. Unlike most of his literary peers, Nabokov was born into what might be called the "service aristocracy" in Russia: his grandfather had been minister of justice under two tsars, and his father was a noted jurist, a member of the first Russian Duma. We can contrast this family background with that of most of the other figures of Nabokov's generation who would rise to prominence in Russian literature. Pasternak's father was an artist and the director of an art school; Tsvetaeva's and Bulgakov's fathers were professors (as was Alexander Blok's father). Other writers, including Esenin, Mayakovsky, and Olesha came from even more modest origins. Brought up in a cosmopolitan household, Nabokov learned to read in English before he could do so in Russian, and he soon added French to his repertoire;[9] we shall see the enduring impact of this multi-nationalism on his self-image later. Yet like the others mentioned above, Nabokov also belonged to a generation that, as Robert Wohl has put it, was the first to grow up "*within* modernism in a way that no previous generation could have."[10] In a letter to Edmund Wilson he proudly asserted his ties to that era; referring to Russian literature during the period from 1905–1917, he declared: "Blok, Bely, Bunin and others wrote their best stuff in those days. And never was poetry so popular –

not even in Pushkin's days. I am a product of that period. I was bred in that atmosphere."[11]

Raised at a time when Symbolism reigned supreme, to be followed in quick succession by Acmeism and Futurism, Nabokov, like many of his fellow modernists, was acutely interested in the workings of human consciousness, and in particular, in the way the creative mind attends to and places its unique stamp upon experience and perception. In his interviews and lectures he repeatedly expressed his admiration for Joyce's *Ulysses* and Proust's *A la recherche du temps perdu*, especially their treatment of perception, time, and memory. These two works, along with Bely's *Petersburg* and Kafka's *Metamorphosis*, made up Nabokov's own list of the best works of the twentieth century (see *SO*, 57).

Yet perhaps because of his profound involvement in a very different type of intellectual pursuit – lepidoptery (and specifically, the classification of butterflies and moths) – Nabokov did not share of the anti-scientific bias of some of his peers, and he laid special emphasis on a particular approach to the representation of experience. Highly impatient with vague, impressionistic evocations of consciousness,[12] he stressed above all an attention to *detail*, to the smallest, most minute attributes of a given phenomenon. "In high art and pure science detail is everything," he declared; "Only myopia condones the blurry generalizations of ignorance" (*SO*, 168; see also *SO*, 7). This, of course, was a principle he followed in his teaching as well: "In my classes, readers had to discuss specific details, not general ideas" (*SO*, 128); a former student recalls him saying "Caress the details ... the divine details."[13] Thus, while he was deeply interested in the way the individual consciousness perceives and transforms experience, he remained devoted to the belief that a central concern of this consciousness should include concrete, sensual experience itself – textures, smells, fine gradations of color.

Like Virginia Woolf, Nabokov sharply criticized a writer's readiness to settle for vague platitudes, lifeless descriptions, or bland clichés.[14] He constantly strove to find fresh ways of describing the world and its experiences, and he deployed a dazzling array of devices to achieve this effect. These include the personification of inanimate objects, unexpected combinations of concrete detail and abstract concepts, the depiction of phenomena from striking angles of perception, surprising metaphors, and even phrases in which words appear at first glance to be linked by sound more than sense (though closer scrutiny always discloses an inner-bond). Despite his appreciation for unusual perspectives and bold detail, however, he was representative of what might be called the anti-avant-garde wing of European modernism, and rejected much of the work of the avant-garde. His comments on Russian art are indicative: "I prefer the experimental decade that coincided with my boyhood – Somov, Benois... Vrubel, Dobuzhinski, etc. Malevich and Kandinsky mean nothing to me and I have always found Chagall's stuff intolerably primitive and grotesque" (*SO*, 170). Nabokov welcomed art that presented a new way of seeing life, but he had little interest in art that veered off into abstraction or deformed the world beyond any hope of recognition or reconstitution. As Ellen Pifer has noted, the function of art and artifice in Nabokov's own work was not to "*oppose*" life but rather "to *renew* the reader's perception of reality – by estranging that perception from habitual formulations."[15]

Nabokov's aversion to the avant-garde also showed up in his views on modern poetry. For example, among the Russian poets, he preferred Ivan Bunin, Vladislav Khodasevich, and the early Blok to the Blok of "The Twelve" and the work of the Futurists; his tastes here were not unusual within the Russian émigré community. Attending Cambridge during the very years that Pound and Eliot were forging new paths in Anglo-American poetry, Nabokov recalls his fondness for the "Georgians," and specifically Rupert Brooke (see *SM*, 266, 268 [Ch. 13]). His lack of interest in Eliot or Pound (and his outright hostility toward them in later years)[16] is noteworthy, but it may have been inspired by a number of factors. For one thing, at the very heart of Nabokov's view of life was an undiluted appreciation for the notion of the individual and the particular. He could never have written, as Eliot once did in connection with his editorial work on *The Criterion*: "I am not an individual but an instrument."[17] More important in terms of art, Nabokov viewed with disfavor any attempt to use what Eliot termed "the mythical method" as an organizing principle in writing. Eliot introduced the term in an article on Joyce's *Ulysses*,[18] and it suggests the type of approach Nabokov had in mind when he declared that "*Ulysses*... is a divine work of art and will live on despite the academic nonentities who turn it into a collection of symbols or Greek myths" (*SO*, 55).[19]

He was also profoundly suspicious of the tendency of some modernist figures to espouse a socio-political agenda in their writings: "I never could admit that a writer's job was to improve the morals of his country, and point out lofty ideas from the tremendous height of a soapbox, and administer first aid by dashing off second-rate books."[20] Having witnessed first-hand the havoc wreaked on Russia by the Communists, and the rising ugliness of Fascism in Hitler's Germany, he felt a special antipathy toward those who endorsed either Fascism or Communism, an activity that a fair number of European modernists engaged in, including Pound, Céline, Wyndham Lewis, Eliot, and Malraux (though not Forster, noted for his liberal humanism, or Woolf, known for her anti-militarism). What is more, Nabokov was particularly aware of the degree to which demands for political tendentiousness had crippled Russian literature in the Soviet Union from the late 1920s on, and he deplored the heavy-handed imposition of political ideology on literary creation: "I have despised ideological coercion instinctively all my life" (*SO*, 64).[21] Again and again, he would return to the simple formula: "there can be no question that what makes a work of fiction safe from larvae and rust is not its social importance but its art, only its art" (*SO*, 33). In brief, he was less interested in reforming the present world than in refining the worlds created in his art.[22]

Nabokov's aversion to the pursuit of political goals in art had even deeper roots. Throughout his life, he tried to discourage attempts to identify him with any larger, communal group, whether it be a social class, a generational category (including such entities as Wohl's "generation of 1914" discussed above), or even nationality. So, in addition to declaring "I have never belonged to any club or group. No creed or school has had any influence on me whatsoever" (*SO*, 3), he could answer an interviewer's question about national identity by saying: "I am an American writer, born in Russia and educated in England where I studied French literature, before spending fifteen years in Germany" (*SO*, 26).[23] Again, his stress is on individual talent, not national origin: "I have always maintained ... that the nationality of a worthwhile writer is of secondary importance ... The writer's art is his real passport" (*SO*, 63).

Such a stance not only accorded well with Nabokov's insistence on appreciating the individual over the general, it also had a second, perhaps more pervasive significance. Nabokov once stated that he felt an affinity for the "type of artist who is always in exile even though he may never have left the ancestral hall or the paternal parish" (*SO*, 117). Having been forced from his homeland, and having witnessed the untimely loss of cherished friends and family members over the years, Nabokov placed great store in self-reliance, and in the maintenance of a singular, ever-renewing, personal sense of self. Having created this specific self-image, he might have felt less vulnerable to the inevitable depredations of time and contingency. In Jessica Feldman's formulation, exile offered Nabokov a clear choice: "purposeful self-creation or defeat by external events."[24] At times, Nabokov's seeming aloofness struck outside observers as snobbery, but closer inspection suggests that his detachment was more of a protective device than an expression of disdain for the general public.

Nabokov's response to the question of national identity has additional implications. It serves as a reminder that those who would seek to delineate Nabokov's position within literary modernism[25] need to be aware of a number of contexts – Russian, Anglo-American, French, and yes, even German. Nabokov's art presents an intriguing blend of literary perspectives and echoes. Multilingual and multilayered, his fiction draws upon an immense variety of sources from the literature of the past and from literature of his day (including Russian, French, German, British, and American literature, both high-brow and mass-market). Nabokov's readers and scholars alike face significant challenges in their quest to understand the full range of Nabokov's creative imagination.

II

The present collection, prepared in anticipation of the centenary of Nabokov's birth, attempts to make its own contribution to this endeavor. The eleven essayists whose work is represented here were asked to move beyond the existing body of work on Nabokov and to offer a fresh appraisal of his artistic legacy. The resulting work falls broadly into two categories. Several of the essays delve into Nabokov's central artistic strategies and comment on the reflection of his personal experience in his art, while others explore the relationship of Nabokov's work to the literary and cultural traditions in which it was generated.

One of Nabokov's more famous declarations has to do with his sense of control over the created world: "every character follows the course I imagine for him. I am the perfect dictator in that private world insofar as I alone am responsible for its stability and truth"

(*SO*, 69). A number of the essays in this volume investigate the specific ways in which the author attempts to manifest such control. Gavriel Shapiro's essay opens this line of inquiry by offering a close examination of Nabokov's remarkable penchant for elaborate forms of auto-allusion or self-reference. After acknowledging Nabokov's familiar device of encoding his name anagramatically in his work, Shapiro shows that the writer utilized a wide-range of techniques not only to refer to himself, but also to pay coded homage to those he admired and loved. Turning to Nabokov's autobiographical writings, Galya Diment investigates the subtle interplay of remembrance and invention in the telling of one's story. In contrast to Proust, who valorized the workings of involuntary memory, Nabokov highlighted the considerable role of the creative imagination in the recovery of details from the past. Diment's essay underscores the degree to which the writer's stress on the role of imagination in memory may point to an under-appreciated element of the autobiographical genre itself. Maurice Couturier interrogates Nabokov's work from a different angle. Squarely addressing the issue of authorial control in the novel *Pale Fire*, Couturier finds that there is a reservoir of implication that eludes the author's attempt at control. In an intriguing series of analyses he argues that an interpretive strategy which investigates the text in terms of "desire" permits access to this reservoir and discloses meaning that the author may wish to suppress or evade.

Other contributors to this volume are interested in refining our understanding of basic ethical principles conveyed in Nabokov's work. Maxim Shrayer tackles the difficult question of what specific role Nabokov's life-long acquaintance with Russian Jews had on his work, and he indicates that the effects were both palpable and far-reaching. Leona Toker looks at the seminal importance of individualism in Nabokov's work, but she approaches it from a new tack. She probes the consequences of an individual's contact with the crowd, and she examines the promises and pitfalls of one's involvement with another, even if the other is a lover. Finally, in an essay with extensive implications, Gennady Barabtarlo examines the very foundation of Nabokov's art, and he uncovers in an early Nabokov piece, *The Tragedy of Mr. Morn*, the core elements of an artistic philosophy that Barabtarlo believes runs throughout the fiction. His analysis of two interlinked trinities – space, time, matter; imagination, memory, love – ends with a call for a reconsideration of Nabokov's entire oeuvre.

The essays devoted to Nabokov's relationship to the literary and cultural traditions in which he wrote provide just a small indication of the breadth of his interests as a writer and critic. Although the early émigré critics argued that Sirin's work lay outside the Russian tradition, subsequent research by such figures as Simon Karlinsky, G. M. Hyde, Vladimir Alexandrov, and others have tried to show how Nabokov's work emerges from the heritage of Anton Chekhov, Leo Tolstoy, Ivan Bunin, and the writers of the Russian Silver Age.[26] Here, I too deal with Nabokov's relationship to the Russian literary tradition, this time attempting to sort out the contentious issue of Nabokov's attitude toward Fedor Dostoevsky's work and reputation. Also in this volume are two articles that explore connections between Nabokov's work and English literature. Taking issue with the notion that Nabokov felt an entrenched dislike for literature by women, Ellen Pifer uncovers intriguing links between *Lolita* and Mary Shelley's *Frankenstein*. D. Barton Johnson considers Nabokov's years at Cambridge, and he examines the effect that Nabokov's interest in Rupert Brooke may have had on the subsequent evolution of his work. Passing beyond the borders of fiction proper, John Burt Foster, Jr., investigates the ways in which Nabokov's modest position as a critic of culture resonates and contrasts with that of other contemporary European thinkers such as Adorno and Malraux. Alexander Dolinin also contemplates Nabokov's European experience, and he demonstrates how staunchly opposed the individualist writer was to the determinist historical theories of many of his contemporaries. Although Nabokov expressed scorn for didactic literature, his own writings reveal him to be a pointed critic of contemporary culture and thought.

These essays, along with the intense flurry of international activities honoring Nabokov during this centennial year, testify to the writer's vibrant legacy. In the memorable opening lines of *Speak, Memory* Nabokov wrote that "common sense tells us that our existence is but a brief crack of light between two eternities of darkness" (*SM*, 19). He went on to assert the he "rebel[s] against this state of affairs" (20). While his physical presence may be gone, his life's work continues to cast bright beams throughout the reading world. This work, and the extraordinary individual who created it, will continue to attract the attention of devoted readers for generations to come.

NOTES

1 Vladimir Nabokov, *Strong Opinions* (1973; New York: Vintage International, 1990), 107. (Hereafter *SO*.)
2 In the original poll, *Lolita* tied for first place with *Ulysses, The Great Gatsby, A Portrait of the Artist as a Young Man,* and *Brave New World.* When the members of the editorial board were asked to rank the five novels, *Lolita* finished in fourth place.
3 After translating his novel *Otchaianie* into *Despair* in 1935 and *Kamera obscura* into *Laughter in the Dark* in 1937, Nabokov felt confident enough to write *The Real Life of Sebastian Knight* in English from December 1938 through January 1939.
4 Jane Grayson, *Nabokov Translated: A Comparison of Nabokov's Russian and English Prose* (Oxford University Press, 1977), 216.
5 For a discussion of the émigré response to Sirin's work, see Ludmila A. Foster, "Nabokov in Russian Emigré Criticism" in *A Book of Things about Vladimir Nabokov,* ed. Carl R. Proffer (Ann Arbor: Ardis, 1974), 42–54. A brief survey of émigré criticism that complements Foster's study is Marina T. Naumann's article, "Nabokov as Viewed by Fellow Emigrés," *Russian Language Journal* 28, no. 99 (1974): 18–26. Ironically, a similar debate about Nabokov's "Russianness" broke out in the late 1980s in the Soviet Union when the conditions of *glasnost'* made it possible for Nabokov's work to be published there. See Aleksei Zverev, "Literary Return to Russia" in *The Garland Companion to Vladimir Nabokov,* ed. Vladimir E. Alexandrov (New York and London: Garland, 1995), 291–305.
6 Vladislav Khodasevich, "On Sirin," trans. Michael H. Walker, ed. Simon Karlinsky and Robert P. Hughes, *TriQuarterly* 17 (1970): 96–101; reprinted in *Nabokov: Criticism, Reminiscences, Translations and Tributes,* ed. Alfred Appel, Jr., and Charles Newman (Evanston: Northwestern University Press, 1971); also reprinted in *Nabokov: The Critical Heritage,* ed. Norman Page (London: Routledge and Kegan Paul, 1982). Just the year before, in a review of Nabokov's work, Weidle had voiced a similar view: "The theme of Sirin's art is art itself – this is the first thing one must say about him;" see "Vladimir Weidle on Sirin," in *The Complection of Russian Literature,* compiled by Andrew Field (New York: Atheneum, 1971), 239.
7 Alter's reading of the novel *Invitation to a Beheading* for a special issue of the journal *TriQuarterly* disclosed Nabokov's crucial point: "that it is life rather than art alone that is inexhaustible, and that art's ability to renew itself, to be infinitely various and captivating, finally depends on its necessary inadequacy in the face of the inexhaustible enigma of conscious life." See Robert Alter, "*Invitation to a Beheading*: Nabokov and the Art of Politics," *TriQuarterly* 17 (1970): 57; reprinted in *Nabokov: Criticism, Reminiscences, Translations and Tributes,* ed. Appel, Jr., and Newman, 57; and in *Nabokov's* Invitation to a Beheading*: A Critical*

Companion," ed. Julian W. Connolly (Evanston: Northwestern University Press, 1997), 63. Nabokov himself may have welcomed the attention to the ethical implications of his work. In materials prepared for an interview in 1971, he asserted: "I believe that one day a reappraiser will come and declare that, far from having been a frivolous firebird, I was a rigid moralist kicking sin, cuffing stupidity, ridiculing the vulgar and cruel – and assigning sovereign power to tenderness, talent, and pride" (*SO*, 193).

8 See, *inter alia*, Jonathan Borden Sisson, "Cosmic Synchronization and Other Worlds in the Work of Vladimir Nabokov" (Ph.D. diss., University of Minnesota, 1979); Sergej Davydov, *"Teksty-Matreshki" Vladimira Nabokova* (Munich: Otto Sagner, 1982); D. Barton Johnson, *Worlds in Regression: Some Novels of Vladimir Nabokov* (Ann Arbor: Ardis, 1985); Brian Boyd, *Nabokov's Ada: The Place of Consciousness* (Ann Arbor: Ardis, 1985), and Vladimir E. Alexandrov, *Nabokov's Otherworld* (Princeton University Press, 1991).

9 See Nabokov, *Speak, Memory* (1967; New York: Vintage International, 1989) [ch. 4], 79 (hereafter *SM*), and *SO*, 5.

10 Robert Wohl, "The Generation of 1914 and Modernism," in *Modernism: Challenges and Perspectives*, ed. Monique Chefdor, Ricardo Quinones, and Albert Wachtel (Urbana and Chicago: University of Illinois Press, 1986), 73.

11 *The Nabokov-Wilson Letters: Correspondence between Vladimir Nabokov and Edmund Wilson 1940–71*, ed. Simon Karlinsky (New York: Harper Colophon Books, 1980), 220. (Hereafter *NWL*.)

12 He even expressed reservations about Joyce's use of the stream of consciousness technique by reminding his students the device does not reflect the fact that "we do not think continuously in words – we also think in images." Vladimir Nabokov, *Lectures on Literature*, ed. Fredson Bowers (New York: Harcourt Brace Jovanovich / Bruccoli Clark, 1980), 363. (Hereafter *LL*.)

13 Ross Wetzsteon, "Nabokov as teacher," *TriQuarterly* 17 (1970): 245; reprinted in *Nabokov: Criticism, Reminiscences, Translations and Tributes*, ed. Appel, Jr., and Newman, 245.

14 Cf. Woolf's complaint about the literary conventions utilized by the Edwardians – H. G. Wells, Arnold Bennett, and John Galsworthy – in, for example, her essay "Mr. Bennett and Mrs. Brown" (1924) in Virginia Woolf, *Collected Essays*, vol. 1 (London: The Hogarth Press, 1966), 319–37.

15 Ellen Pifer, *Nabokov and the Novel* (Cambridge, MA: Harvard University Press, 1980), 25 (emphasis added).

16 He ultimately called each writer a "fake" and a "fraud." On Eliot, see *NWL*, 237; on Pound, see *SO*, 102 and 136.

17 T. S. Eliot to Wyndham Lewis, January 31, 1925, in *The Letters of Wyndham Lewis*, ed. W. K. Rose (London: Methuen, 1963), 151.

18 See Eliot's essay "*Ulysses*, order, and myth," *The Dial* 75 (1923): 483.
19 For a discussion of Nabokov's response to Eliot's approach in *Pale Fire*, see John Burt Foster, Jr., *Nabokov's Art of Memory and European Modernism* (Princeton University Press, 1993), 224–31.
20 Vladimir Nabokov, "The Art of Literature and Commonsense" (*LL*, 376).
21 For additional detail, see his remarks in "Russian Writers, Censors, and Readers" in his *Lectures on Russian Literature*, ed. Fredson Bowers (New York: Harcourt Brace Jovanovich / Bruccoli Clark, 1981). (Hereafter *LRL*.)
22 His criticism of the concept of the "modern world" was characteristic: "What I feel to be the modern world is the world the artist creates, his own mirage, which then becomes a new *mir* ('world' in Russian) by the very act of his shedding, as it were, the age he lives in" (*SO*, 112). On the other hand, he was a staunch opponent of bigotry and cruelty in all forms, and his fiction was not oblivious to political developments occurring around him. He termed his novels *Invitation to a Beheading* and *Bend Sinister* "final indictments of Russian and German totalitarianism" (*SO*, 156).
23 Putting it another way, he wrote: "I see myself as an American writer raised in Russia, educated in England, imbued with the culture of Western Europe; I am aware of the blend, but even the most lucid plum pudding cannot sort out its own ingredients" (*SO*, 192).
24 Jessica R. Feldman, *Gender on the Divide: The Dandy in Modernist Literature* (Ithaca: Cornell University Press, 1993), 225.
25 Some critics have argued that Nabokov, at least in his late novels (*Pale Fire*, *Ada*), should be seen as a postmodernist rather than as a modernist writer; see, e.g., Brian McHale, *Postmodernist Fiction* (London and New York: Routledge, 1993), 18–19. Herbert Grabes offers an engaging presentation of arguments for viewing Nabokov both as a modernist and as a postmodernist writer in his essay, "A Prize for the (Post-)Modernist Nabokov," published in *Cycnos* 12.2 (1995): 117–24; this issue of the journal bears the title *Nabokov at the Crossroads of Modernism and Postmodernism*.
26 See, *inter alia*, Simon Karlinsky, "Nabokov and Chekhov: The Lesser Russian Tradition" in *Nabokov: Criticism, Reminiscences, Translations and Tributes*, ed. Appel, Jr., and Newman, 7–16; G. M. Hyde, *Vladimir Nabokov: America's Russian Novelist* (London: Marion Boyars, 1977), and Vladimir E. Alexandrov, *Nabokov's Otherworld* (Princeton University Press, 1991).

PART I

Artistic strategies and themes

CHAPTER 1

Setting his myriad faces in his text: Nabokov's authorial presence revisited

Gavriel Shapiro

"Setting his myriad faces in his text" is a paraphrase of Vladimir Nabokov's paraphrase of a passage from James Joyce's *Ulysses* which Nabokov discusses in his Cornell lectures. In his examination of *Ulysses*, Nabokov demonstrates his fascination with authorial presence, a device known from time immemorial and customarily employed in various creative media, such as literature, fine arts, and cinema.[1] In particular, Nabokov draws his students' attention to Joyce's "Man in the Brown Macintosh," whose identity Nabokov interprets as follows:

> Do we know who he is? I think we do. The clue comes in chapter 4 of part two, the scene at the library. Stephen is discussing Shakespeare and affirms that Shakespeare himself is present in his, Shakespeare's, works. Shakespeare, he says, tensely: "He has hidden his own name, a fair name, William, in the plays, a super here, a clown there, as a painter of old Italy set his face in a dark corner of his canvas . . ." and this is exactly what Joyce has done – *setting his face in a dark corner of this canvas* [emphasis added]. The Man in the Brown Macintosh who passes through the dream of the book is no other than the author himself. (*LL*, 319–20)[2]

As this passage suggests, Nabokov was fascinated with manifestations of authorial presence in the works of his predecessors and contemporaries, such as Shakespeare and Joyce. At the same time, Nabokov tended to encode his own presence as author in his texts, a habit which has long been noted by Nabokov scholars.[3] In this article, I revisit the issue of Nabokov's self-representation in his work and focus on his more intricate and heretofore unnoticed modes of self-encodement. In addition, I discuss the reasons for Nabokov's strong propensity toward this device.

THE SURNAME

Although Nabokov believed that his family name was derived from a legendary Nabok (see *SM*, 52 [ch. 3]), he was also aware that it lent itself to another interpretation more suited to Russian language etymology: *na bok* ("on[to] the side").[4] Scholars have also noticed that Nabokov often encoded his authorial presence in his works through these "asides."[5]

Concomitant with the use of these rather obvious "asides" is the writer's far more surreptitious self-encodement via references to string instruments, such as the violin and viola, which a musician holds *na boku* ("sideways"). We may recall that Nabokov characterizes *Invitation to a Beheading* as "a violin in a void."[6] In *Lolita*, he includes among the class list of Lolita's peers the name of Viola Miranda – an anagram of Vladimir N.[7] *Mirando* in Italian means "wonderful." Thus, "viola miranda" can be seen, first and foremost, as a sign of Nabokov's high artistic self-esteem. This interpretation is supported in the foreword to the novel, when John Ray, Jr. (of whose "impersonation" of himself Nabokov speaks in the opening of the postscript) calls the reader's attention to the magic of Humbert Humbert's "singing violin" (*AnL*, 5 ["Foreword"] and 311, 324).[8]

FATIDIC DATES

Throughout his life, Nabokov attributed great significance to fatidic associations. The writer admits: "I am the subject of embarrassing qualms of superstition: a number, a dream, a coincidence can affect me obsessively" (*SO*, 177). Nabokov often encodes his authorial presence by means of fatidic dates: commonly his birth day (April 23) or birth year (1899).[9] In such cases, however, he at times introduces them indirectly, through works of literature or art, or historic events contemporaneous with these dates. We come across a rather intricate example of fatidic self-encodement through works of literature in *The Gift*. There, the name of Shahmatov (in Nabokov's transliteration; the Library of Congress system transliterates the surname as Shakhmatov), a fleeting character in the novel, calls to mind Aleksei Shákhmatov, an eminent linguist, known in particular for his edition of the *Primary Chronicle*. This chronicle is contained in a number of codices, of which the Hypatian codex is among the most ancient and best known. The Hypatian codex is mentioned in

The Gift, in connection with Nikolai Chernyshevsky, who compiled *A Tentative Lexicon* for this literary monument.[10] The allusion to the *Primary Chronicle* as well as the mention of the Hypatian codex are significant: the latter is the only existing written source which dates the beginning of Igor's campaign to April 23, 1185. (Nabokov was well aware of this: in the foreword to his translation of *The Song of Igor's Campaign*, he points out that the campaign started on that date.)[11] In this way, Nabokov subtly alludes to his authorial presence by linking his birthday (April 23) to Russia's greatest epic, a work that signifies the dawn of Russian literature.

In addition, with the names of Sha(k)hmatov and his fellow writer Shirin, Nabokov alludes to Pushkin's juvenile epigram which begins: "Ugriumykh troika est' pevtsov / Shirinskii, Shakhovskoi, Shishkov" ("There is a gloomy triumvirate of bards / Shirinsky, Shakhovskoi, Shishkov").[12] The subjects of young Pushkin's ridicule here were clearly his older contemporaries: the literati Sergei Shirinsky-Shikhmatov, Alexander Shakhovskoi, and Alexander Shishkov.[13] Although written in 1815, the epigram was not published until 1899. Thus, Nabokov intricately encodes his presence through his birth year (1899) and at the same time once again fatidically ties himself to Pushkin.[14]

By means of two dates – one (April 23) associating him with *The Song of Igor's Campaign* through his birthday, and the other (1899) through his birth precisely one century apart from Pushkin's (two of the highest pinnacles of Russian literature) – Nabokov apparently viewed himself fatidically destined to become a great Russian writer. Many years later, he evidently saw himself as having been chosen by Providence to translate both *The Song of Igor's Campaign* and *Eugene Onegin* (Pushkin's *magnum opus*) into English; all the more, since he was also acutely aware that he shared his birthday with Shakespeare (see *SM*, 13–14 ["Foreword"]). For example, in Nabokov's untitled poem, which begins: "Here is what we call the moon" ("Vot eto my zovem lunoi," 1942), he mentions Shakespeare and Pushkin side by side.[15] In this way, Nabokov not only claims his literary ancestry, but also encodes his presence through his birth date: April 23 (identical with Shakespeare's), and 1899 (exactly a century after Pushkin's).

Another such birth-year related manifestation of the authorial presence can be found in *The Enchanter*. In this work, Nabokov makes reference to his birth year through Maria, the only character named in the novella – an important marker indeed.[16] Maria, a maidservant, who is described as "shooing the chicks in",[17] is reminiscent of Marina, a servant in Anton Chekhov's *Uncle Vanya*, who also "walks near the house and calls the chickens."[18] When asked which fowl she is after, Marina responds: "The speckled hen has walked off with her chicks ... The crows might steal them" (*ibid.*), which, in the context of Nabokov's novella, sends out a metaphorical warning about the protagonist. The play, we may recall, premiered at the Moscow Art Theater in 1899.

Nabokov's authorial presence, this time through a work of art, is evident in *The Gift*, in the reference to Pan (*Gift*, 335 [ch. 5]). The mention of the Greek god of shepherds is an example of complex authorial presence which I shall discuss at the end of this article. Suffice it to say at this point that Pan paronomastically suggests Nabokov's pen name, Sirin, by way of a syrinx, or Pan-pipe. More important for our purposes here, however, is that Nabokov's mention of Pan apparently alludes to Mikhail Vrubel's 1899 painting of the same name. Incidentally, Vrubel is implied earlier in the novel when Fyodor Godunov-Cherdyntsev, the author's *alter*-ish, if not *alter*, ego recalls Yasha Chernyshevski's "rather pathetic reference to 'Vrublyov's frescoes' – an amusing cross between the two painters (Rublyov and Vrubel)" (*Gift*, 39 [ch. 1]). It is also noteworthy that Nabokov lists Vrubel among his most favorite artists of "the experimental decade that coincided with my boyhood" (*SO*, 170).

Another example of labyrinthine birth-year related self-encodement through a work of art appears in *Invitation to a Beheading*, which Nabokov composed while working on *The Gift*. Here we come across the description of a photohoroscope which M'sieur Pierre concocted for Emmie "by means of retouching and other photographic tricks" (*IB*, 170 [ch. 16]). In particular, it shows the 12-year-old Emmie "already in her bridal veil, the groom at her side was tall and slender, but had the round little face of M'sieur Pierre" (*ibid.*). This description evokes, albeit by way of parody, the self-portrait of Gertrude Käsebier: the turn-of-the-century American pioneer of photography and originator of photomontage. In this self-portrait, very much like in the photohoroscope, Käsebier attached her photographed face and hands to her ink-drawn, dress-clad figure.[19] Through this photohoroscope description, aside from poking fun at photomontage, Nabokov encodes his authorial presence, since Käsebier's self-portrait dates, in all likelihood, from 1899. This assumption is supported by reference to the artist, thinly disguised, in *The Gift:* Käsebier is the surname of one of the directors of the Berlin law firm Traum, Baum and Käsebier (*Gift*, 189-90 [ch. 3]). Many years later, Nabokov also describes Käsebier's "photographic masterpiece 'Mother and Child' (1897)."[20] Although Nabokov refers to the 1897 photograph, it is quite possible that he alludes, by association, to Käsebier's eponymous and better known work of 1899 (The Metropolitan Museum of Art, New York City).

Nabokov's authorial presence through a historical event that took place in his birth year can be found in "The Return of Chorb." In this earlier story, Nabokov points out that Keller, the protagonist's father-in-law, "closely resembl[ed] Oom Paul Kruger".[21] This mention undoubtedly refers to Paul Kruger (1825-1904), the South African statesman and President of Transvaal whose ultimatum provoked the outbreak of the Anglo-Boer War in 1899. It is noteworthy that this surname also appears in *The Gift*, in a letter in which Fyodor's mother advises him, in preparation for writing his father's biography: "be sure to get into touch with Vasiliy Germanovich Krüger, search him out if he's still in Berlin, they once traveled together" (*Gift*, 97 [ch. 2]).

An important period in Nabokov's life was the time of his study at the Tenishev School; doubly so because the school was founded in 1899, the year of his birth.[22] Therefore, Nabokov occasionally encodes his authorial presence through the names of personalities who are connected to the school in one way or another. One such example apppears in *The Gift*. There, we come across a character named Strannolyubski: Chernyshevsky's fictitious biographer whom Nabokov apparently endows with his own opinions and who, therefore, can be viewed as a distinctive manifestation of Nabokov's authorial presence. His actual namesake was Alexander Nikolaevich Strannoliubsky: a notable pedagogue and mathematics teacher whose most outstanding student was the renowned mathematician Sof'ia Kovalevsky. Strannoliubsky was a member of the Tenishev School's Board of Trustees.[23]

In addition to his personal fatidic dates, Nabokov at times encodes his presence through important familial dates, such as the birth years of his dear ones. An example of this kind of fatidic date use can be found in *Invitation to a Beheading*. In the novel's episode of the supper held before the scheduled execution, there is mention of "a white rose that distinctly adorned his [Cincinnatus's] place" (*IB*, 182 [ch. 17]). The most prominent white rose in fine arts is evident in El Greco's *The Burial of the Count of Orgaz* (Church of Santo Tomé, Toledo), in which it adorns the garment of St. Stephen, the first Christian martyr. Aside from hinting at Cincinnatus's martyrdom, El Greco's masterpiece commands interest in another important respect: the boy in the left-foreground, who is pointing to the white rose, is assumed to be El Greco's son. The handkerchief protruding from his pocket bears the painter's signature followed by the date of the boy's birth.[24] (This is all the more remarkable since artists commonly date their paintings' completion.) Therefore, this likely allusion to El Greco's masterpiece by way of the white rose could be viewed as an intricate manifestation of a very momentous event in Nabokov's life: the birth of *his* son, Dmitri, in 1934; the year in which the writer composed *Invitation to a Beheading*.

SIRIN

Nabokov commonly encodes his authorial presence through various meanings attached to Sirin, the pen-name the writer used throughout his "Russian years."[25] Nabokov unveiled some of the meanings of his pen-name in his second interview with Alfred Appel, Jr., in August 1970:

In modern times *sirin* is one of the popular Russian names of the Snowy Owl, the terror of tundra rodents, and is also applied to the handsome Hawk Owl, but in old Russian mythology it is a multicolored bird, with a woman's face and bust, no doubt identical with the "siren," a Greek deity, transporter of souls and teaser of sailors. (*SO*, 161)

Nabokov employs for self-encodement all of the following associations of the name: Sirin as an owl; Sirin as a mythical Russian bird of Paradise; Siren as "a Greek deity." Let us consider some less apparent examples of Nabokov's authorial presence associated with each one of these three meanings of the writer's pen-name to which he relates in the interview.

First, the owl. The owl as a manifestation of authorial presence can be found at the close of the story "A Bad Day." There, it finds expression in the form of "a baby owl" (*Stories*, 276), whose image Nabokov employs as his "signet" with which he "seals" this story. Here, this helpless "baby owl," detached from its nest, seems to convey metaphorically the child-protagonist's feelings of loneliness and desperation. Another indication of such authorial presence can be found in Nabokov's first English novel in the image of "an owl hooting."[26] The owl- and, therefore, Sirin-marked authorial presence is reinforced in the ensuing paragraph iconically, through Nabokov's first initial, by the mention of "a V-shaped flight of migrating cranes" (*RLSK*, 137; see iconicism discussed below).

It is commonly known that Nabokov frequently encodes his presence through the image of Sirin as a legendary bird of Paradise: a mythical land believed to have been located in the East. Therefore, the mention of "the paradisian Orient" (*Stories*, 338) in the description of medieval maps in the story "Perfection" can be seen as a subtle manifestation of the authorial presence. In another, more intricate example, the caption of one Russian *lubok* tells about Sirin appearing in India, where, to avoid temptation by the bird's singing and to scare it away, the people fire a cannon.[27] This explains why in *Korol', dama, valet*, Martha's dancing partner, Blavdak Vinomori – a full anagram of Vladimir Nabokov – is described as "student s indusskimi glazami" ("a student with Indian eyes"), thereby additionally implying the authorial presence, this time by the allusion to Sirin, the bird of Paradise.[28] (In *King, Queen, Knave*, the English rendition of the novel, this phrase is omitted.)

An intricate example of self-encodement by way of Siren, "a Greek deity," is evident in *The Gift*. There, the reference to Zina as "half-Mnemo*syne*" (*Gift*, 157 [ch. 3]) points to Memory not only as a crucial aspect of Nabokov's poetics, but also "genealogically" alludes to Nabokov's pen name: Mnemosyne was the mother of the Muses, and the Sirens were believed to be the daughters of Melpomene, the muse of drama, or of Terpsichore, the muse of dance and light verse.[29] The same intricate reference to Nabokov's *nom de plume* is contained perhaps by way of Mnemosyne, the Sirens' "grandmother," in the appellation of Nabokov's memoirs, *Speak, Memory*, which he initially intended to entitle *Speak, Mnemosyne* (see *SM*, 11 ["Foreword"]).

Another less apparent instance of Nabokov's self-encodement via his *nom de plume*, this time through paronomastic and multilingual wordplay, can be seen through his mention of canaries – *serin* in French. (In English, "serin is a small European finch [*Serinus canarius*], related to the canary."[30]) An example of such typically Nabokovian authorial presence by way of multilingual punning is manifest in *The Gift*. In the episode clearly inspired by Gogol's

"Overcoat," the shoemaker, who refuses to mend Fyodor's worn-out shoes, thus prompting him to buy a new pair, bears the surname Kanarienvogel, which means "canary bird" in German. Furthermore, to underscore the meaning of the shoemaker's last name, the narrator points out that in his (the shoemaker's) window "there actually was a bird cage, although minus its yellow captive" (*Gift*, 57 [ch. 1]). And toward the end of this long paragraph, the bird is mentioned once again in the title of the painting – "Four Citizens Catching a Canary." The two "canary" episodes are then tied together by the remark that the bird in the painting was "perhaps the one that had escaped from my shoemaker's cage" (*Gift*, 58–59 [ch. 1]).

ANAGRAMMATIC ENCODING

It has become commonplace throughout Nabokov scholarship to speak of the author's self-encodement via full or partial anagrammatization of his name.[31] The most oft-quoted examples are the earlier mentioned Blavdak Vinomori, as well as Mr. Vivian Badlook (*King, Queen, Knave*), Vivian Darkbloom (*Lolita*), Vivian Bloodmark (*Speak, Memory*), Baron Klim Avidov (*Ada*), Adam von Librikov (*Transparent Things*), Van Bock (*Strong Opinions*), and V. Irisin (*Look at the Harlequins!*).[32]

As we have already seen, Nabokov tends to manifest his authorial presence through the titles of his works, such as *Speak, Memory*, and at times does it by implanting his name in them anagrammatically. Thus, the original title of Nabokov's novella *The Enchanter*, *Volshebnik*, contains Nbkovl, a partial anagram of the writer's surname and given name. This anagrammatized self-encodement is supported by Nabokov's self-referential allusion through the meaning of the title which undoubtedly implies the magic art of the novella's creator and not the repulsive perversity of its pedophile-protagonist. (As we may recall, Nabokov considered enchantment the main component of a writer's gift when he remarked that "it is the enchanter in him [a writer] that predominates and makes him a major writer" [*LL*, 5].) Similarly, the original title of the story "Cloud, Castle, Lake," "**Obla**k**o**, **o**zero, **b**ash**n**ia,"[33] contains Naboko(v), a partial anagram of the writer's surname. Our supposition that this title implies Nabokov's authorial presence is reinforced by the trisyllabic nature of its first two words and the disyllabic nature of its third. Despite the difference in the stress pattern, the title nevertheless apparently alludes to Vladimir Nabokov Sirin.

No less common, however, are cases in which Nabokov employs anagrammatized self-encodement in the text itself, rather than in the title, without resorting to his characters' names. Thus, his poem "In Memory of Gumilev" ("Pamiati Gumileva," 1923): "**Go**r**do** i **ias**no ty **um**er, kak **M**uza **u**chi**la**. / **N**yne, **v** **ti**sh**i** **Eli**seisk**oi**, s **to**boi govo**r**it o **letia**shchem / me**dn**o**m** **P**et**re** **i** o d**ikikh** **ve**t**r**akh **afri**kan**s**kikh – **P**ush**kin**" (*Stikhi*, 95) ("Proudly and serenely you died, as the Muse had taught [you]. / Now, in the Elysian quiet, Pushkin speaks with you of the flying / bronze Peter and of the wild African winds"), contains the dedication: Pamiati Nikolaia Stepanovicha Gumileva Vladimir Sirin (In memory of Nikolai Stepanovich Gumilev – Vladimir Sirin).[34] Another good example is Nabokov's poem "Ut pictura poesis," which bears an inscription to his former drawing master, the celebrated Mstislav Dobuzhinsky (see *Stikhi*, 181–82). Each of the poem's three stanzas contains the anagrammatized dedication: Mstislavu Dobuzhinskomu Vladimir Nabokov Sirin (To Mstislav Dobuzhinsky – Vladimir Nabokov Sirin).

In these two examples, the title of the first short poem and the inscription in the second poem allude to a possibility of self-encodement coupled with dedication. The authorial presence is less apparent, however, in a "plain" text without such signposts, in which case both contextual and metatextual inklings, no matter how subtle, could assist in its discovery. For example, the final quatrain of the previously mentioned poem "The Skater," "**Ost**a**vil** ia o**din** uzo**r** s**lovesn**yi, / **m**g**n**o**v**e**nn**o **r**askruzh**i**vsh**i**isia ts**ve**tok. / **I** za**v**tra s**n**eg **b**esshu**mn**yi i **otv**es**n**yi / zapo**r**o**s**h**it is**cherche**nn**yi kat**ok**" (*Stikhi* 162) ("I left a verbal design / an instantly uncircled flower. / And tomorrow the noiseless and vertical snow / will powder the rink, crossed with lines"), anagrammatically indicates that this "uzor slovesnyi" ("verbal design"), which the skater left on the ice, contains the dedication: Vere Evseevne Slonim Vladimir Nabokov Sirin (To Véra Evseevna Slonim – Vladimir Nabokov Sirin). The poem was written on February 5, 1925, that is a little over two months before Vladimir and Véra were married (April 15).[35] Thus, the date of the poem's composition assists in establishing that Véra Slonim was the addressee of this piece which Nabokov intended as a gift to his bride.

Earlier, I suggested that in *Korol', dama, valet* the phrase describing Martha's dance partner Blavdak Vinomori – an oft-quoted full anagram of Vladimir Nabokov – as "a student with Indian eyes," alludes to Sirin by way of the *lubok* caption. This context helps to determine that the whole sentence, which includes this phrase: "Eia **kaval**e**r**, stud**e**nt s **in**dussk**imi** glazami, ot**ryv**is**to** i tikho ei o**b**″ias-**n**ialsia v liu**bv**i" (*Kdv*, 237) ("Her partner, a student with Indian eyes, was abruptly and quietly declaring his love to her"), contains the anagram: Vladimir Nabokov Sirin. Furthermore, in the English rendition of the novel, the corresponding sentence: "Her p**a**rt**n**er in full e**recti**o**n** aga**i**nst her leg was **d**ecl**ar**in**g** h**i**s **l**o**v**e in p**a**nting sentences fr**om** some lewd **b**oo**k**"[36] contains the anagram: Vladimir Naboko(v) Sirin.

In addition to self-encodement by way of anagrams in both the titles and bodies of his works, Nabokov, as I previously mentioned, employs his authorial presence as a "sealing" device at their close. To this effect, it should be added, the writer frequently uses anagrams of his name. Thus, the last sentence in *King, Queen, Knave*, both in the Russian original and the English translation, contains, respectively: Vladimir Nabokov Sirin and Vladimir Nabokov Siren. We find the same technique in *Invitation to a Beheading*: the last clause of the novel in both Russian and English contains, again respectively: Vladimir Nabokov Sirin and Vladimir Sirin. And the concluding sentence of *Lolita*'s Russian version, "**I** eto – ed**i**nst**venn**oe be**ssm**e**rti**e, **ko**t**o**r**o**e my mozhem s to**b**oi r**az**d**e**lit', m**o**ia Lol**ita**"[37] ("And this is the only immortality which we can share, my Lolita"), incorporates the anagram that indicates the authorial presence: Vladimir Naboko(v) Sirin. This sentence, of course, contains a double entendre: contextually it appears that it is Humbert Humbert who is addressing Lolita, the object of his obsession, but metatextually, it is the author who is bidding farewell to his book and its title-heroine.

CHROMESTHESIA

Nabokov also customarily encodes his authorial presence chromesthetically, drawing on his ability to see letters and their representative sounds in colors.[38] Thus, in *King, Queen, Knave* we come across the sentence, "Three rackets, each in a differently colored cloth case – maroon, blue, and mulberry – protruded from under his arm" (*KQK*, 32 [ch. 2]). Interpreted in Nabokov's "alphabetic rainbow," the colors of the cloth cases of the tennis rackets – maroon, blue, and mulberry (the berry originally appears as waxen yellowish-white) –

respectively point, by way of the color groups red, blue, and white, to "V," "S," and "N" – the initials of the writer's first name, pen-name, and surname: Vladimir Sirin Nabokov. The sentence does not exist in the Russian original, but the corresponding sentence reads: "On byl **v** pr**o**stornom pal′to, **na** shee, spe**red**i, puch**i**los′ **bel**oe **k**ashne, **iz** p**odm**yshk**i** torch**a**la **r**aketa **v** chekhle, kak muzykal′nyi **instr**ument, **v** ruke on nes chemodan**chik**" (*Kdv*, 34) ("He was in an ample overcoat, on his neck a white scarf was bulging out the front, a racket in a cloth case was protruding from his armpit, he was carrying a valise in his hand"), suggesting the author's same presence, even though anagrammatic – Vladimir Vladimiro(vi)ch Nabokov Sirin.

Nabokov resorts to the analogous technique of self-encodement in *Invitation to a Beheading*. In speaking about Cincinnatus's world, Nabokov refers to it as "blue" (*IB*, 93 [ch. 8]) (or, in Russian, "sinii mir"),[39] thereby alluding to Sirin through the initial "s," which belongs to the blue group in Nabokov's chromesthetic system. This seems all the more plausible if we consider that the phrase "**sin**ii m**ir**" contains Sirin, an anagram of Nabokov's pen name. (Nabokov's choice of pen name, with its sky-blue initial denoting creativity and poetic inspiration, can be viewed as a self-affirming gesture on the part of the young aspiring writer.)[40]

Nabokov employs a similar device in the episode in which Cincinnatus, presuming that he has escaped from captivity, observes the landscape: "In the rosy depths of the sky, stood a chain of translucent and fiery cloudlets, and there stretched a long violet bank with burning rents along its lower edge" (*IB*, 164 [ch. 15]). Since in the writer's chromesthetic system "V" belongs to the red group and "S" to the blue, "the rosy depth of the sky" and "fiery cloudlets," together with the "violet bank," chromesthetically suggest "V" and "S" (the initials of Nabokov's first name and pen-name) and should be perceived as a "heavenly sign" that foreshadows Cincinnatus's salvation by the God-like author. Our assumption is strengthened by the fact that in Russian this passage, "no nad ne**vidim**ymi s**adam**i, **v** roz**o**voi gl**ub**i**n**e neba, stoia**li** tsep′iu proz**r**achno og**n**ennye **o**bla**chk**a, i tianulas′ odn**a** dlinnaia lil**ov**aia tucha s go**ri**ashch**im**i p**ro**rezami po **n**izhnemu kraiu" (*Pnk*, 164), set within dashes to draw the reader's special attention, once more anagrammatically contains the writer's full name: Vladimir Vladimirovich Nabokov Sirin. An example of a related chromesthetic device appears in *The Gift:* "Fyodor sat between the novelists Shahmatov and Vladimirov, by a wide window behind which the night gleamed wetly black, with two-toned (the Berlin imagination did not stretch to any more) illuminated signs – ozone-blue and oporto-red" (*Gift*, 320 [ch. 5]), the latter two hues, despite the attention-distracting ironic "Berlin" disclaimer, suggest the authorial presence through the color groups of Nabokov's initials, "S" and "V."

Nabokov employs a similar technique, albeit in a more intricate manner, when he encodes his authorial presence by means of red-and-blue objects, such as balloons, balls, and pencils. As we may recall, aside from being anagrammatic (the combination "red-and-blue," or "**kras**n**o**-s**ini**i" in Russian, contains the word Sirin), the phrase chromesthetically points to the initials of Nabokov's first-name and pen-name: Vladimir Sirin. We come across the red and blue balloons in the *kursaal* episode of the penultimate chapter of *Korol', dama, valet,* which marks the earliest *persona* appearance of the author, together with his wife, for his "visits of inspection" as he put in the foreword to the English version of the novel (*KQK*, viii ["Foreword"]). Nabokov's authorial omnipresence is underscored through Martha's perspective, when she observes that "v kazhdom byla vsia zala, i liustra, i stoliki, i ona sama" ("each [balloon] contained the entire ballroom, and the chandeliers, and the tables, and herself") (*Kdv*, 237; *KQK*, 252 [ch. 12]). (In the English rendition of the novel this perception is somewhat blurred by the addition of green balloons.)

A red-and-blue ball is rolling through the pages of *Invitation to a Beheading.* If we take into account the narrator's emotional involvement in the fate of the protagonist, whom he calls "my poor little Cincinnatus" and whom he occasionally admonishes against oncoming danger by imploring him to "be careful" (*IB*, 65 [ch. 5] and 155 [ch. 14]), we shall realize that this authorial presence, in the context of the novel, suggests once again that the hero will be rescued in the *deus ex machina* fashion by his omnipotent creator.[41]

The authorial presence is also manifest in *The Real Life of Sebastian Knight,* in the narrator's remark that "[t]he child came up to me and silently showed me a new red-and-blue pencil" (*RLSK*, 140 [ch. 15]). This authorial presence signals the importance of this whole episode: the artistic propensity of the child and his uncle, and specifically, the latter's ability to write his name upside down, of which the narrator learns at the time, returns later in the novel and assists him in revealing Madame Lecerf's true identity (cf. *RLSK*, 142 [ch. 15] and 169 [ch. 17]).

ICONICISM

Nabokov, who possessed an exceptional visual acuity, displays great fascination with alphabetic iconicism and occasionally thus encodes his authorial presence.[42] We come across a curious example of this in *Invitation to a Beheading*, where the narrator remarks that "Okruzhaiushchie ponimali drug druga s poluslova, – ibo ne bylo u nikh takikh slov, kotorye by konchalis' kak-nibud' neozhidanno, na izhitsu, chto-li, obrashchaias' v prashchu ili ptitsu, s udivitel'nymi posledstviiami" ("Those around him understood each other at the first word, since they had no words that would end in an unexpected way, perhaps in some archaic letter, an upsilamba, becoming a bird or a catapult with wondrous consequences") (*Pnk*, 38; *IB*, 26 [ch. 2]). As D. Barton Johnson has perceptively observed, in the Russian original, "The Church Slavonic *izhitsa*, in its turn derived from the Greek upsilon (v), has the form and, as Nabokov suggests, physically resembles a slingshot ('catapult' in British English) or the head-on view of a bird in flight."[43] One important component should be added to this observation, however: namely, that the Roman letter "V," Nabokov's first initial, iconically resembles the Church Slavonic *izhitsa*. As the novel's context suggests, the world surrounding Cincinnatus is predictable and *izhitsa*-less, whereas the secret world of the protagonist includes this seldom-occurring letter, the paragon of unexpectedness and, thus, the quintessence of creativity. Its visual resemblance to the author's Roman initial not only alludes to Nabokov's authorial presence but also suggests that Cincinnatus's inner-world is akin to that of his creator. In the English translation, Nabokov substitutes "an upsilamba" for "*izhitsa*," which not only creates "a blend of the letter upsilon (v) which indeed visually mimics a flying bird, and lambda which in its lower case form (λ) resembles the inverted 'Y'-fork of a slingshot",[44] but also twice points to the authorial presence through the resemblance of these two Greek letters to the writer's Roman initial.

Another example of Nabokov's authorial presence encoded through the shape of his first initial can be found in *The Real Life of Sebastian Knight*. It originally appears rather inconspicuously in the description of the plot-line of Sebastian's novel *Success*, where "[t]he two lines which have finally tapered to the point of meeting are really not the straight lines of a triangle which diverge steadily towards an unknown base, but wavy lines, now running wide apart, now almost touching" (*RLSK*, 95 [ch. 10]). While on the surface this butterfly-wing fluttering description speaks of Sebastian's novel's plot-line (although, on the other hand, lepidoptery is another very telling device of Nabokov's self-encodement), contextually it iconically alludes to the presence of the narrator V., but more importantly, to the presence of the author, his "initialsake."[45] Later in the novel, Nabokov's authorial presence is manifest iconically once again, more overtly, through the image of the writer's first initial in the form of "a V-shaped flight of migrating cranes; their tender moan melting in a turquoise-blue sky" (*RLSK*, 137 [ch. 14]). In addition to indicating the authorial presence, this sentence also expressively conveys the sorrowful atmosphere which surrounds the love-lorn Sebastian of his "Russian years." This sorrowfulness is achieved by means of auditory imagery – the cranes' moan, preceded by "an owl hooting" (*RLSK*, 137 [ch. 14]; cf. our discussion above) – that is coupled with visual imagery – "an abyss of darkness" and the "trunk of a felled tree" [*ibid.*]). It is noteworthy that this whole flashback episode portends the name of Sebastian's last unrequited love: "A **Cam**berwell Beauty ski**m**s past and sett**le**s on the **k**erf, **f**a**nni**ng her velvety wings" – Mme Lecerf, flighty like a butterfly, with her first name (Nina) and the time span implied in the last clause by *anni* (Latin "years"). Her previous full married name: Nina Rechnoy (under which she was known to Sebastian), is suggested in the subsequent sentence: "**B**a**c**k to tow**n** to-mo**rr**ow, s**ch**ool b**e**g**inn**ing **o**n Monda**y**" (*RLSK*, 137 [ch. 14]). These two examples of anagrammatization underlie the narrator's supposition that "There seems to have been a law of some strange harmony in the placing of a meeting relating to Sebastian's adolescent romance in such close proximity to the echoes of his dark love" (*RLSK*, 137 [ch. 14]).

Several years later, this crane imagery reappears in Nabokov's poem "An Evening of Russian Poetry": "On mellow hills the Greek, as you remember, / fashioned his alphabet from cranes in flight."[46] In this programmatic poem, however, Nabokov imbued the imagery of "cranes in flight" with a new and very telling meaning – *nomen est omen*. This fatidic imagery seems to intimate that Nabokov was destined to become a writer, as his first initial, "V," that resembles "cranes in flight" from whom "the Greek" "fashioned his alphabet," lies at the base of verbal creation.

COMPLEX ENCODING

I have already pointed out Nabokov's use of complex self-encodement in which he combines various modes of authorial presence. Now, I would like to focus on one of the most striking examples of this kind. It appears in *Pnin*, in the episode of the protagonist's house-warming party. In this scene, we come across a description of Jan van Eyck's *Madonna of Canon van der Paele* (Groeninge Museum, Bruges), seemingly because Laurence Clements, Pnin's university colleague and former landlord, bears a "striking resemblance" to the "ample-jowled, fluff-haloed Canon" (*Pnin*, 154 [ch. 6]). Elsewhere I suggested that Nabokov's mention of Jan van Eyck's masterpiece intricately alludes to Nabokov's authorial presence in the novel. We may recall that the painting contains the image of, as Nabokov put it, "a super, rigged up as St. George" (*ibid.*), in whose armor a reflection of the artist can be seen.[47] In this context, van Eyck's self-portrait as a reflection in the armor of St. George also implies the authorial presence by way of birthday, since Nabokov celebrated his birthday on St. George's Day (April 23).[48] In addition, van Eyck's self-representation could also draw Nabokov's attention as it appears on the side (*na boku*) of St. George's armor. Further, by mentioning van Eyck's painting, Nabokov implies his own authorial presence both chromesthetically and anagrammatically: van Eyck's vermilion hat and hose and a dark blue mantle in the image that is reflected in St. George's armor, could also attract Nabokov, since "V" and "S," the initials of his first name, Vladimir, and of his pen-name, Sirin, belong, in the writer's chromesthetic system, as I have already mentioned above, to the red and blue groups, while the Russian rendition of the color combination, red-and-blue, *krasno-sinii*, anagrammatically suggests Sirin.

The authorial presence is reinforced in this same episode when Joan Clements, Laurence's wife, ostensibly speaks of some unidentified writer who is clearly Nabokov himself. And Joan's "fetching way" "of interrupting her speech, to punctuate a clause or gather new momentum, by deep hawing pants" is designed to underscore the importance of the pronouncement and to draw the reader's attention to it. As Gennady Barabtarlo has aptly commented, the sentence itself sums up "the principal feature of *Pnin*'s composition and of Nabokov's novelistic art in general."[49] The sentence in its English original, "**B**ut d**o**n't you thi**nk** – haw – that what he **is** trying to **do** – haw – p**r**a**c**tically in **a**ll **h**is **n**ov**e**ls – haw – is – haw – to exp**r**ess the fantastic recurrence of certain situations?" (*Pnin* 159) contains the anagram of Nabokov's abbreviated first name, surname, and pen name: Vlad. Naboko(v) Sirin. Rendered into Russian as: "A **v**y ne **d**u**ma**ete,[50] **ch**to to, chto on pytaetsia sde**lat**′ prak**ti**ches**ki** **v**o **v**sekh svo**i**kh **r**o**m**an**a**kh, eto peredat′ **n**e**b**yval**o**e p**o**v**t**or**e**n**i**e **o**p**red**e**l**ennykh s**i**tuatsii," the sentence, once again, anagrammatically, but this time in the Russian translation, contains the writer's first, patronymic, last, and pen names: Vladimir Vladimirov(i)ch Nabokov Sirin.

How to explain, then, Nabokov's strong predilection for the diverse and deeply-embedded art of self-encodement? First, in his manifestations of authorial presence, Nabokov followed a cultural tradition, well established in various media, such as literature, fine arts, and cinema. Further, Nabokov, who viewed himself as "an anthropomorphic deity"[51] in his fictional universe, would display this notion by leaving "divine signs" that pointed to his authorial appearance. Occasionally, he would reveal his empyrean presence at the close of his works by sealing them with one of its manifestations – a "signet," as it were. When employing complex self-encodement techniques, Nabokov would resort to the strategy concomitant with that of composing charades and chess problems whose solution commonly necessitates a number of "moves." *Homo ludens* to the extreme, Nabokov encoded his authorial presence in a great number of ways as a fun game which he enjoyed playing with his "good readers" (*LL*, 1–6), but first and foremost, with "the person he sees in his shaving mirror every morning" (*SO*, 18).[52] Finally, the exploration of Nabokov's self-encodement yields unique access to the creative laboratory of this incomparable verbal magician whose authorial presence is so multifariously embossed throughout his oeuvre.

NOTES

1 Thus Cicero reports in his *Tusculanae disputationes* (I.xv.34) that "Phidias inserted his likeness on the shield of Minerva, though not allowed to inscribe his name on it." See Cicero, *Tusculan disputations*, trans. J. E. King (Cambridge, MA: Harvard University Press, 1966), 41.

On authorial presence in literature, see Bruce E. Chaddock, "Authorial Presence and the Novel" (Ph.D. diss., Cornell University, 1974); and more recently, G. R. Thompson, *The Art of Authorial Presence: Hawthorne's Provincial Tales* (Durham and London: Duke University Press, 1993). On various aspects of the artist's self-representation in fine arts, see Matthias Winner (ed.), *Der Künstler über sich in seinem Werk* (Weinheim: VCH, Acta Humaniora, 1992).

Nabokov, a movie aficionado, was undoubtedly familiar with manifestations of the authorial presence in the works of his coeval, the film director Alfred Hitchcock. Thus, while in the foreword to the *Lolita* screenplay Nabokov humorously refers to his persona as having "the placid profile of a stand-in for Hitchcock" (*Lolita: A Screenplay* [1974; New York: Vintage International, 1997], xii ["Foreword"] [hereafter *LoScreen*]), he briefly enters the scene under his own name in the screenplay itself, subsequently envisioning this episode acted out in the movie (see *ibid.* 127–28 [Act 2]). Such self-representation is very much in keeping with Hitchcock's "walk-on" technique. See Alfred Appel, Jr., *Nabokov's Dark Cinema* (New York: Oxford University Press, 1974), esp. 249–52; and Pekka Tammi, *Problems of Nabokov's Poetics: A Narratological Analysis* (Helsinki: Suomalainen Tiedeakatemia, 1985), 315–17.

2 See also Tammi, *Problems of Nabokov's Poetics*, 317.
3 For the most extensive discussion, including the bibliography on the subject, see Tammi, *Problems of Nabokov's Poetics*, esp. 314–59. For more recent references to Nabokov's self-encodement, specifically in *Despair*, see Julian W. Connolly, *Nabokov's Early Fiction: Patterns of Self and Other* (Cambridge University Press, 1992), 157–60 and Alexander Dolinin, "The Caning of Modernist Profaners: Parody in *Despair*," *Zembla*, online available at http://www.libraries.psu.edu/iasweb/nabokov/doli1.htm, 6 n.7.
4 Vladimir Nabokov, *Drugie berega* (Ann Arbor: Ardis, 1978), 43. (Hereafter *DB*.) For the meaning of Nabok, see Alexander Lehrman, "An Etymological Footnote to Chapter Three of *Speak, Memory*," *The Nabokovian* 24 (1990): 32–33.
5 See Tammi, *Problems of Nabokov's Poetics*, 327; Connolly, *Nabokov's Early Fiction*, 157; Dolinin, "The Caning of Modernist Profaners," 6, n. 7. Nabokov was also undoubtedly aware that the meaning of his surname corresponds to his position as an émigré writer: an outsider who looks at things *sboku* ("from the [out]side").
6 *Invitation to a Beheading*, trans. Dmitri Nabokov in collaboration with the author (1959; New York: Vintage International, 1989), 7 ("Foreword"). (Hereafter *IB*.)
7 *The Annotated Lolita*, ed. and introd. Alfred Appel, Jr. (1970; rev. edn. New York: Vintage International, 1991), 52 (pt. 1, ch. 11). (Hereafter *AnL*.)
8 Also see Gavriel Shapiro, "*Lolita* Class List," *Cahiers du Monde russe* 37 (1996): 327.

9 For Nabokov's use of fatidic dates, see Tammi, *Problems of Nabokov's Poetics*, 327–29, and Priscilla Meyer, *Find What the Sailor Has Hidden: Vladimir Nabokov's* Pale Fire (Middletown, CT: Wesleyan University Press, 1988), 88. On the significance of birthdays in the works of Nabokov's contemporaries, specifically in the poetry of Marina Tsvetaeva and Velimir Khlebnikov, see Barbara Lönnqvist, "K znacheniiu dnia rozhdeniia u avangardnykh poetov" in *Readings in Russian Modernism. To Honor Vladimir Fedorovich Markov*, ed. Ronald Vroon and John E. Malmstad (Moscow: Nauka, 1993), 206–11.
10 *The Gift*, trans. Michael Scammell in collaboration with the author (1963; New York: Vintage International, 1991), 288 (ch. 4). (Hereafter *Gift*.)
11 *The Song of Igor's Campaign*, trans. Vladimir Nabokov (1960; New York: Vintage International, 1989), 1 ("Foreword"). (Hereafter *Song*.)
12 Here and henceforth, all unattributed translations are mine.
13 Cf. Annelore Engel-Braunschmidt's commentary in Vladimir Nabokov, *Die Gabe* (Reinbek bei Hamburg: Rowohlt, 1993), 785.
14 For more on the subject, see Gavriel Shapiro, "Nabokov's Allusions: Dividedness and Polysemy," *Russian Literature* 43 (1998): 329–38.
15 See Vladimir Nabokov, *Stikhi* (Ann Arbor: Ardis, 1979), 269. (Hereafter *Stikhi*.)
16 Cf. Gennady Barabtarlo, "Those Who Favor Fire (On *The Enchanter*)," *Russian Literature Triquarterly* 24 (1991): 91.
17 *The Enchanter*, trans. Dmitri Nabokov (1986; New York: Vintage International, 1991), 61. (Hereafter *En*.)
18 Anton Chekhov, *Plays*, trans. Eugene K. Bristow (New York: Norton, 1977), 61.
19 See Barbara L. Michaels, *Gertrude Käsebier. The Photographer and Her Photographs* (New York: Abrams, 1992), 65, ill. 40.
20 *Pnin* (1957; New York: Vintage International, 1989), 95 (ch. 4). (Hereafter *Pnin*.)
21 *The Stories of Vladimir Nabokov* (1995; New York: Vintage International, 1997), 147. (Hereafter *Stories*.)
22 See Osip Mandel'shtam, *Sobranie sochinenii*, 3 vols. (New York: Mezhdunarodnoe Literaturnoe Sodruzhestvo, 1967–71), II:576.
23 See L. S. Zhuravleva, *Kniaginia Mariia Tenisheva* (Smolensk: Poligramma, 1994), 17–18.
24 See Francisco Calvo Serraller, *El Greco: The Burial of the Count of Orgaz* (London: Thames and Hudson, 1994), 19.
25 For a detailed discussion of Nabokov's pen name and its multilayered connotations, see B. Ostanin, "Ravenstvo, zigzag, trilistnik, ili o trekh rodakh poezii" and "Sirin: 22 + 2," *Novoe literaturnoe obozrenie* 23 (1997): 300–02 and 305; A. Fomin, "Sirin: dvadtsat' dva plius odin," *Novoe literaturnoe obozrenie* 23 (1997): 302–04; and Gavriel Shapiro, *Delicate Markers: Subtexts in Vladimir Nabokov's* Invitation to a Beheading (New York: Peter Lang, 1998), 9–29.

26 *The Real Life of Sebastian Knight* (1941; New York: Vintage International, 1992), 137 (ch. 14). (Hereafter *RLSK*.)
27 See Iurii Ovsiannikov, *The Lubok: Seventeenth- and Eighteenth-Century Russian Broadsides* (Moscow: Sovetskii khudozhnik, 1968), ill. 81.
28 Vladimir Nabokov, *Korol', dama, valet* (New York: McGraw-Hill, 1969), 237. (Hereafter *Kdv*.)
29 See Pierre Grimal, *The Dictionary of Classical Mythology* (New York: Blackwell, 1987), 293 and 421. Nabokov paid tribute to both Muses: he wrote several plays and was not above composing light verse. For the latter, see, for example, *Selected Letters, 1940–1977*, ed. Dmitri Nabokov and Matthew J. Bruccoli (New York: Harcourt Brace Jovanovich / Bruccoli Clark Layman, 1991), 246, 324, and 383. (Hereafter *SL*.) Nabokov mentions Terpsichore in his poem "The Skater" ("Kon'kobezhets," 1925); see *Stikhi*, 162.
30 *Webster's New Dictionary*, 2nd edn. (Springfield, MA), s.v. "serin".
31 For the sake of conciseness I will use the term "anagram" to include partial or incomplete anagrams as well as exact anagrams.
32 For the most recent discussion of anagrams of Nabokov's name, see Laurence Guy, "Les anagrammes cosmopolites de l'auteur dans son oeuvre, ou l'identité renversée de Vladimir Nabokov," *Cahiers du Monde russe* 37 (1996): 337–48.
   On the use of anagrammatic encodement and alphabetic iconicism in Nabokov's native Russian literature, and specifically in the works of Nabokov's literary ancestors Pushkin and Gogol, cf., respectively, A. A. Kandinskii-Rybnikov, *Uchenie o schast'e i avtobiografichnost' v "Povestiakh pokoinogo Ivana Petrovicha Belkina, izdannykh A. P."* (Moscow: Feniks, 1993); Lauren G. Leighton, *The Esoteric Tradition in Russian Romantic Literature* (University Park: The Pennsylvania State University Press, 1994); and Gavriel Shapiro, "Nikolai Gogol' i gordyi gogol': pisatel' i ego imia," *Russian Language Journal* 43, no. 144 (1989): 145–59.
33 In several of these passages there is an excess of letters that could be chosen to make up the target name or phrase. I have chosen a representative selection of these letters.
34 "Serenely" as well as "quiet," synonymous with "serenity," are perhaps additional, paronomastic, allusions to the authorial presence by way of Sirin/Siren. "The flying bronze Peter" suggests, of course, the Falconet monument of Peter I in St. Petersburg and Pushkin's poem *The Bronze Horseman*. "African" refers to Pushkin's ancestry and Gumilev's journeys to the continent.
35 For the date of the poem's composition, see D. Barton Johnson with Wayne C. Wilson, "Alphabetic and Chronological Lists of Nabokov's Poetry," *Russian Literature Triquarterly* 24 (1991): 365; for the date of the Nabokovs' wedding, see Brian Boyd, *Vladimir Nabokov: The Russian Years* (Princeton University Press, 1990), 239–40.
36 *King, Queen, Knave*, trans. Dmitri Nabokov in collaboration with the

author (1968: New York: Vintage International, 1989), 252 (ch. 12). (Hereafter *KQK*.)
37 Vladimir Nabokov, *Lolita* (New York: Phaedra, 1967), 287. (Hereafter *LoR*.)
38 See D. Barton Johnson, *Worlds in Regression: Some Novels by Vladimir Nabokov* (Ann Arbor: Ardis, 1985), 7–46.
39 Vladimir Nabokov, *Priglashenie na kazn'* (Ardis: Ann Arbor, 1979), 99. (Hereafter *Pnk*.)
40 Cf. Nabokov's own admission: "I saw Sirin with an 's' being a very brilliant blue, a light blue ... I thought it was a glamorous, colorful word." Cited in Andrew Field, *Nabokov: His Life in Part* (New York: Viking, 1977), 149.
41 For a detailed discussion of the red-and-blue ball as a manifestation of Nabokov's authorial presence in the novel, see Shapiro, *Delicate Markers*, 67–70.
42 On Nabokov's employment of alphabetic iconicism, specifically in *Invitation to a Beheading*, see Johnson, *Worlds in Regression*, 28–46 and Shapiro, *Delicate Markers*, 32–55.
43 Johnson, *Worlds in Regression*, 35. Both images, a bird in flight and *prashcha* ("slingshot" or "catapult") are very telling: the former, of course, connotes freedom, and the latter alludes to King David's victory over Goliath; they foretell, respectively, Cincinnatus's liberation and his triumph over the world around him.
44 Johnson, *Worlds in Regression*, 35.
45 Cf. Susan Elizabeth Sweeney, "The V-Shaped Paradigm: Nabokov and Pynchon," *Cycnos* 12.2 (1995): 173–80.
46 *Poems and Problems* (New York: McGraw-Hill, 1970), 158. (Hereafter *PP*.)
47 For the most recent discussion of Jan van Eyck's self-representation in the painting, see John L. Ward, "Disguised Symbolism as Enactive Symbolism in Van Eyck's Paintings," *Artibus et historiae* 29 (1994): 43–44.
   It is noteworthy that earlier in the novel Nabokov refers to such practice of self-representation, common among Early Netherlandish painters: "In the chrome plating, in the glass of a sun-rimmed headlamp, he [Victor] would see a view of the street and himself comparable to the microcosmic version of a room (with a dorsal view of diminutive people) in that very special and very magical small convex mirror that, half a millennium ago, Van Eyck and Petrus Christus and Memling used to paint into their detailed interiors, behind the sour merchant or the domestic Madonna" (*Pnin* 97–98 [ch. 4]).
48 See Gavriel Shapiro, "Two Notes on *Pnin*," *The Nabokovian* 29 (1992): 36–37.
49 Gennady Barabtarlo, *Phantom of Fact: A Guide to Nabokov's* Pnin (Ann Arbor: Ardis, 1989), 246.
50 Cf. the reverse translation of this phrase in, respectively, *Dar* (Ann Arbor: Ardis, 1975), 327 and *Gift*, 293 (ch. 4).

51 *Bend Sinister* (1947; New York: Vintage International, 1990), xviii ("Introduction"). (Hereafter *BS*.)
52 On Nabokov as *homo ludens*, see A. M. Liuksemburg and G. F. Rakhimkulova, *Magistr igry Vivian Van Bok (Igra slov v proze Vladimira Nabokova v svete teorii kalambura* (Rostov-on-Don: Rostovskii gosudarstvennyi universitet, 1996).

CHAPTER 2

Vladimir Nabokov and the art of autobiography
Galya Diment

Anyone can create the future but only a wise man can create the past.
Vladimir Nabokov, *Bend Sinister*

Brian Boyd calls Nabokov's *Speak, Memory,* "the most *artistic* of all autobiographies,"[1] and it is true that before Nabokov's work the whole notion of the "art of autobiography" could be considered something of a misnomer. But Russian literature, in which Nabokov was so well grounded, thrived on apparent misnomers. Pushkin called his major work in verse, *Eugene Onegin,* "a novel," while Gogol proclaimed his long work in prose, *Dead Souls,* "a poem." (And Dostoevsky, following in Gogol's footsteps in more senses than one, christened his early prose tale – and the only work of his that Nabokov admired – *The Double,* "a Petersburg poem.") Nabokov labeled his work "a memoir" in 1951 and "an autobiography" in 1966, but many critics, noticing the unusually high level of artistry involved, chose to remain unconvinced. "Autobiography as Fiction" was Dabney Stuart's 1978 verdict for *Speak, Memory.*[2] "*Speak, Memory* must be regarded as a work of fiction," G. M. Hyde admonished us in *Vladimir Nabokov: America's Russian Novelist.*[3]

As innovative as Vladimir Nabokov may have been as a novelist or a translator, nowhere, it seems to me, was the truly original nature of his art revealed more profoundly than in his published autobiographies. Alfred Kazin, who, writing in 1964, was one of the first critics to call Nabokov's *Speak, Memory* fiction, pointed out that the writer's autobiographical narrative "is designed, even when the author does not say so, to make a fable of his life, to tell a story, to create a pattern of incident, to make a dramatic point." "Autobiography," Kazin remarked, "like other literary forms, is what a gifted writer makes of it."[4] What Nabokov, one of the most gifted writers of his generation, made of his autobiography was not, however, "fiction." What Nabokov made of it was a highly crafted and introspective autobiographical narrative which he himself described in an unpublished introduction to *Conclusive Evidence* as "the meeting point of an impersonal art form and a very personal life story."[5] Between the "invented facts" of fiction and the "real facts" of one's personal life there appears to have been enough creative space for Nabokov to fashion an autobiography based on what he himself would call the "imagined facts."[6]

In his *On the Theory of Prose*, Victor Shklovsky shocked many readers by declaring that Sterne's *Tristram Shandy*, considered by many a very unusual novel if a novel at all, may be, in fact, "the most typical novel in the history of world literature."[7] By that he meant that Sterne bared many novelistic devices which other novelists equally employ but try to keep hidden. Like Sterne's *Tristram Shandy*, Nabokov's *Speak, Memory* is a work of heightened artistic self-consciousness. What Shklovsky calls "the baring of the device" occurs everywhere in the autobiography as Nabokov attempts not only to make his memory speak but also forces it to analyze itself. "I witness with pleasure the supreme achievement of memory," he writes in the chapter devoted to the tutors of his youth,

which is the masterly use it makes of innate harmonies when gathering to its fold the suspended and wandering tonalities of the past ... In the place where my current tutor sits, there is a changeful image, a succession of fade ins and fade outs ... And then, suddenly, just when the colors and outlines settle at last to their various duties ... some knob is touched and a torrent of sounds comes to life: voices speaking all together, a walnut cracked, the click of a nutcracker carelessly passed, thirty human hearts drowning mine with their regular beats ...[8]

As Elizabeth Bruss comments in her excellent analysis of this passage, "The optical tricks, the description of a memory which feeds on and is fed by the imagination – composing rather than resurrecting the setting – ... leave little doubt about the status of this scene. It will not be forgotten by any reader of these memoirs that the memory summoned by the title's epic invocation is the mother of all other arts."[9] But was that mechanism of "composing rather than resurrecting," or of "imagining" rather than "reproducing," just true for Nabokov? Or did he, like Sterne – "I love Sterne," Nabokov confessed to an interviewer in 1967 (*SO*, 74) – skillfully and artfully uncover the otherwise concealed devices present in other works of the same genre?

I believe he did. It may be quite sensational to suggest that Nabokov's *Speak, Memory*, which, as we have seen, some consider not at all an autobiography, could be, after all, "the most typical autobiography in the history of world literature." And yet, as this article will attempt to show, there may be excellent reasons for doing just that, especially if one follows Shklovsky's line of argument that the revolutionary technique of "baring devices" merely exaggerates and underscores what is otherwise passed in silence in less self-conscious and thus more "traditional" works.

In 1951, the same year that *Conclusive Evidence*, the first incarnation of Nabokov's autobiography, was published in the United States, a prominent English poet, Stephen Spender, complained in his own autobiography, *World Within World*, that many literary works of that genre irritated him. While he "wanted to read about the writer's achievements," Spender wrote there, most autobiographies began, instead, "with a detailed account of [the writer's] early days ... a morass of ancestors, nurses, governesses, first memories ... Certainly masterpieces have been written about childhood," Spender continued, "but these are chiefly important for the light they throw on childhood in general, and they are not especially illuminating as the autobiography of particular individuals ... That autobiographers have to begin by plunging into their earliest memories is surely an unnecessary convention."[10]

Nabokov could not have disagreed with Spender more. "I may be inordinately fond of my earliest impressions," he wrote in *Conclusive Evidence*, "but then I have reason to be grateful to them. They led the way into a veritable Eden of visual and tactile sensations ... Nothing is sweeter or stranger than to ponder those first thrills. They belong to the harmonious world of a perfect childhood and, as such, possess a naturally plastic form in one's memory, which can be set down with hardly any effort" (*CE*, 6).[11] When it came to the art of autobiography, Nabokov and Spender, appear, in fact, to have disagreed on virtually every aspect of it. Comparing these two works published the same year can, I believe, serve as an excellent catalyst for revealing Nabokov's artistic intent in *Speak, Memory* and for re-assessing the writer's unique contributions to the genre of self-writing.

If prior to writing their autobiographies (Nabokov started his in 1946, Spender in 1947) Nabokov and Spender had sought a common definition of "autobiography," they probably would have read something like this: "Facts are as necessary to autobiography as they are to biography ... for on them truth, the greatest quality of art, is founded."[12] As one critic observed recently, back in that era, when "very few people even thought about th[e] question [of what is autobiography]," those who did "generally agreed that an autobiography had to offer an at least ostensibly factual account of the writer's own life – that it had to be, in short, a self-written biography."[13] Since the author-cum-subject of one's autobiography supposedly knew everything about his or her "real" life and personality and was, therefore, as close to being "omniscient" as any author could be, it was widely assumed that autobiographies contained pure "facts" and "truth" unless the author was intentionally lying.

Despite Spender's professed dislike for convention, *World Within World* is devoid of "excessive" artistry and progresses, for the most part, in a strictly chronological and spiral manner. It often does read like what many critics and readers expect an autobiography to be, namely, a "self-written biography." As many biographies do, it deals primarily with the subject's trials, tribulations, and occasional triumphs as he faces the many conflicts and contradictions which, according to many biographers, it is one's destiny in life to face (not unlike the "tests" in the earlier genre of the Lives of Saints, on which the first secular biographies were often modeled). In Spender's case those were the conflicts of his origin (German on the one side, Jewish on the other), sexuality (he appears to have been drawn emotionally to women but physically to men), and political views (his father was a liberal; his uncle, who became a father figure to Spender after his father's death, a conservative. Spender himself became a Marxist during his Oxford years, yet was always repelled by the Marxist propagandistic view of art and later became disillusioned with the Marxist doctrine in general.). Stephen Spender seems to have taken the convention that autobiographies should reveal "truth and nothing but the truth" quite seriously as well. "Autobiography sets ... a very special problem," he wrote in 1955 in "Confessions and Autobiography." "The theme of [the autobiographer's] book is himself. Yet if he treats this theme as though he were another person writing about himself, then he evades the basic truth of autobiography which is 'I am alone in the universe.'"[14]

Even now, almost half a century after *World Within World* and *Conclusive Evidence* were published, autobiography is still one of the most poorly defined of all genres. Modern definitions run the full gamut from very general, like "an account of a man's life by himself"[15] to quite restrictive, as in Elizabeth Bruss's formulation: "Autobiography as we know it is dependent on distinctions between fiction and nonfiction, between rhetorical and empirical first person narration."[16] On the other hand, there also exist definitions which are virtually unlimited. William Spengemann, for one, refuses even to distinguish between autobiography and fiction, suggesting that any work which deals with the "over-riding concern with the realization of [the writer's] self" should be considered autobiography.[17] He then describes different "forms of autobiography" – "Historical," "Philosophical," "Poetic" – which would make both Nabokov's *Speak, Memory* and his largely autobiographical novel *Dar* (*The Gift*) equally "poetic" autobiographies.

Ironically, as Avrom Fleishman astutely points out, readers appear to have fewer problems with identifying the genre than do critics. "[A] wide audience of modern readers," Fleishman states in *Figures of Autobiography*, "has reached a higher sophistication in regard to autobiography than some members of the critical fraternity, so that it welcomes displays of fictionality, artfulness and even tailoring of the fact in behalf of skilled performance in an autobiographical role." Fleishman's footnote to this sentence refers his reader to Elizabeth Bruss's chapter on Nabokov and thus leaves little doubt as to which author – and which argument among the "critical fraternity" – he may have in mind here.[18]

Francis R. Hart may be right when he states that the problem of "fact" and "fiction" in autobiography is in itself a largely fictional, invented problem. Those who debate that question, Hart writes in "Notes for an Anatomy of Modern Autobiography," "are continually preoccupied with a question which, while inescapable, is in part a pseudo-problem: the relation in autobiographical writing of the fictive and historical, 'design' and 'truth,' *Dichtung und Wahrheit*."[19] The more crucial questions for the genre, it would seem, are the ones which go below the surface and probe not whether the account is linear, spiral, or circular, chronological or random, ornamental or documentary, but how this account has come into being, how one's memory facilitated it, and how the distance in years between the described events and the act of writing them down has colored and transformed the original scenes and the so-called "facts." Few common wisdoms of the nature of autobiography ever go to the essence of the process of writing the autobiography, and what this process inevitably does to "facts" that long ago ceased being immediate or even "real."

"The more one ponders this enchanting book," writes Robert Alter of *Speak, Memory*,

> the more evident it becomes that Nabokov's conception of memory is profoundly – and appropriately – ambiguous. In the same breath, he intimates that he has recovered or somehow reconstituted the past in his prose, and that he has rather reinvented a past forever lost in the vanishing perspective of time. To affirm merely the former would be to succumb to self-indulgent delusion; to affirm merely the latter would be to concede that autobiography is impossible because it must always turn into fiction."[20]

But where the critic sees an appropriate ambiguity, Nabokov, it appears, saw none. What makes Nabokov not just a great practitioner of the art of autobiography but also its great theoretician is that he goes straight to the heart of what is autobiographical "fact" and "fiction" and, in the process, both challenges the existent assumptions and bares – nay, flaunts! – the narrative devices which others use either secretively or unconsciously.

"*Speak, Memory* is strictly autobiographic," he stated to Alfred Appel in 1966:

> I would say that imagination is a form of memory... An image depends on the power of association, and association is supplied and prompted by memory. When we speak of a vivid individual recollection we are paying a compliment not to our capacity of retention but to Mnemosyne's mysterious foresight in having stored up this or that element which creative imagination may use when combining it with later recollections and inventions. In this sense, both memory and imagination are a negation of time. (*SO*, 77, 78)

If imagination is a "form of memory," then facts remembered are, indeed, facts "imagined." "[B]are facts," Nabokov wrote in 1943, "do not exist in a state of nature, for they are never really quite bare."[21] Perfect memories do not exist either. "I am an ardent memorist with a rotten memory," he confessed to the same Appel in 1960, "a drowsy king's absent-minded remembrancer. With absolute lucidity I recall landscapes, gestures, intonations, a million sensuous details, but names and numbers topple into oblivion with absurd abandon like blind men in file from a pier."[22] Since pure facts and instant recall are usually not available, the "imagined" facts and selective memories may be as close as any autobiographer can get to the utmost truthfulness. "I tend more and more to regard the objective existence of *all* events as a form of impure imagination," Nabokov stated in a 1969 interview. "Whatever the mind grasps, it does so with the assistance of creative fancy" (*SO*, 154; his emphasis).

With that as a background, let us compare how in their 1951 autobiographies Nabokov and Spender record conversations which took place in the past. In a characteristic admission that he is more than aware of the natural limitations of his human memory, Nabokov hardly ever tries to reproduce them. As he describes his memories, they are often akin to silent movies: "Through a tremulous prism, I distinguish the features of relatives and familiars, mute lips serenely moving in forgotten speech" (*CE*, 122; *SM*, 171). When there are rare exceptions and the sound injects itself into a remembered scene, the conversations we hear tend to further highlight Nabokov's thoughtful approach as to what is autobiographical "truth" and what is "fiction."

One such incident occurs when, while in Germany with Vladimir and his brother Sergei in 1910, Nabokov's father learns of Tolstoy's death: "'Tolstoy vient de mourir,'" he suddenly added, in another stunned voice, turning to my mother. 'Da chto ty [something like 'good gracious']!' she exclaimed in distress, clasping her hands in her lap. 'Pora domoj [Time to go home],' she concluded, as if Tolstoy's death had been the portent of apocalyptic disasters" (*CE*, 145; *SM*, 207–08; his brackets). The event described was, obviously, such a pivotal moment in the life of the 11-year-old boy – and his country – that a reader should have little reason to doubt that the whole scene was likely to have forever etched itself into the autobiographer's memory.

In contrast, Spender demands of his reader much more credulity if one is to assume, for example, that in 1951 the autobiographer would still remember verbatim the following casual conversation with two acquaintances which took place (also in Germany) in 1929:

Dr. Jessell came up to me and said: "I think it's about time we went home."
"All right," I said. "But I want first of all to say good night to Willi."
"He's just gone out of the room, I think."
Dr. Jessell gazed at me with a scrutinizing smile which seemed posted like a sentry at the outskirts of his face, ready to open fire at a sign from me. He went away and came back with Willi. "What do you want, Stephen?" Willi asked, smiling broadly. "I only want to say good night to you, Willi."

"Oh, is that all!" he burst out laughing and took my hand. "How very funny! Good night!" (*WWW*, 112)

Spender offers no explanation as to why his memory of the conversation has remained so vivid. He does mention a diary which he kept at the time but the sample entry he gives has no recorded conversations in it (*WWW*, 104–05). His only published journals begin in 1939,[23] so there is no way one can reasonably establish the accuracy of this account. By failing to provide explanations, Spender therefore chooses to ask his reader to take the autobiographer at his word that he can still remember lengthy conversations which took place many years ago. In doing so, he seems to endanger the "factual" side of his narrative to the point where his allegedly "real" facts are quickly becoming "invented," "fictional" facts. The irony is, of course, that so far not a single critic, including those who believe that autobiographies have to be strictly "factual," has doubted the status of *World Within World* as an autobiography, as opposed to "fiction," while, as we have seen earlier, with Nabokov, who appears to this reader to have been much more careful not to cross the line between memory and invention, critical arguments still rage.

Next to "factuality," the convention that autobiographies ought to be "confessional" is probably the most common one. An autobiographer, it is often believed, creates his narrative primarily for himself, driven by an overwhelming need to re-examine and re-think his life in the privacy of his inner world. The autobiography as a genre, according to John N. Morris, "values the private and the inward in experience more highly than the public and the outward ... 'self' is the modern word for 'soul.'"[24] That Nabokov's autobiography is not "revealing" or "confessional" enough has been frequently noted by critics, beginning with his first biographer, Andrew Field, who suggested that in *Speak, Memory* Nabokov's past "is not searched out" but, instead, "carefully selected."[25] Spender, on the other hand, is often seen by critics as, if anything, overly "confessional." And yet, the comparison is, once again, not as simple as it may first appear.

Spender's ever-present uncertainty – whether about his origins, sexuality, or political views – prompted many critics to pronounce his autobiography a failure. "The real drift of the book," writes A. O. J. Cockshut in *The Art of Autobiography*, "and the cause of the curiously vague impression it makes as a whole, despite some sharp episodes, is that he never knew what he had become. Whether among respectable burghers in Hampstead or in homosexual brothels in Berlin he was always watching himself in puzzlement, wondering who he was."[26] In order to write a successful autobiography, Cockshut seems to be saying – and few would disagree – the subject should know himself well enough to convince readers that he is telling them the truth about what he is and what has made him that particular person. He also has to convince them that they want to get to know him and his world better, otherwise they will never finish the book. No one, on the other hand, ever reproached Vladimir Nabokov for a lack of self-knowledge or ability to suck his readers into the fascinating world of his past. Of the two works, then, Spender's *World Within World* may appear more "confessional," but Nabokov's *Conclusive Evidence* is infinitely more "omniscient" and thus perhaps closer to the conventional autobiographical ideal of "truthful revelation."

When critics maintain that autobiographies are written primarily for writers themselves, they also usually fail to take into account that autobiographers who have intentions of seeing their narratives published fashion and structure them in ways that should be most appealing to their readers. Rejecting the false pretense that concerns for readers should not exist if one is to be truthful and honest about his life, Nabokov actually "dramatizes" his reader within his text and makes him a frequent presence in the narrative. He talks to his reader, plays with his expectations, teases him. Sometimes he even insults him. "The following passage," he writes in a decidedly unlyrical digression half way through chapter 3, "is not for the general reader, but for the particular idiot who, because he lost a fortune in some crash, thinks he understands me." After explaining that what he misses and longs for has nothing to do with the property and wealth he lost, the narrator gives his approval for "the general reader" to "resume" (*CE*, 40; *SM*, 73).

Even when Nabokov appears to be adhering to common autobiographical conventions, he often does so by redefining them first. It has been a widely held critical belief, for example, that autobiographies should feature a distinct character development, with setbacks and triumphs, and thus, like *Bildungsromane*, progress in some kind of a spiral fashion. "The ideal autobiography," writes Jerome H. Buckley, "presents a retrospect of some length on the writer's life and character, in which the actual events matter far less than the truth and depth of his experience. It describes a voyage of self-discovery, a life-journey confused by frequent misdirections and even crises of identity but reaching at last a sense of perspective and integration. It traces through the alert awakened memory of continuity from early childhood to maturity or even to old age."[27] Spender's autobiography is, as we discussed earlier, an excellent example of the autobiography Buckley describes here, since "crises" and "misdirections" truly abound. Apparently full of confidence and self-knowledge from his early childhood, Nabokov, for his part, is fairly alien to developmental turbulence and, in his autobiography, he chooses to give us his own definition of what "a spiral" represents:

The spiral is a spiritualized circle. In the spiral form, the circle, uncoiled, unwound, has ceased to be vicious; it has also been set free. I thought this up when I was a schoolboy, and I also discovered that Hegel's triadic series expressed merely the essential spirality of all things in their relation to time. (*CE*, 204; *SM*, 275)

An ardent and almost mystical believer in fate's "patterned" and repetitive nature, Nabokov at times appears to take his notion of "a spiritualized circle" to an extreme, making some readers suspect that he is pulling their leg. "Sometimes Nabokov teases us with such artificial relations between the past and the present," writes Georges Nivat in *The Garland Companion to Vladimir Nabokov*, "that it looks like a mere joke, a retreat into sarcasm." The critic gives as an example the recurring pattern of flight from political trouble: "[Nabokov's] greatgrandmother helped Louis the XVI to flee to Varennes (thus provoking the King's ruin), and a century and a half later his father gives his old Benz to Kerensky so that he might flee from the Winter Palace."[28]

But Nabokov's use of this motif here is hardly "sarcasm" or even a "joke." In describing the event (Kerensky apparently ended up not using "our debile old Benz," as Nabokov describes it), the narrator remarks: "if I treasure the recollection of that request ... it is only from a compositional viewpoint – because of the amusing thematic echo of Christina von Korff's part in the Varennes episode in 1791" (*SM*, 183).[29] In admitting, rather unabashedly, that in attempting to present a possible "pattern" of history he was governed, at least in this particular instance, by his "compositional" needs, Nabokov flaunts the device once again and virtually challenges autobiographers like Spender to confess that in structuring their lives in a conventionally defined spiral manner they are often governed not by their "true" experiences but by equally compositional demands.

Nabokov's use of the theme of childhood is another instance where he appears to use an autobiographical convention only to redefine it. "The fascination with childhood as a subject of contemporary narratives," writes Kazin, "derives, I think, from the esthetic pleasure that the writer finds in substituting the language of mature consciousness for the unformulated consciousness of the child."[30] In *When The Grass Was Taller: Autobiography and the Experience of Childhood*, Richard N. Coe makes a similar point: "The former self-as-child is as alien to the adult writer as to the adult reader. The child sees differently, reasons differently, reacts differently."[31] Not, however, if that child is Vladimir Nabokov. There is nothing "unformulated" or "alien" about the child's consciousness that the author of *Conclusive Evidence* and *Speak, Memory* attempts to remember, re-imagine, and reproduce. That probably helps to explain why in Coe's book, devoted solely to childhoods in autobiographies, Nabokov's depiction of his childhood, indisputably among the most famous in the history of written autobiographies, receives but a couple of very brief mentions while the discussion of Konstantin Paustovsky's quite mediocre *Story of a Life* occupies many pages.[32]

"In probing my childhood (which is the next best to probing one's eternity)," Nabokov tells us in his autobiography, "I see the awakening of consciousness as a series of spaced flashes, with the intervals between them gradually diminishing until bright blocks of perception are formed, affording memory a slippery hold" (*CE*, 3; *SM*, 20–21). As in his rendering of the distant-in-time conversations, Nabokov never pretends here that his memory retained more than it has. If things remain "unformulated" (but never "alien"!), it is largely a function of his faulty human memory, not at all an attribute of his childhood. The child's world view, as that of an adult, is often based on the knowledge available to him. When the knowledge expands, the formulations may change, yet, since as much knowledge is lost as gained as one matures, it is never a given that a child's perception of the life around him is any less complete or accurate than the perception of an adult.

In a poignant passage at the end of chapter 3, Nabokov writes:

I see again my classroom, the blue roses of the wall-paper, the open window. Its reflection fills the oval mirror above the leathern couch where my uncle sits, gloating over a tattered book. A sense of security, of well-being, of summer warmth pervades my memory. That robust reality makes a ghost of the present. The mirror brims with brightness; a bumblebee has entered the room and bumps against the ceiling. Everything is at it should be, nothing will ever change, nobody will ever die. (*CE*, 44; *SM*, 76–77).

It may be a scene perceived by a child, and formulated for him by an adult, but what is more important here is that it is a vision shared by them both, the vision so "robust" and so "real" that all knowledge to the contrary acquired in later years pales in comparison. In writing his autobiography, in trying to achieve what John Pilling astutely describes as "a recovery of lost time, a monument designed to withstand time and to bring time to a halt,"[33] Nabokov's mature consciousness gains, step-by-step, what his child consciousness knew without much effort to be true. Preserved in his memory, in his imagination, in his art, in his reverence, in his continued sense of joy, security, and well-being, for which such a firm foundation had been laid in his childhood, everything and everyone he describes here, including the bumblebee, is indeed immortal and will never change.

It would be tempting to quote Wordsworth here and suggest that, as in "Intimations of Immortality," Nabokov's child is, indeed, "Father of the Man." There is, however, a crucial difference between Wordsworth's well-known sentiment and Nabokov's. It is true that in his ode, Wordsworth presents a vision of childhood which is every bit as joyous and colorful as Nabokov's:

> There was a time when meadow, grove, and stream,
> The earth, and every common sight,
>   To me did seem
>   Apparelled in celestial light,
> The glory and the freshness of a dream.

The movement in the recollection, however, quickly drifts into a comparison between the past and the present, and the sense of joy is soon replaced by the sense of grief:

> It is not now as it hath been of yore; –
>   Turn whereso'er I may
>   By night or day,
> The things which I have seen I now can see no more.[34]

In Nabokov, child is not so much "Father of the Man" as his intellectual, artistic, and philosophical "twin," albeit at times a more precocious one since it takes him less time to create than for his grown-up counterpart to re-create. There is also no sharp contrast between past and present, but a continuum instead, and even the grammatical tense Nabokov uses is present in contrast to Wordsworthian past.

Great art is sometimes measured by its ability to establish a "tradition" which, in turn, is judged by the caliber of artists who attempt to follow in the footsteps of the innovative practitioner. There have been many autobiographies written since the publication of *Conclusive Evidence* yet it is hard to establish, with any certainty, a definite case of literary influence. Nabokov's autobiography may be "the most typical" one "in the history of world literature," if we apply Shklovsky's criteria to it, but, like *Tristram Shandy*, it still remains one of the very unique works of literature as well. It may be that while conventional "devices" are easy to imitate, baring them is not quite as simple, and may require that rare Sterne-like or Nabokov-like talent. There exists, however, at least one – and, as far as I know, as yet critically unexplored – instance where Nabokov's influence as an autobiographer might have been appreciated and felt by an author whose original talent was quite akin to Nabokov's. That author was Yury Olesha.

Like Nabokov, Olesha was born in 1899. As a child he moved to Odessa and then, following the revolution which split his family to Moscow (his parents, Polish Catholics, emigrated to Poland). A writer of relatively few works – especially after the 1930s when he was virtually silenced by the literary and government establishments – Olesha nevertheless managed to establish himself as one of the most fascinating Russian writers of the century. In his artistic temperament he was among the purest and most skillful of Russian modernists. In his works, most notably his novel *Envy* (1927) and a number of excellent short stories also written in the late 1920s – Olesha, like Nabokov, is always a supreme craftsman in full control of his creation. He likes to bare the artifact, shock his reader into seeing routine things in a new light, and paint the narrative with bold colors.

It should come as no surprise, then, that even Nabokov, who was not overly generous with praise towards other writers, considered Olesha's works "absolutely first-rate fiction" (*SO*, 87). In a rare instance of what Brian Boyd calls "a spirit of homage rather than scorn" towards a Soviet author, Nabokov even translated excerpts from Olesha's story "The Cherry Stone" for his classes at Cornell.[35] While we thus know that Nabokov was well aware of Olesha, Olesha's awareness of – and, in fact, indebtedness to – Nabokov cannot be documented as easily. Olesha's *No Day Without a Line* was edited and published with the major assistance of Victor Shklovsky in 1965, five years after Olesha's death. It mentions Proust and even Freud (with much more respect than Nabokov did) but it could not possibly evoke Nabokov since in the former Soviet Union Nabokov, whom many intellectuals secretly read, was officially banned. I believe, however, that Olesha's autobiography may bear visible signs of Nabokov's influence, and it was probably not just a coincidence that Olesha started writing *No Day Without a Line* in 1954, the very same year that the Russian version of Nabokov's autobiography, *Drugie berega* (Other Shores), was published in the United States.

"The act of memory is an astonishing thing," Olesha writes in *No Day Without a Line*:

We remember things for reasons completely unknown to us ... A picture lights up, switched on by something like engineers in the back of your mind ...

Science says that in infancy we perceive the world turned on its side. If that is true, then it means that I too saw the world on its side. I don't recall that picture of a tipped-over world, so it follows that my first impression of the world has vanished forever. I must therefore be satisfied with the later ones, considering them as if they were first.

I am eating watermelon under a table, and I am wearing a girl's dress. The red slices of watermelon ... This is what rises before me as my earliest recollection. Until then all is darkness, darkness unrelieved.[36]

"Darkness, darkness unrelieved" is, of course, reminiscent of Nabokov's opening of his autobiography where "a young chronophobiac" experiences panic when contemplating "the prenatal abyss" (*CE*, 1; *SM*, 19).[37] Several pages later Olesha evokes the image of the prenatal darkness in terms even closer to Nabokov's: "The golden years of childhood! But were they really so golden? What about proximity to still recent non-existence?" (*NDWL*, 51).

Olesha's autobiography is more fragmented and less polished than *Drugie berega* (it is also unfinished) but it is every bit as self-conscious. He confesses that he inevitably shapes and packages his memories: "I must admit ... that I'm writing all this more like a professional writer than like one who is merely recalling something from his past" (*NDWL*, 77). He also constantly questions whether his recollections are "real" or "imagined": "My grandmother took me to Rishelevsky Gymnasium in Odessa to take the entrance examination for the beginning class ... My grandmother brought not a writer, but a little boy like the others. And he didn't see everything the writer remembers now. Perhaps none of it ever happened! No, of course it happened!" (*NDWL*, 78–79).

As in Nabokov, Olesha's child is not "Father of the Man" but a precocious twin of the adult:

[T]he boy did see all of this, and the writer, drawing upon other recollections, now only remembers what the boy brought by his grandmother actually saw.

So, she did bring a writer after all, a poet, albeit a very young one. And where is the border really? Where indeed did the boy begin to see as a writer? At what point was he simply a boy, and then suddenly a poet? For on that morning he unquestionably did look and he did see." (*NDWL*, 79)

Judson Rosengrant, in the excellent introduction to his 1979 translation of Olesha's autobiography, notices the same distinction between Olesha's and Wordsworth's "children" as the one discussed earlier in connection with Wordsworth and Nabokov: "Indeed, it may be that 'child' and 'man' is a false distinction. Rather, in Olesha's view, a life should be regarded not as first one and then the other, but as a continuum in which adult consciousness is potential in the child's view of the world, and in which the child's view is latent in adult perception" (*NDWL*, 24).

Also like Nabokov, Olesha strives not merely to remember his childhood but to imagine it, or, as Rosengrant puts it, "he wants the past to live again as it was *then*, to be reborn in art" (*NDWL*, 22; Rosengrant's emphasis). In a letter to his mother, written in 1954, Olesha calls his new project "deeper than memoirs": "I am ... now writing a book of memoirs, at least in form, although it is much deeper than memoirs. Odessa during my childhood figures in it, so that I find myself within the sphere of childhood and in proximity to you ..." (*NDWL*, 20). Olesha's memoir also placed him in proximity to Nabokov, and, in all likelihood, it was the kind of proximity that Olesha deliberately sought to attain.

Knowing the particulars of Nabokov's artistic vocabulary and his views on memory, we can legitimately reword Nabokov's dictum – "Anyone can create the future but only a wise man can create the past" – into the assertion: "Anyone can invent the future but only a wise man can imagine the past." Imagining the past, as Nabokov does so skillfully in *Speak, Memory*, may be a sign of wisdom – but, even more so, it is a sign of how well Nabokov understood the genre which so many have had so much trouble defining for so long. And this, together with his original strategies as a novelist, will forever remain Vladimir Nabokov's supreme artistic achievement as well as his indispensable contribution to the craft of creating literature.

NOTES

1 Brian Boyd, *Vladimir Nabokov: The American Years* (Princeton University Press, 1991), 149 (emphasis in the original).
2 Dabney Stuart, *Nabokov: The Dimensions of Parody* (Baton Rouge: Louisiana State University Press, 1978), 163.
3 G. M. Hyde, *Vladimir Nabokov: America's Russian Novelist* (London: Marion Boyars, 1977), 192.
4 Alfred Kazin, "Autobiography as Narrative," *The Michigan Quarterly Review* 4 (1964): 211.
5 Boyd, *The American Years*, 149.
6 "[Gogol] was in the worst plight that a writer can be in," Nabokov wrote in his 1943 study of Gogol reflecting on the writer's creative drought one hundred years earlier. "He had lost the gift of imagining facts and believed that facts may exist by themselves." In Vladimir Nabokov, *Nikolai Gogol* (1944; New York: New Directions, 1961), 119. (Hereafter *NG*.)
7 Viktor Shklovskii, *O teorii prozy* (On the Theory of Prose) (Moscow: Federatsiia, 1929), 204 (my translation).
8 Vladimir Nabokov, *Conclusive Evidence: A Memoir* (New York: Harper, 1951), 121, 122, 123. (Hereafter *CE*.) Also in *SM*, 170, 171.
9 Elizabeth W. Bruss, *Autobiographical Acts: The Changing Situation of a Literary Genre* (Baltimore: Johns Hopkins University Press, 1976), 135.
10 Stephen Spender, *World Within World* (London: Faber, 1951), vii-viii. Subsequent citations from this edition will be noted in the text with a parenthetical reference containing the abbreviation *WWW* and the page number. That Nabokov was well aware of Spender's autobiographical writings at the time became clear just recently when the *New Yorker* published what had been originally intended to be the last chapter of *Conclusive Evidence*. In it, a fictional "reviewer" contrasts "Nabokov's rather gruesome impressions of Berlin between the two wars" and "Mr. Spender's contemporaneous but far more lyrical recollections" (December 28, 1998 and January 4, 1999, p. 128).
11 See also *SM*, 24 (ch. 1).
12 Joseph Collins, "Autobiography" (1925). Quoted in William C. Spenge-

mann, *The Forms of Autobiography: Episodes in the History of a Literary Genre* (New Haven: Yale University Press, 1980), 191.
13 *Ibid.*, xi.
14 Stephen Spender, *The Making of a Poem* (London: Hamish Hamilton, 1955), 65–66.
15 J. A. Cuddon, *A Dictionary of Literary Terms* (Harmondsworth: Penguin, 1976), 42. For a more detailed discussion of various definitions of the genre, see my *The Autobiographical Novel of Co-Consciousness: Goncharov, Woolf, and Joyce* (Gainesville: University Press of Florida, 1994), 52–56.
16 Bruss, *Acts*, 8.
17 Spengemann, *Forms*, 122.
18 Avrom Fleishman, *Figures of Autobiography: The Language of Self-Writing* (Berkeley: University of California Press, 1983), 18–19.
19 Francis R. Hart, "Notes for an Anatomy of Modern Autobiography," *New Literary History* 1 (1969–1970): 485. "Design" and "truth" are in reference to Roy Pascal's pioneering work *Design and Truth in Autobiography* (Cambridge: Harvard University Press, 1960).
20 Robert Alter, "Nabokov and Memory," *Partisan Review*, 58 (1991): 627.
21 *NG*, 21.
22 Alfred Appel, Jr, "Conversations with Nabokov," *Novel* 4 (1971): 214. While most of the interview is reprinted in *Strong Opinions* this part was curiously omitted.
23 See Stephen Spender, *Journals 1939–1983*, ed. John Goldsmith (New York: Random, 1986).
24 John N. Morris, *Versions of the Self: Studies in English Autobiography from John Bunyan to John Stuart Mill* (New York: Basic Books, 1966), 3, 6.
25 Andrew Field, *Nabokov: His Life in Art* (Boston: Little, Brown, 1967), 36.
26 A. O. J. Cockshut, *The Art of Autobiography in Nineteenth- and Twentieth-Century England* (New Haven: Yale University Press, 1984), 95.
27 Jerome Hamilton Buckley, *The Turning Key: Autobiography and the Subjective Impulse since 1800* (Cambridge: Harvard University Press, 1984), 39–40.
28 Georges Nivat, "*Speak, Memory*," in *The Garland Companion to Vladimir Nabokov*, ed. Vladimir Alexandrov (New York: Garland, 1995), 683.
29 This passage was a later addition to the autobiography and thus is not found in *Conclusive Evidence*.
30 Kazin, "Autobiography as Narrative," 214.
31 Richard N. Coe, *When The Grass Was Taller: Autobiography and the Experience of Childhood* (New Haven: Yale University Press, 1984), 1.
32 Coe's stunning lack of interest in Nabokov, whose autobiography refuses to conform to the critic's more conventional notions of what a portrayal of a childhood should read like, is further underscored by the wrong patronymic he gives him in the index, confusing Nabokov with his father, Vladimir Dmitrievich Nabokov; see Coe, *When the Grass Was Taller*, 309.

33 John Pilling, *Autobiography and Imagination: Studies in Self-Scrutiny* (London: Routledge, 1981), 105.
34 William Wordsworth, "Ode: Intimations of Immortality From Recollections of Early Childhood," st. 1, ll. 1–9.
35 Boyd, *American Years*, 507.
36 Yury Olesha, *No Day Without a Line*, trans. and ed. Judson Rosengrant (Ann Arbor: Ardis, 1979), 35–36. (Hereafter *NDWL*.)
37 In *Conclusive Evidence*, it is "a sensitive youth," not a "chronophobiac."

CHAPTER 3

The near-tyranny of the author: Pale Fire
Maurice Couturier

Few contemporary novels have continued to baffle readers for so long as Nabokov's *Pale Fire*, an authentic *tour de force*. Joyce's *Ulysses* has, from the start, teased the annotators to elucidate the many linguistic and intertextual enigmas it teems with, and challenged critics from all walks of academia to provide inspired interpretations, but it remains largely open structurally and encourages the reader to appropriate it creatively and to apply to it the methodological grids at his disposal. One might say that *Ulysses*, which has proven to be an inexhaustible source of high-flown gnoses, is reader-friendly, whereas *Pale Fire*, more than a generation after its first publication, remains durably reader-resistant. The latest row in 1997–98 on the electronic Nabokov Forum (NABOKV-L) over the question of who invented whom in the novel bears evidence that, no matter how many of its so-called secrets have been cracked, it remains as disturbing as it was when it first came out, as if its author, before departing upon his aeonian crusade on Anti-Terra, had safely locked it in a poetic belt and catapulted the key into inter-galactic space on his way.

Since Mary McCarthy's celebrated "Bolt from the Blue," each new exegete who has tried to tackle this difficult novel, the present one included, has paused more or less as a lucky space-traveler who would have stumbled upon the magic key, until someone came around and told him or her that he or she had obviously brought back the wrong key, since the belt – the text – remained hermetically locked. The first article I published on Nabokov some twenty-three years ago dealt precisely with this novel;[1] and so did, in large part, the paper I read behind the Iron Curtain in 1977.[2] Looking back upon the obstinate research that I have been carrying out on the modern novel these last twenty-five years, I realize that, all the time, I have been trying to find that devilish key, perhaps in a hopeless attempt to outwit Nabokov. This acknowledgment, too painfully reminiscent of Kinbote's arrogance, is unlikely to gain approval among fellow Nabokovians, I fear; but having undertaken to deconstruct the mechanisms of bad faith, I prefer to show my cards (or should I say "my map," both words being translations of the word *"carte"* in French?) right away, especially as the present essay constitutes a report of my latest, hopefully my last, expedition into the intergalactic space separating Kinbote's Zembla from Shade's Sybilland.

Beyond the ludic view of the text promoted by Mary McCarthy, Robert Alter, Julia Bader, and many others, myself included, beyond Page Stegner's Kinbotian interpretation, or Andrew Field or Brian Boyd's Shadean reading of the novel, there is room, I propose, for a third, intratextual (and mildly intersubjective) approach which balances one text, one text-based author, against the other, and allows the reader-critic to free himself from the real author's hold on his text without running the risk of emulating Kinbote's unscholarly stance. This approach, which is in no way based on intentionality,[3] implies that one overlook Nabokov's statements concerning his novel (at first, at least) and test the various reading contracts proposed in the text itself, and that one pay close attention to the various elements of overdetermination which bespeak the desire of the real author as "dictator" and constitute paradoxical and problematic points of contact between real author and real reader, the only genuine subjects, beyond the narrators and characters, involved in textual exchange.

Of the five main functions of literary criticism as I see them – formalist (linguistic, narratological, generic), genetic (biographical, historical), hermeneutic (mimetic, psychoanalytical, didactic, metaphysical, etc.), esthetic, and pragmatic (perlocutionary, affective ...)[4] – I am aware of putting more emphasis on the first, third, and fifth, than on the other two, though I realize that an intersubjective approach (any approach, perhaps) often leads one to cross borders. Since many of the misunderstandings between the exegetes of this difficult novel come, I am convinced, from a fuzzy definition of one's critical objectives, I felt it necessary to take these methodological precautions before launching upon my textual quest, my eventual goal being to analyze the reader's response to the author's "tyranny," and to propose a possible strategy, based on psychoanalysis (which, in the circumstances, may go all the way back to

Aristotle's catharsis), that will enable the reader-critic to free himself with profit and pleasure from the textual belt.[5]

THE READING CONTRACTS

Kinbote proposes a reading contract of the whole book in his "Foreword" when he advises the reader to consult the notes first "and then study the poem with their help, rereading them of course as he goes through its text, and perhaps, after having done with the poem, consulting them a third time so as to complete the picture."[6] Yet, this recommendation appears some sixteen pages into his Foreword in which he has crammed enough damning elements to make us doubt his words and laugh at his presumptions that assume unscholarly proportions when, in an oft-quoted aphorism, he claims that "for better or worse, it is the commentator who has the last word" (29 ["Foreword"]). It is because Kinbote appears as a disagreeable and arrogant character in this Foreword, and also because we tend to obey the law which intimates that we read a book page after page, that we naturally tend to disregard his recommendations and to read the book in the order in which it is presented.

There are a number of data provided by him, however, which have a favorable influence on the way we read the poem: the fact that the poet died the very day he ended or nearly ended his poem, that Kinbote virtually stole the manuscript, that the poet's wife wanted to retrieve it, that a campaign was launched about it on campus, etc. Before we even start reading the poem (at least the first time), we know that it has been the object of a petty feud between people struggling to appropriate it. This "battle of the poem" encourages us to read it with an open mind, without any of the preconceptions or prejudices that Kinbote and, indirectly, his opponents have tried to plant in us. This clever strategy, which contradicts the reading contract Kinbote was trying to impose in his Foreword, must indeed be attributed to a higher narrative instance. That is how, I suggest, the authorial figure appears for the first time in the novel: in the hiatus between Kinbote's restricted (and crazy) reading contract, which gives precedence to the commentary, and the more open contract which gives precedence to the poem, at least for the time being.

The poem does not seem, at first, to raise any problem in terms of narrative reliability: we take on trust everything it says about the poet himself, his parents, his wife, his daughter, his metaphysical views about death, his methods of composition and his esthetic theory. We blissfully absorb its lexical and specular virtuosity, we sympathize with the tortured parents who are painfully aware of their daughter's absence of a love life, with their grief after she commits suicide. As we do so, we totally overlook Kinbote's pretensions, nay his existence even, realizing that we are here in the presence of a highly sincere and sensitive man who needs to exorcise his fear of death and his affliction after his daughter's disappearance. At no time are we tempted to look up the annotations, having realized by now that Kinbote was much too unreliable to be trusted.

Indeed, we may be tempted to consider John Shade as the author's mouthpiece, or rather his ideal self, in view of the accepted fact that lyrical poetry is always the expression of the author's feelings, opinions or emotions. Yet, the poem is not signed "Vladimir Nabokov" but "John Shade," and since its thematics depend so much on the word games this name lends itself to, as in the very first line, for instance ("I was the shadow of the waxwing slain ..."), we gradually begin to view Shade as another persona, different – to what extent, we don't know – from the real author, but expressing opinions and feelings that the real author (narcissistic at heart, like all authors) would, we assume, readily make his own. Hence the impression that the authorial figure is hovering over the poem more authentically than it does over the Foreword, though that figure remains terribly elusive. So, it is not the text of the poem itself which raises any problem in terms of narrative contract but the fact that it is attributed to an "invented poet." Nabokov crosses the boundaries here (as he also does in *Lolita* and *Ada*) between two literary genres, lyrical poetry on the one hand and the modernist novel on the other: the poem expresses genuine feelings, intense emotions, but we are prompted to believe that those feelings and emotions are not those of the actual poet, Nabokov, but of one of his puppets. The authorial figure, whose hidden purpose and desires still remain inaccessible, looms larger than in the Foreword, because the literary genre involved here leaves less room for lying or simulating than does the critical genre mimicked in the Foreword.

The commentary lends itself to at least three, and probably four, simultaneous reading contracts. The first one, indirectly suggested by the Foreword, consists in identifying the traces of Kinbote's unreliability and megalomania, in viewing the text as a madman's delirious fantasy with no other purpose than to bolster a shaky identity. We take it almost for granted that the commentary has nothing to do, or practically nothing to do, with the poem, that it is the invention of a madman, a parasitic text only tangentially related to Shade's poem – a text somewhat similar to Daniel Paul Schreber's *Denkwürdigkeiten eines nervenkranken* which Freud analyzed in a 1911 article. This reading contract will be given additional legitimacy when Professor Botkin appears in a parenthesis, one step behind Professor Pnin: "Speaking of the Head of the bloated Russian Department, Professor Pnin, a regular martinet in regard to his underlings (happily, Professor Botkin, who taught in another department, was not subordinated to that grotesque 'perfectionist')" (155 [line 172 n.]). The name's spurious etymology had been parenthetically mentioned earlier ("one who makes bottekins, fancy footwear" [100]); it becomes a common noun later in an oblique reference to Shakespeare (220 [line 493 n.]). The autotextual reference (that is, the reference to Nabokov's previous novel) has rarely been exploited in the study of *Pale Fire*. In *Pnin*, there are two conjuring tricks: firstly, the heterodiegetic narrator is supplanted by a homodiegetic one who was once Pnin's rival; and, secondly, the protagonist is supplanted professionally by Cockerell who, despite the fact that he is represented in the third person till the end, seems to be the most likely (and the least likeable because the most prejudiced) homodiegetic narrator. This game of substitution is carried on from *Pnin* to *Pale Fire*; it is in fact one of Nabokov's most consistent narrative ploys, from *Despair* to *The Real Life of Sebastian Knight* and *Lolita*. Amorous rivalry of one kind or the other is often at the root of this game.

The second reading contract turns the commentary into a fable, not unlike a medieval romance, which contains some elements of suspense, not the least of which concerns the dénouement, that is, the way this incredible story will merge with Kinbote's American "reality." From this perspective, the commentary contains a gothic story in reverse. Whereas, in a gothic story, the narrative takes its roots in reality and gradually grades into the supernatural, the story here starts as a sheer fantasy but gradually becomes anchored in reality as the King (and later Gradus himself) leaves implausible Zembla, travels across reality's antechamber (that is, Western Europe), and parachutes down to earthy America. In accordance with this contract, suggested as early as the Foreword ("imagine a historical personage whose knowledge of money is limited to the abstract billions of a national debt; imagine an exiled prince" [17 ("Foreword")]), we believe or feign to believe that Kinbote is indeed Charles Xavier, King of Zembla; after all, romances and novels contain many implausible stories and it does not occur to us to question their "truth" as stories. Paradoxically, it is Shade's poem, firmly anchored as it is in modern-day America, which prevents us from sticking throughout to this reading contract. Kinbote cannot be both Shade's colleague and neighbor and the deposed King of Zembla – unless, of course, we assume that he has invented Shade and written the poem himself, but this reductionist interpretation does not do justice to the virtuosity of the text, as I am trying to show. We are led to conclude that the story told in the commentary cannot be true to facts the way the story told in the poem probably was; nonetheless, we gradually consider that, no matter how implausible it may be, it is far more exciting and imaginative than Shade's own banal story. We are even tempted to consider Kinbote's imagination as stronger than Shade's.

The third reading contract is the one openly proposed by Kinbote himself, namely that the notes offer a more or less enlightening commentary on Shade's poem. Having previously read the foreword, we are now strongly biased against Kinbote who reasserts his pretensions in the first note: "Incidentally, it is curious to note that a crested bird called in Zemblan *sampel* ('silktail') . . ." (73 [lines 1–4 n.]). It is all too obvious that he is trying to foist his Zemblan allegorical interpretation of the poem upon us. In the second note, he avails himself of a variant, unreferenced in the index, to launch the king's story proper; later, however, he will confess that the two lines in the variant "are distorted and tainted by wistful thinking," but he will refuse to erase them, alleging the following reasons: "I could strike them out before publication but that would mean reworking the entire note, or at least a considerable part of it, and I have no time for such stupidities" (227–28 [line 550 n.]). Indeed, striking them out would not simply mean "reworking the entire note" but canceling out the whole saga which largely hangs upon this very tenuous thread.

Kinbote gives us, indeed, enough elements to question his sanity and to consider him as an unscrupulous critic who wants to smuggle the King's story (or his own fantasy) into Shade's poem, stealing the latter in the process. But what if he can prove that the poem is a metaphorical rendering of the King's story? There are indeed plenty of echoes between the poem (not only the variants) and the commentary which the critics have patiently tabulated and which gradually suggest that Kinbote's pretensions may not be as extravagant as they seemed at first. I will take only one example which I analyzed in my 1976 article: the poetic parallel between the opening lines of the poem and the "limpid tintarron" passage of the commentary. Through the waxwing parable, John Shade represents the suicide of Narcissus, the waxwing dying at the very moment when it meets its reflection in the windowpane; the poet, borrowing its wings phoenix-like, pursues the fatal trajectory, and duplicates himself and his furniture outside on the grass or the snow: "The windowpane is no longer a cutting edge: it does not separate life from death, day from night, but makes for greater fluidity of the inside and the outside, of the 'real' and the imaginary."[7] This windowpane, as I suggested then, is more or less a replica of the printed page as an interface between the elusive author and the inquisitive reader who seeks to make contact with him, the dead waxwing representing as it were the absent and dead author who, from his distant nothingness, continues to assert his law upon us and therefore upon Shade as well, though to a lesser degree.

This beautiful opening is magically reflected by Kinbote in his commentary when he describes the King's fleeting confrontation with one of his conniving impersonators:

In its limpid tintarron he saw his scarlet reflection but, oddly enough, owing to what seemed to be at first blush an optical illusion, this reflection was not at his feet but much further; moreover, it was accompanied by the ripple-warped reflection of a ledge that jutted high above his present position. And finally, the strain on the magic of the image caused it to snap as his redsweatered, red-capped doubleganger turned and vanished, whereas he, the observer, remained immobile. He now advanced to the very lip of the water and was met there by a genuine reflection, much larger and clearer than the one that had deceived him. (143 [line 149 n.])

The word "tintarron," a rare noun in English, is presented as a Zemblan word in the index: "a precious glass stained a deep blue, made in Bokay, a medieval place in the mountains of Zembla" (314 ["Index"]). This passage suggests, indeed, that Zembla is a metaphorical representation of the more ordinary world represented poetically in Shade's poem. This passage as a whole magically reflects the opening lines of the poem, the receding images of the

King mirroring the receding images of Shade and his furniture in the poem; it appears in the note to line 171 which refers to the "great conspiracy" concerning "the truth / About survival after death" (39), which suggests that this specular game, like the one described in the opening lines, refers not to death as a tragedy of loss, but to death as the extinction of the self.

Such beautiful passages – and there are many more in the commentary – induce the reader to disregard the referential value of Kinbote's commentary and to privilege its imaginary and poetic value on a par with the poem which, at first, it simply seemed to caricature. This interpretation leads us to adopt a fourth reading contract: to test the commentary against the poem and the poem against the commentary, not only in terms of poetic value, however, but also in terms of reference: if there are so many echoes between the poem and the commentary, is it because Kinbote playfully (poetically?) drew upon the poem's most tenuous suggestions to invent his extravagant saga, or because Shade could not help echoing the story Kinbote was telling him at the time when he was composing his poem? Both interpretations are acceptable, in my view. The first one would probably imply that Kinbote/Botkin, far from being only a megalomaniac or a madman, is also and above all a gifted writer in his own right; the second would naturally be less in his favor. Having no way to decide which of these two interpretations is correct, and being rather inclined to accept them both at the same time, I play one text against the other as if they were mirror images of each other and try to recompose them, to "refigure" them as Paul Ricoeur would put it, as one single text reflecting one single authorial figure.

METATEXTUALITY

This twin-faced interpretation, which eventually conflates all the three reading contracts of the commentary mentioned above, amounts to putting Shade on the same level, both as protagonist and "narrator," as Kinbote himself, and to view *Pale Fire* as a highly elaborate metatextual novel in the tradition of *Pamela*, *Bleak House*, or *The Sound and the Fury*, to mention only a few. The metatextual novel, like the fragmented novel *à la* Beckett, is a highly daunting text which forces the reader to enter its black box and compels him to try and recompose or refigure it in an attempt to free himself from it.

But there are sometimes inconsistencies in the text which providentially allow us to make contact with the author as a fallible craftsman. Such is the case in *Pamela*, for instance. The editor who, in the preface, had listed the reasons which had induced him to publish this collection of letters, does not disappear completely from the text once the exchange of letters begins but continues to intervene throughout the novel. The first time he allows his voice to be heard is in a long footnote following a poem which begins as follows:

Here it is necessary the reader should know, that when Mr B. found Pamela's virtue was not to be subdued, and he had in vain tried to conquer his passion for her, he had ordered his Lincolnshire coachman to bring his travelling chariot from thence, in order to prosecute his base designs upon the innocent virgin; for he cared not to trust his Bedfordshire coachman, who, with the rest of the servants, so greatly loved and honoured the fair damsel.[8]

As all the letters which had been exchanged since the opening of the book had been written by either Pamela or by her parents, there was apparently no other way for the author to inform the reader of Mr. B.'s evil design and of his intention to sequestrate Pamela. It is in the above footnote that we learn how Mr. B. intercepts Pamela's letters and that we are given to read the letter he sent to her father; after Mr. B.'s letter, the footnote continues with another letter written by Pamela and addressed to Mrs. Jervis. Richardson was unable to stick to the narrative contract he had adopted at the start and felt it necessary to give his reader information no other plausible letter-writer could have provided. Later, the epistolary scheme will turn into a mere diary, Pamela being unable to communicate with her parents anymore.

As this obvious example shows, it is when the narrative contract changes that the authorial figure, the author's desire to guide his reader, appears in the text. In *Pale Fire*, there are indeed many more narrative contracts at work than in *Pamela* but they are so cleverly combined that it is difficult, often impossible, to pinpoint the exact moment when a shift is made. Let us list these contracts again:
- the commentary (Foreword included) is a madman's fantasy with no other purpose than to bolster a shaky identity
- the commentary is a fable, no less extravagant than many medieval romances

- the notes offer a more or less enlightening commentary of Shade's poem
- commentary and poem are mirror images of each other

Each contract implies a different relationship between Shade and Kinbote:
- in the first, Kinbote is the madman and Shade the sane man
- in the second, Kinbote's text is an inflated, referentless fable, whereas Shade's poem is a lyrical text which takes its roots in the poet's life and experience
- in the third, the poem takes precedence over the commentary, and therefore the poet over his commentator
- in the fourth one, which conflates the previous three, poem and commentary, poet and commentator are more or less on the same level, the authorial figure looming prominently over the novel as a whole

In all four readings, the intratextual writers take precedence over their respective texts, defining themselves as they do in terms of their opposition to each other. Here are some of the main points on which they radically differ:
- Kinbote is a homosexual, Shade a heterosexual
- Kinbote is left-handed, Shade right-handed
- Kinbote had many lovers, Shade only one
- Kinbote is childless, Shade has a daughter
- Kinbote is a Christian, Shade an agnostic
- Kinbote is a music lover, Shade is not
- Kinbote is a vegetarian, Shade is not
- Kinbote is tall and erect, Shade short and twisted
- Kinbote is athletic, Shade is clumsy
- Kinbote is bearded, Shade is clean-shaven ...

On the other hand, they also have many points in common, as Michael Long pointed out: "Shade and Kinbote are both liberal in opinion. Both are haters of violence. Both are lovers of literature. Both are scorners of orthodoxy. Both are scholars of a sort and poets of a sort. Both love wine and word-games. Each has his own kind of arrogance and irascibility, and his own little bundle of Strong Opinions, on trivial matters as well as serious ones."[9] Bringing all these things together, Long concludes: "Their deepest points of contact have to do with the centre of the Nabokovian world," and he points out, for instance, that they both "lost their fathers in infancy."[10] Long, who only refers to the "centre of the Nabokovian world," refrains in part from surrendering to intentional fallacy; his interpretation remains text-based rather than biography-based, but it presupposes that the text contains elements whose roots are grounded in the real author.

If we now put together the many reading contracts that can be applied to the commentary and, indirectly, to the whole novel, as well as the similarities and dissimilarities between Shade and Kinbote, we begin to realize that we have been the victims of an illusion, the illusion that the text is inhabited by two full-fledged subjects who are both endowed with an individual unconscious. In point of fact, I would suggest, these two text-based subjects reflect two complementary facets of one single but schizoid subject who is preoccupied with his sexual identity and with death, and who tries to unburden himself of these obsessions by generating a kind of paranoia in us, hoping to divert our attention from himself, the primary enunciator of the text. It is this partially reconstructed subject with his conflicting desires and inhibitions but also with his virtuosity in composing such a poetic and intricately woven text, that I call the authorial figure. It is the evocation of this figure that allows me to shift from a formalist description of the text in terms of contracts to an interpretation in terms of desire, and thus to get out of the black box of the text. So long as I remain within the text, I am merely describing the novel but remain unable to interpret it. Shade and Kinbote are not the prime enunciators of the text but the author's paradoxical masks. Interpreting the text requires that we identify the author's desire to impose the tyrannical law of his ideal self upon us and his determination to prevent us from having access to his unconscious self.

THE AUTHORIAL FIGURE

There is in fact nothing revolutionary in this communication-based approach to fiction and fiction-writing. In *Tristram Shandy*, Sterne humorously explained that writing is a form of conversation:

Writing, when properly managed (as you may be sure I think mine is) is but a different name for conversation: As no one, who knows what he is about in good company would venture to talk all, – so no author, who understands the just boundaries of decorum and good breeding, would presume to think all. The truest respect which you can pay to the reader's understanding, is to halve this matter amicably, and leave him something to imagine, in his turn, as well as yourself.[11]

There is, perhaps, no better presentation of a truly intersubjective theory of the novel: the matter must be "halved ... amicably" between the author and the reader; if the writer is too complacent and does not make sufficient attempts to communicate with his reader, the book will remain a kind of unread and unreadable blank, as some of Beckett's later texts, like "Ping," are; if, on the other hand, the reader does not do his share of the work, the book will remain an intimidating or a boring puzzle. To be sure, there are large differences between oral and literary communication, as Marshall McLuhan and Walter Ong have pointed out, but the similarities are important, too. In daily conversation the speaker can monitor his discourse upon the verbal and non-verbal reactions of his interlocutor; each, though, strives to free himself from the other's law while trying to promote the best possible image of himself in the other's eyes. They both labor under the law of the Lacanian Other of which they, each in turn, claim to be the interpreters when passing judgment on their interlocutor's discourse. In a conversation between two lovers, each speaker addresses the other's ideal ego, an attitude which naturally fosters an illusion of fusion and identification and gives the lovers the impression that they have freed themselves from the law of the Other; they are mistaken, of course, since, as Lacan intimates, the Other also orders the subjects to desire, if only to play their role in the perpetuation of the race.

Textual exchange is, in many respects, a conflation of oral and literary exchange,[12] a form of communication in which the two interlocutors, the author and the reader, both love and hate each other, both passionately depend upon each other but also resent the other's intervention which can lead to dramatic disclosures. They are never face to face, except in such exceptional situations as poetry readings. The author has no other instruments at his disposal than those ciphered into his text to guide or mislead his reader, even though, at times, as we shall later see in the case of Nabokov, he makes belated attempts to put his reader on the "right" or the "wrong" track in his non-fictional pronouncements. And the reader, wary of the intrinsic differences in terms of truth and sincerity between fictional and non-fictional discourse,[13] cannot ask him any question, supposing he was in a position to; neither can he summon biographical data, which, if they might provide a genetic explanation of the text, would not guarantee the legitimacy of one's interpretation of it. The author asserts his superiority over his reader, adopting a one-up position, as Gregory Bateson's disciples' would put it.[14] But, as he tries to indulge his desires, to gain admiration and promote the best possible image of himself (three contradictory priorities, as it were), he unmistakably feels that he is surrendering too much of himself and exposing himself to the analyses that will be proposed by his readers. The complex narrative strategies used in modernist and post-modernist fiction serve all these contradictory purposes at one and the same time: they dazzle the reader and make him wish to commune with the magician who invented them, but they also constitute shrewd denials and indirectly invite the reader to decipher the unwritten, somewhat guilty, pages of the text, and to play the part of the compassionate or complicitous analyst. The reader resents the authorial law ciphered into the text; he would like to appropriate the literary object and use it as the lame depository of his intellectual, aesthetic, or erotic desire, but, if he does not want to be an impostor and purloin the text as Kinbote purloins Shade's text, he must refrain from indulging himself too much in that way. It is in this complex interplay of desires and challenges that the web of the text which Barthes writes about in *The Pleasure of the Text* is woven. A novel is an interface that brings together and keeps apart the author and the reader, compelling them to change places all the time and to enter the black box of the text.

Why speak of the authorial figure, though? And wouldn't it be simpler to speak only of the real author? To me, the real author is a dead subject who once desired and created works of art, and whom the text represents here for me in my act of reading. Biographical criticism attempts to resurrect the dead author and to read the text as he meant it, without taking into acount the fact that the subject is inevitably cleft (he is the subject of his unconscious, to borrow Lacan's theory) and therefore capable of bad faith. Formalist criticism is aware of this bad faith, though it makes little use of it, but it refuses to take into account the author's will to say, seeking to establish the meaning-within-a-given-interpretative-grid of the text; it largely depends, therefore, on the methodological tools it mobilizes: literary conventions, narratology, intertextuality, linguistics, etc.

The two chief anchorings of critical reading are indeed, as Wolfgang Iser claims, the text and the reader as signifying subject.[15]

Yet, whereas Iser considers the text as a disembodied signifying object, I consider it as an interface between two subjects, separated temporally and spatially, who passionately desire each other, seeking, and running away from, each other at one and the same time. It is this meshing of desires that I would totally miss were I to propose a purely formalist analysis of the text; the analysis would betray my intellectual desire to master the restive object, but it would speak less of the author's ciphered desire than of the semiotic grid used for the purpose. Meaning, in a literary text, cannot be an ideal, disembodied object: it is necessarily a meaning for a subject who, within the black box of a novel, can temporarily be a character or a narrator. Reading a novel requires therefore that the instances in which the transitional meanings are anchored be identified.

Those instances being themselves embedded at various levels, as I have shown throughout *La Figure de l'auteur*,[16] one eventually reaches the authorial instance which is not at all Booth's implied author. That concept was invented precisely in order to keep the real author totally out of the text: it is invoked mostly in reference to third-person novels where there is no intratextual enunciator; the homodiegetic narrators in novels like *Tristram Shandy*, *Lolita*, or *Pale Fire* are considered therefore as the ultimate enunciators, which, naturally, they are not. It is a fuzzy concept which has neither narratological, nor linguistic, nor psychological foundation. The authorial figure, on the other hand, is an enunciation-based construct: it is the prime enunciator of the text as reconstructed by the reader in the act of reading. This reconstruction depends on various elements of the text: some are linguistic, others narratological, others again thematic. The authorial figure takes its roots in the over-determination of the text on the one hand, and, on the other hand, in the analytic work done by the reader and the chords that the themes of the text strike in him, which naturally (and fortunately) leaves room for misunderstanding. The author's insistence upon over-determining his text and promoting the reader's aesthetic admiration, as well as his need to make of it an efficient screen to keep the reader at a safe distance, lead him to project his ideal self onto the text. It is the ideal self's desire (the ideal self being always to some extent the reversed image of the unconscious, as Freud pointed out) that the reader identifies and that allows him to start constructing the authorial figure – a figure who, from the reader's perhaps limited point of view, stands here and now for the real author who is absent or dead.

The authorial figure, being reader-based, can naturally be at variance with the real author, either because, in his reading practice, the reader has overlooked important clues and allowed his desires and fantasies to overrule the text, or because the author managed after all to fool his ideal self. The latter possibility is much less plausible: no matter how imaginative and poetically inventive a writer may be, it is most unlikely that he could project into his work a self and therefore an unconscious totally disconnected from his own, though he can distribute it in various ways among his fictional characters or narrators, as Freud explained in a lecture given in 1907: "The psychological novel in general no doubt owes its special nature to the inclination of the modern writer to split up his ego, by self-observation, into many part-egos, and, in consequence, to personify the conflicting currents of his own mental life in several heroes."[17]

The evocation of the "Viennese witch doctor" may sound sacrilegious, considering Nabokov's countless forays against him, but, in my view, this approach is the only way to get out of the black box of the text, to avoid being forever bogged down in the marshes of description (and annotation), and therefore to free oneself from the author's tyranny. Nabokov was right, of course, to denounce many of the gross simplifications that psychoanalysis has been guilty of, but he shared many of Freud's preoccupations as the superb psychological acumen that he displays throughout his fiction testifies. It is Freud's theory of the unconscious, of course, that he rejected, being passionately convinced that he exerted full control over himself and his literary inventions; and he certainly did, more than most writers, but his obsessions, sexual and otherwise, show that he had a powerful unconscious and a very creative one (thank goodness for that), and that he was using his marvelous talent to cope with it. After dealing with nympholepsy in *Lolita*, he dealt with homosexuality in *Pale Fire*, and with incest in *Ada*. I personally interpret his clever narrative ploy in all three novels both as a strategy to confuse his readers by putting them in a paradoxical situation and as an attempt to blind them to his intense preoccupation with the question of sexual identity, which is central to these three masterpieces and many of his other novels. This interpretation, if it accounts for the complexity of the text as a mask and allows one to free oneself from its black box by cracking the Shade–Kinbote enigma, does not in any way reduce the magnitude of the author's achievement. Nabokov's (near)-tyranny or aesthetic desire was, I presume, proportional to the intensity of his erotic desire, but this conviction, grounded in psychoanalysis as much as in my refusal to surrender to the intentional fallacy, does not entitle me in any way to shout "Eureka!" and to claim that I have discovered *the* meaning of the text, the Shade–Kinbote enigma being only one element – though very important – of this clever novel.[18] The concept of the authorial figure, based on an interactive theory of the text, provides, I think, a useful key to solve some of the problems that the critics have been asking themselves since Forster, Lubbock, Booth, Barthes, Genette, and Stanzel, and that contemporary theoreticians like Iser, Banfield, and Fludernik still attempt to tackle. It does not replace previous theories but neatly complements them by showing that author and reader belong to the same system and try to negotiate their respective places.

POSTSCRIPTS

Indirectly, Nabokov himself demonstrates that the text of his novel is not entirely self-sufficient. Besides the references to poet John Shade elsewhere in his writings, in the unpublished introduction mentioned by Boyd or again in *Ada*, he made a number of declarations about *Pale Fire* in his letters and interviews which confirm his desire to guide or influence his reader further as if he wished to amend or to complete his text. He claimed, for instance, in a letter written a few months before the publication of *Pale Fire*, that the "commentary *is* the novel" (*SL*, 332). How does Shade's poem fit in the book? He does not explain. Perhaps he means that the plot of the book is hatched in the commentary and the commentary only, but, to be sure, it depends a great deal upon the existence of the poem itself, as I have tried to show in my presentation of the four reading contracts. This aside suggests that Nabokov himself, Frankenstein-like, was not too sure how to consider his own book and wondered whether his creation had not started to have a life of its own that he could not fully control any longer.

There are two main enigmas in the novel that no one had been able to solve until Nabokov pointed out the solution. To Alfred Appel's question, "Where, please, are the crown jewels hidden?" Nabokov answered tongue in cheek: "In the ruins, sir, of some old barracks near Kobaltana (q.v.); but do not tell it to the Russians"

(*SO*, 92). Kobaltana appears in the index but in a cryptic entry which ends with the words: "not in the text" (310). In this case, the author has clearly been playing a little game with the reader, taking him on a merry-go-round of cross-references, and prompting him to look for "fictitious" jewels as if they were real ones. He is as unreliable in this case as Humbert Humbert was when he discovered from Lolita the name of his rival but flippantly declined to tell us, claiming that we must have guessed long ago. Nabokov clearly wants us to believe that he is the one and only keeper of the book's secret.

The same reasoning would apply in the case of the coded message taken down by Hazel Shade in the barn. Many "translations" had been proposed by the critics but none were as satisfactory as the one given by Nabokov himself to Andrew Field on September 26, 1966:

> As Nabokov has noted privately, the message can be decoded as a garbled warning via Hazel "to her father and hint at the title of the poem to be written many years later. *Padre* should *not go* to the *lane* to be mistaken for *old Goldswart* (worth) after finishing his *tale* (pale) *feur* (fire) [which in Shakespeare is accompanied by] the word 'arrant' (*farant*) [and this] with '*lant*' makes up the Atalanta butterfly in Shade's last scene. It is '*told*' by the spirit in the barn."[19]

Curiously, Field does not communicate this information to his reader as if he were afraid that Nabokov was pulling his leg. The message makes sense, however, but, as far as I know, there is no built-in code in the novel that could have allowed us to decipher it. Of course, we may wonder if the whole passage is not Kinbote's invention rather than Hazel's transcription, which prompts us to resume the annotation game within the black box. Nabokov made another remark concerning Kinbote which projects us outside the limits of the book:

> I think it is so nice that the day on which Kinbote committed suicide (and he certainly did after putting the last touches to his edition of the poem) happens to be both the anniversary of Pushkin's *Lyceum* and that of "poor old man Swift"'s death, which is news to me (but see variant in note to line 231). (*SO*, 74–75)

He did not mean to refer to Pushkin or Swift, but he did mean to say that Kinbote committed suicide on October 19, the date on which, we assume, the demented commentator finished his Foreword and his editorial work.

Should Nabokov's statements about his novel be taken seriously? Or wouldn't they constitute another facet of the demented mask games that he plays with us in his fiction? Deception, as he explains to Allene Talmey in one of his interviews, is as essential to his art as it is to nature:

> Deception is practiced even beautifully by that other V. N., Visible Nature. A useful purpose is assigned by science to animal mimicry, protective patterns and shapes, yet their refinement transcends the crude purpose of mere survival. In art, an individual style is essentially as futile and as organic as a fata morgana. The slight-of-hand you mention is hardly more than an insect's sleight-of-wing. A wit might say that it protects me from half-wits. A grateful spectator is content to applaud the grace with which the masked performer melts into Nature's background. (*SO*, 153)

Shade apparently shares his view on the subject; he says to Kinbote: "when I hear a critic speaking of an author's sincerity I know that either the critic or the author is a fool" (156 [l. 172 n.]).

In all his postscripts to the novel, Nabokov continues to play with us, but he also claims emphatically that the reader will never be able to crack all the novel's secrets without his help, that he is or has the final key that can open all the doors. He obviously wants to make sure that we will never be able to get out of the black box of the text and have access to his desire and his real self behind or beyond the text. These afterthoughts, no matter how much they owe to Nabokov's forethoughts, only confirm the interpretation I have proposed in the present essay: they show the author trying to reassert his authority over us and confirm his total control over his text and his masks; indirectly, also, they betray his doubts about his sanity and his sexual identity. In his last novel, *Look at the Harlequins!*, he was to undertake a last titanic struggle against one of his caricatural doubles, ending his text upon a gaping sentence or a snore.

NOTES

1 Maurice Couturier, "Nabokov's *Pale Fire*, or the Purloined Poem," *Revue Française d'Etudes Américaines*, 1 (April 1976): 55–69.
2 See "The Subject on Trial in Nabokov's Novels" in *Proceedings of a Symposium on American Literature*, ed. Marta Sienecka (Poznan University Press, 1980). That symposium, which took place in September 1977, was the first on American literature to be held behind the Iron Curtain.
3 At the second Nice conference on Nabokov, David Lodge accused Brian Boyd of intentional fallacy in his interpretation of *Pale Fire*. See David Lodge, "What Kind of Fiction did Nabokov Write? A Practitioner's View," *Cycnos* 12.2 (1995): 142–43, and *The Practice of Writing*

(London: Secker & Warburg, 1996), 162. The problem of "intentionality" is obviously very complex and cannot be as easily shrugged off as it could a generation ago.
4   I am currently preparing a book in which I examine the endless crossovers between these five functions.
5   The title of this article is of course an oblique reference to the subtitle of my second book on Nabokov, *Nabokov ou la tyrannie de l'auteur* (Paris: Ed. du Seuil, "Coll. Poétique," 1993).
6   *Pale Fire* (New York: Vintage International, 1989), 28, ("Foreword"). All subsequent citations appear in the text.
7   Couturier, "Nabokov's *Pale Fire*, or the Purloined Poem," 58.
8   Samuel Richardson, *Pamela* (Harmondsworth: Penguin Books, 1980), 123.
9   Michael Long, *Marvell, Nabokov: Childhood and Arcadia* (Oxford: Clarendon Press, 1984), 181.
10 *Ibid.*
11 Laurence Sterne, *Tristram Shandy* (1760–67; Boston: Houghton Mifflin Co., 1965), 83.
12 Monika Fludernik largely confirms this theory in her recent book, *Towards a 'Natural' Narratology* (London and New York: Routledge, 1996). She does not include the author in the enunciative game, however.
13 A point cleverly analyzed by Peter Lamarque and Stein Haugom Olsen in *Truth, Fiction and Literature* (Oxford: Clarendon Press, 1994), 11–14.
14 See Paul Watzlawick, et al., *Pragmatics of Human Communication* (New York and London: W. W. Norton and Co., 1967), 67ff.
15 Wolfgang Iser, *The Act of Reading* (Baltimore: The Johns Hopkins University Press, 1978), 169.
16 See *La Figure de l'auteur* (Paris: Ed. du Seuil, "Coll. Poétique," 1993).
17 Sigmund Freud, "Creative Writers and Day-Dreaming," *Standard Edition of the Complete Psychological Works of Sigmund Freud*, ix (London: The Hogarth Press, 1959), 150.
18 See Geoffrey Green, *Freud and Nabokov* (Lincoln: University of Nebraska Press, 1988).
19 Quoted by Brian Boyd in *Vladimir Nabokov: The American Years* (Princeton University Press, 1991), 454.

CHAPTER 4

Jewish questions in Nabokov's art and life
Maxim D. Shrayer

> Man dieth, and wasteth away: yea, man giveth up the ghost, and where is he?
>
> Job 14:10
>
> What nonsense. Of course there is nothing afterwards.
>
> Nabokov, *The Gift*
>
> ...the brown wigs of tragic old women who had just been gassed.
>
> Nabokov, *Lolita*

INTRODUCTION

Although this essay will only consider two major novels and a short story, Jewish characters, as well as authorial reflections on anti-Semitism, appear in much of Nabokov's fiction.[1] In addition to a series of remarkable Jewish characters, Nabokov also populated his works with non-Jewish characters who exemplify an entire spectrum of attitudes toward the Jewish Other, from anti-Semitism to Philo-semitism. Nabokov's interest in the Jewish question increased gradually under the influence of his upbringing, his marriage, and his contacts with Russian-Jewish exiles. His Jewish themes had evolved in his Russian fictions by the early 1930s to reach a crescendo in his third American novel, *Pnin* (1957). These themes were intensified by the rise of Nazism and given their ultimate shape by the Holocaust. Jewish characters are assigned distinct functions in Nabokov's works. Faced with peripeties of exile and catastrophes of the modern age, they confront death, ponder the post-mortem realm, and model immortality. They also enjoy a special relationship with art and facilitate the process of writing. Finally, the deaths of Jewish characters in the Nazi Holocaust, as well as encounters with anti-Semitism, compel their non-Jewish friends to modify their ethical and metaphysical beliefs.

JEWISH QUESTIONS IN NABOKOV'S BIOGRAPHY

Nabokov's father, V. D. Nabokov, was an outspoken opponent of anti-Semitism in pre-1917 Russia, famous for his reporting on the Beilis trial (*SM*, 176 [ch. 9]).[2] In the Constitutional-Democratic Party (CD), his close comrades-in-arms were Jews: Iosif Gessen, Avgust Kaminka, and Maksim Vinaver. Nabokov reminisced in *Speak, Memory* (1966) that growing up he "[had gotten] quite used to the... cartoons which appeared from time to time – [his] father and Milyukov [the leader of the CD Party] handing over Saint Russia on a plate to World Jewry" (*SM*, 188 [ch. 9]). Prior to entering high school, one of Nabokov's tutors was Filipp Zelensky, a convert to Lutheranism like many Russian Jews trying to surpass anti-Semitic quotas. In 1911–17, Nabokov attended the cosmopolitan Tenishev School, where two of his close friends in high school were Jewish, Samuil Rosoff and Savely Grinberg (*SM*, 180–88).[3] The great Russian poet Osip Mandelshtam, a Jew by birth, studied at the Tenishev School in 1900–07.

In exile, much more so than in Russia itself, Nabokov got to know a wide-variety of Jewish characters and types, from penniless poets and philosophers to unbending *Geschäftmacher*. There were two main reasons for Nabokov's proximity to the Russian-Jewish community. One was historical: the high proportion of Jews among Russian expatriates. Russian Jews were active in émigré politics and education, and were particularly visible in publishing. Three figures among Russian-Jewish littérateurs were instrumental in launching Nabokov's literary career: Iosif Gessen who showcased Nabokov's early writing in Berlin's *Rul'* (The Rudder); the satirical poet Sasha Cherny who showed much kindness to the young Nabokov; Yuly Aikhenval'd who encouraged Nabokov's talent in reviews. Other notable Russian-Jewish littérateurs and intellectuals whom Nabokov came into contact with in Europe and America included Mark Aldanov, Il'ia Fondaminsky, Roman Grinberg, Abram Kagan, Solomon Krym, Grigory Landau, Sofiia Pregel', Anna Prismanova, Marc Szeftel, Savely Sherman (A. A. Savel'ev), Mark Tsetlin (Amari), Mark Vishniak. Russian by culture, some of the above converted to Christianity, others continued practicing Judaism, others yet were secularized but retained symbolic affiliations with Jewish traditions. In the United States, Nabokov befriended a number of Jewish academics, including Harry Levin and M. H. Abrams.

The second reason for Nabokov's heightened interest in the Jewish question was personal: his marriage in 1925 to Véra Slonim. Nabokov witnessed Russian anti-Semitism in his childhood and youth, ranging from his aunt's aristocratic condescension to his tutor's Jewish origins (*SM*, 160 [ch. 8]) to his Cambridge room-mate's trying to "foist upon him" a copy of *Protocols of The Elders of Zion*.[4] However, a marriage to a Jew truly opened Nabokov's eyes and awarded him a personal connection with the Jewish past and present. Although raised in St. Petersburg – in financial comfort and relative privilege as compared to the vast majority of Russia's Jews of the Pale – Véra Nabokov experienced anti-Semitism full well. Following the 1889 ukase barring Russia's Jews from practicing law, Véra's father Evsei Slonim refused to convert to Christianity and left the legal profession.[5]

Commentators both objective and racially biased emphasize that Véra's Jewishness had an impact on Nabokov's career. While some have regarded Véra as Nabokov's Jewish muse, others have charged her with ruining Nabokov's talent or converting him into an "un-Russian" author. Vengefully settling her scores with the Nabokovs, Zinaida Shakhovskoy wrote of Nabokov's talent "withering" under Véra's Jewish influence.[6] An émigré correspondent of Shakhovskoy emphatically described how shortly after his marriage, Nabokov had become "sovershenno *enjuive*" ("completely *Jewified*," my italics).[7] Encumbered as it is by a chronic lack of Nabokov's own statements concerning religious beliefs, the question of Véra's impact on Nabokov's faith is a rather complex one, deserving of a separate investigation. It would suffice to say here that Nabokov's marriage to a Jewish woman most likely completed the cycle of his separation from organized Christianity.

The marriage to a Jewish woman who, it seems, could not and would not embrace Christianity, most likely called for a practical compromise, resulting in a secular matrimony. As for Nabokov's metaphysics, the impact of his Jewish muse might have been such that by the end of the 1920s Nabokov had embraced a *sui generis* system of cosmological beliefs combining features of Old Testament monotheism and pantheism. Central to Nabokov's metaphysical vision is the existence of a timeless otherworldly realm that hosts idealized memories and provides personal immortality.[8] Also crucial for Nabokov's beliefs is the intuition that souls of the deceased inhabit a parallel world, communicate with the living, and participate in their lives.

While by the end of the 1920s, vestibules of any organized religion had become too narrow for Nabokov's talent and sensibility, he was far from indifferent to cultural history of religious ideas.[9] Just as his protagonist Krug in *Bend Sinister* (1947), Nabokov probably regarded Judaism and Christianity as a single religious continuum:

> Incidentally in one compact sentence [Krug] had referred to several religions (not forgetting that wonderful Jewish sect whose dream of the gentle young rabbi dying on the Roman *crux* had spread over all Northern lands), and had dismissed them together with ghosts and robolds. (*BS*, 193 [ch. 16])

What might have intrigued Nabokov in Judaic thought?

Much more so than other monotheistic religions, the development of Judaism from the Biblical period – through rabbinical writings, the Kabbalah, and Hasidism – to modern-day Jewish theology has been marked by an ongoing modification of the notions of the afterlife and immortality. In fact, Judaic notions of post-mortem survival are still in progress, and the second-half of the twentieth century witnessed a revival of Jewish metaphysics of the afterlife.[10] Before going any further, it is important to make one distinction. I am not speaking about Nabokov's interest in Judaism as a form of religious communal living. There is little doubt that Nabokov was just as indifferent to Jewish religious practices as he admittedly was to Christian or any other organized forms of worship. (In a 1964 interview, Nabokov spoke of his "indifference to organized mysticism, to the church – any church" [*SO*, 39].) I am, however, hypothesizing about a mediated impact of Judaic religious philosophy upon Nabokov's own models of post-mortem existence, the unique models that he cognized through and envisioned in his fictions.

Nabokov's wife became the lifelong source radiating Jewish traditions. Following his marriage, opposition to anti-Semitism became a leitmotif of Nabokov's living.[11] Living in Germany in the 1930s with a Jewish wife and a half-Jewish son, Nabokov observed the advent of Nazism, the Holocaust already in the making. Fleeing Germany for France in 1937, Nabokov had every reason to fear not only for his family's safety, but his own. In 1938, a repugnant anti-Semitic opus in Berlin's pro-Nazi *Novoe slovo* (New Word), placed Nabokov on the same (death) row with Russian-Jewish artists: "There, in the boiling pots, all those 'exercises' by the sirins [Sirin was Nabokov's pseudonym], the chagalls, the knuts, the burliuks [David Burliuk was often mistaken for a Jew], and hundreds of others will be cleansed entirely. And all those 'works of genius' will flow where flows all filth, opening the passage to fresh, national art."[12] Upon his arrival in the United States, Nabokov re-experienced the familiar anti-Semitic ways of a part of the émigré community: "A teacher of Russian at Columbia complimented him ... on his magnificent aristocratic pronunciation: 'All one hears here are Yids'."[13] Nabokov also tasted of the reticent social anti-Semitism of the Anglo-Saxon intelligentsia, as well as of the popular anti-Jewish sentiments, still visible in small-town America well into the 1950s (Boyd, *AY* 311; Field, *Nabokov: His Life in Part* 275).[14] Always watchful for hints of prejudice, he recoiled at restaurant signs "stipulating only 'gentile clientèle'."[15]

Finally, as a Russian émigré writer in Europe, Nabokov received assistance from Russian-Jewish patrons of the art.[16] The Nabokovs sailed to America on board a liner chartered by the Hebrew Immigrant Aid Society (HIAS). For the rest of his years, Nabokov remained grateful for the Jewish support. He made financial contributions to Jewish organizations.[17] He took a passionate interest in the Jewish state and rejoiced over the end of the Six-Day War: "I triumph now, saluting the marvelous victory of Israel."[18]

JEWISH QUESTIONS IN NABOKOV'S LITERARY WORKS

Death, religious conversion, anti-Semitism in The Gift

The Gift offers an in-depth investigation of major themes in Jewish history and thought. I shall examine four issues in the novel: conversion of Jews to Christianity; models of post-mortem survival; anti-Semitism; the impact of the protagonist's half-Jewish Muse.

One of the principal characters, Alexander Chernyshevski, goes insane after the suicide of his son Yasha in Weimar Berlin. Chernyshevski's Jewish grandfather is said to have been baptized and given his last name by a Russian Orthodox priest, the father of the prominent radical Nikolai G. Chernyshevski (1828–89). The fictional Chernyshevski suggests that the protagonist, Fyodor Godunov-Cherdyntsev, write a biography of the historical Chernyshevski. Both husband and wife Chernyshevski try to orient the protagonist toward writing about their family lore, and he worries that in addition to Chernyshevski's biography, he would be "cornered" to undertake a "long short story depicting [their son's] fate" (*Gift*, 40 [ch. 1]).

For Alexander Chernyshevski, as for many more Jews who were converted to Christianity, the acquired religion amounted to an illusory ticket to mainstream Gentile society.[19] Culturally a Russian, and spiritually an agnostic, the exile Chernyshevski hovers between his ancestral Judaic past and his assimilated and displaced present. Despite a seemingly materialist and secularist orientation of his ideas, he becomes the author's agent for exploring the metaphysics of death. The loss of his son plunges Chernyshevski into despair and mental illness. At first he believes that his son exists in some parallel world. Ironically, Godunov-Cherdyntsev, who mourns the loss of his own father, is not indifferent to the daunting task of communicating with the souls of the deceased. During the second stage of his derangement, Chernyshevski rejects the possibility of otherworldly encounters with his son. Temporarily released from the mental institution, Chernyshevski had "grown thinner and quieter after his illness ... but Yasha's ghost no longer sat in the corner" (*Gift*, 195 [ch. 3]).

Godunov-Cherdyntsev calls on Chernyshevski just before the publication of his controversial biography. Full of deliberate ambiguities, the episode of the protagonist's last visit with Chernyshevski opens with a pseudo-philosophical discussion of death and immortality with references to and quotations from Delalande's *Discourse on Shadows*. The French philosopher serves as a fictional disguise allowing Nabokov to expound upon his views of death and the other world. Remarkably, after a page or so of Delalande's discourse, the narrator's philosophizing voice flows into the voice of Chernyshevski, who ponders his own imminent death. So gradual is the transmogrification of the former voice into the latter, that for a while the reader is not sure where one ends and the other starts. Nor is the reader clear whether Delalande's discourse is a product of the narrator's consciousness or a figment of Chernyshevski's inflamed imagination. At a certain point Chernyshevski unequivocally interrupts the rendition of Delalande's discourse by voicing skepticism about Christian notions of the afterlife:

If the poor in spirit enter the heavenly kingdom I can imagine how gay it is there [a parodic evocation of Christ's Sermon on the Mount: "Blessed are the poor in spirit; the kingdom of Heaven is theirs," Matthew 5:3]. I have seen enough of them on earth. (*Gift*, 310 [ch. 5])

Now that he is dying, Chernyshevski confesses, his previous belief in ghosts as well as his experiences of communicating with his son's spectral presence, appear to him as something base. The paradox of Chernyshevski's pre-mortem vision lies in a recognition that "in dying [he gets] farther away from [his son], when the opposite should have been true – ever nearer and nearer" (*Gift*, 311 [ch. 5]). On the eve of his death, in a "moment of lucidity," Chernyshevski utters: "What nonsense. Of course there is nothing afterwards" (*Gift*, 312 [ch. 5]).

What do the words of the dying Chernyshevski mean? That death is not a passage to the other world? That whatever the destiny of the surviving soul, it is only significant for the living, insofar as the living remember the deceased and try to communicate with them? That traditional religious models of salvation are forms of popular communal living, and not at all models of individual immortality? The reader learns that Chernyshevski "had turned out at the last minute to be a Protestant [Lutheran in the Russian]" (*Gift*, 312 [ch. 5]). Chernyshevski's religious affiliation with Protestantism, and not Russian Orthodoxy, highlights his *pro forma* Christianity, his conversion in a minor key.

Godunov-Cherdyntsev finds vexing his own inability to "imagine some kind of extension of [Chernyshevski] beyond the corner of life" (*Gift*, 314 [ch. 15]). As he ponders Chernyshevski's disappearance, "at the same time he [cannot help] noticing through the window of a cleaning and pressing shop near the Orthodox church, a worker with devilish energy and an excess of steam, as if in hell, torturing a pair of trousers" (*Gift*, 314 [ch. 5]). Such a cinematic superimposition of two spaces, an Orthodox church and a cleaning shop, evokes a traditional Christian notion of an anthropomorphic hell where the wicked undergo torment. In their own ways, both Chernyshevski and Godunov-Cherdyntsev have rejected such models. From a "troubled and obscured state of mind," the protagonist passes "with a kind of relief" (*Gift*, 286 [ch. 4]) to a new cosmic awareness:

as if the responsibility for his soul belonged not to him but to someone who knew what it all meant – he felt that all this skein of random thoughts, like everything else as well [...] – was but a reverse side of a magnificent fabric [iznanka velikolepnoi tkani], on the front of which there gradually formed and became alive images invisible to him. (*Gift*, 314 [ch. 5])[20]

This newly arrived *sui generis* model of the other world helps the protagonist, an aspiring author and thinker, to make sense of his own existence. In fact, Godunov-Cherdyntsev's account of his encounters with the Chernyshevskis, culminating in Alexander Chernyshevski's death, intertwines with the narrative of his falling in love with Zina Mertz. Right after the funeral service, Godunov-Cherdyntsev finds himself "on a bench where once or twice at night he had sat with Zina" (*Gift*, 314 [ch. 5]). The parallel unfolding of Chernyshevski's quest for details of post-mortem survival and Godunov-Cherdyntsev's own quest for a transcendent love strongly suggest a linkage. The protagonist needs the spiritual travails of the teetering Jewish convert Chernyshevski to realize that the realm of the afterlife is only meaningful when one believes that it affects one's life in this world, rather than that it is a goal to which one aspires throughout one's life or that it is another chance to make a difference in the universe. Such an understanding permeates the development of Judaism.

Almost at the very end of the novel, when the protagonist and Zina have firmly linked their lives together, Godunov-Cherdyntsev recalls his meetings with the Chernyshevskis. Previously, the protagonist was having a difficult time holding on to the image of the deceased. Now "he was seized by a panicky desire not to allow [all the memories] to close and get lost in a corner of his soul's lumber room .... There is a way ["Est' sposob"] – the only way" (*Gift*, 337 [ch. 5], *SSoch*, III:303). The ultimate suggestion is that memory is a form of postmortem survival, and art awards individual immortality by making Chernyshevski a character in Godunov-Cherdyntsev's nascent novel.

Fyodor Godunov-Cherdyntsev's project might not have been undertaken had it not been for his half-Jewish Muse. The entire novel becomes, in the words of its protagonist and presumed author, "a kind of declaration of love" (*Gift*, 364 [ch. 5]). Nabokov's authorial intention, disguised as fate, brings Zina and Fyodor together as the young writer rents a room in the apartment of the Shchyogolevs. Zina's mother married Boris Shchyogolev after the death of her Jewish first husband and Zina's father, Oscar Mertz. Upon seeing Shchyogolev for the first time, Fyodor thinks that his new landlord has "one of those open Russian faces whose openness is almost indecent" (*Gift*, 143 [ch. 2]). A former prosecutor and a ceaseless imitator of the Yiddish accent, Shchyogolev exemplifies a widespread variety of anti-Semitism, the anti-Semitism of Jewish jokes and of pseudo-sociological meandering on the subject of an international Jewish conspiracy.[21]

Zina is burdened by having to live with her anti-Semitic stepfather. Although he outwardly treats Zina with care, he still manages to remind her of her "alien" Jewish origins. At dinner, after Zina pushes away a plate of borscht, Shchyogolev ventures to change her mind: "Come on, eat, Aïda" (*Gift*, 159 [ch. 3]). The latent anti-Semitism of Shchyogolev's remark become transparent if one considers the sources of the nickname "Aïda." On the one hand, Aïda is the female protagonist of the eponymous opera by Giuseppe Verdi (1871). In the opera, set in Egypt in the age of the Pharaohs, Aïda is a captive Ethiopian girl and a beloved of the commander of the Egyptian army, Radamès. At the end of the opera, Aïda chooses to die in Radamès's arms as both are entombed alive. On the other hand, Aïda points to "aid" (pronounced "ayeed"), the Russianized version of the Yiddish for "a Jew"; when speaking Russian, Russian Jews frequently use the word "aid" as a private code, as in "On aid" ("He is Jewish").

Later in the novel, the narrator provides a lengthy explication of Shchyogolev's anti-Semitism. The reader learns that after the death of Zina's father, her mother married "a man whom Mertz would not have allowed over his threshold, one of those cocky and corny Russians [bravurnykh russkikh poshliakov] who, when the occasion presents itself, savor the word 'Yid' as if it were a fat fig" (*Gift*, 185 [ch. 3]; *SSoch*, III:166). One of Shchyogolev's favorite books is the notorious forgery, *Protocols of the Elders of Zion*. Shchyogolev offers his tenant an analysis of the Jewish impact upon his wife and step-daughter:

My better half ... was for twenty years the wife of a kike and got mixed up with a whole rabble of Jew in-laws [prozhila s iudeem i obrosla tselym kagalom]. I had to expend quite a bit of effort to get rid of that stink. Zina ... , thank God, doesn't have anything specific – you should see her cousin, one of these fat little brunettes, you know, with a fuzzy upperlip. (*Gift*, 187 [ch. 3]; *SSoch*, III:168)

Not finding in Zina any screaming features of a Jewish phenotype, Shchyogolev even speculates that Zina is a progeny of her mother's extra-marital affair with an ethnic Russian:

one can't help being drawn to one's own people, you know. Let her tell you herself how she suffocated in that atmosphere.... And to think that her mother was a lady-in-waiting of the Empress ... and she went and married a yid – to this day she can't explain how it happened: he was rich, she says, and she was stupid, they met in Nice, she eloped to Rome with him.... (*Gift*, 187 [ch. 3])

Zina imparts to Fyodor an image of her deceased father as a Jewish aristocrat, adoring "trotting races and music" and reciting "Homer by heart" (*Gift*, 187 [ch. 3]). She tries to select details of her father's image that might "touch Fyodor's imagination, since it seemed to her she detected something sluggish and bored in his reaction to ... the most precious thing she had to show him" (*Gift*, 187–88 [ch. 3]). Fyodor, who "in general did not give a damn about the classification of people according to race, or racial interrelations" (*Gift*, 188 [ch. 3]), found it embarrassing that Zina would concede that he harbored shades of anti-Semitism. Fyodor realizes that Zina's "morbidly acute pride" is fueled by her daily contacts with household prejudice against her Jewish origins. Zina's sense of her own Jewish identity is not without contradictions; to her a Jewish boss was "a German Jew, i.e. first of all a German" (*Gift*, 188 [ch. 3]). Zina's Jewish identity is a composite image of genetic and historical features (according to Jewish Law, Zina would not even be considered Jewish since her mother is not Jewish). Religion never surfaces in her discussions of her Jewishness. From a cultural standpoint, she is a Russian, brought up on the same poetry and cultural mythology as Fyodor himself. An antidote against Russian xenophobia, Zina's Jewish identity is to a large degree a self-definition by negation. Be that as it may, Zina still transforms Fyodor's attitudes toward the Jewish question. Godunov-Cherdyntsev's changing attitude, formerly an abstractly liberal belief in equality of all men, and subsequently a "personal shame for listening silently to Shchyogolev's [anti-Semitic] rot" (*Gift*, 188 [ch. 3]), mirrors Nabokov's own transformation under the influence of his Jewish wife. Intolerant to even slightest nuances of anti-Semitic behavior, the mature Nabokov fought not only his wife's but his own Jewish battles.

In the middle of the novel, Fyodor Godunov-Cherdyntsev formulates "what [it] was about [Zina] that fascinated him most of all":

Her perfect understanding, the absolute pitch of her instinct for everything that he himself loved? ... And not only was Zina cleverly and elegantly made to measure for him by a very painstaking fate, but both of them, forming a single shadow, were made to the measure of something not quite comprehensible, but wonderful and benevolent and continuously surrounding them. (*Gift*, 177 [ch. 3])

The recognition that Zina and Fyodor complement perfectly the fatidic patterns of their lives, the patterns designed by a transcendent source, amounts to a guiding principle in the composition of Godunov-Cherdyntsev's and Nabokov's novel, *The Gift*. In the novel, Zina the Muse not only inspires the writing and serves as the first reader and judge, but also symbolizes the kind of Russia, both idealized and feminized, that Nabokov strove to preserve in exile. In this immortal and nebulous Russia, half-Slavic and half-Jewish, the Jewish question is harmoniously resolved – Nabokov's perfect if unattainable dream.

Holocaust, remembrance, responsibility in Pnin

The novel *Pnin* (1957) is the pinnacle of Nabokov's Jewish theme. Nabokov reactivates two central themes of *The Gift*, namely the theme of post-mortem survival of consciousness and the theme of love between an ethnic Russian man and a Jewish woman. While in *The Gift* the two lovers are united by a benevolent fate that oversees their lives, in *Pnin* Nabokov pursues a tragic scenario. At first, Timofey Pnin and his beloved Mira Belochkin are separated by the Russian Revolution and Civil War; subsequently, Mira perishes in a Nazi concentration camp while Pnin struggles to preserve the pure memories of his beloved and make sense of his own post-Holocaust existence. He seeks to justify his own survival in view of Mira Belochkin's martyrdom and death.

Pnin is a canonical Russian *intelligent*. Like Godunov-Cherdyntsev, he comes from a St. Petersburg liberal milieu that made no distinctions between Jews and Gentiles.[22] On a park bench in a strange American town, by means of an operation that Nabokov called "cosmic synchronization" (*SM*, 218 [ch. 11]), Pnin travels to his Russian childhood while also contemplating his forthcoming lecture at Cremona Women's Club. The narrator underscores Pnin's near-death experience of remembering: "And suddenly Pnin (was he dying?) found himself sliding back into his childhood" (*Pnin*, 21 [ch. 1]). Having survived the excruciating pain of remembrance, but still remaining under the impact of his "seizure" (*Pnin*, 25 [ch. 1]), Pnin endures a fleeting if "limpid ... vision" (*Pnin*, 27 [ch. 1]) as he is being introduced to his audience. In his vision, in place of the members of the Cremona Women's Club, he imagines a room full of his dead loved ones, including Mira:

Next to [one of his Baltic aunts], shyly smiling, sleek dark head inclined, gentle brown gaze shining up at Pnin from under velvet eyebrows, sat a dead sweetheart of his.... . Murdered, forgotten, unrevenged, incorrupt, immortal, many old friends were scattered throughout the dim hall among more recent people. (*Pnin*, 27–28 [ch. 1])

Before such an audience, Pnin's every word must reverberate with intellectual honesty.

Throughout the novel, Pnin thinks of the afterlife and continues to encounter both Jewish characters and anti-Semitism. He comes in contact with memories of his deceased Jewish friends, including a "Samuil Izrailevich" and an "Ilya Isidorovich Polyanski." In "the course of one of those dreams that haunt Russian fugitives" (*Pnin*, [ch. 4] 109), Pnin sees himself and Polyanski waiting for "some mysterious deliverance to arrive in a throbbing boat from beyond the hopeless sea" (*Pnin*, 110 [ch. 4]). Pnin's dead friend Polyanski has the same first name and patronymic as Nabokov's good friend Fondaminsky, who died in a Nazi concentration camp.[23] Additionally, Samuil Izrailevich shares his name and patronymic with Nabokov's friend Rozoff (Zavyalov-Leving, "Samuel Izrailevich").

Pnin's ex-wife Liza, an immoral and manipulative woman, tells him about her new male friend: "His father was a dreamer, had a floating casino ... but was ruined by some Jewish gangsters" (*Pnin*, 56 [ch. 2]). Uncomfortable with traditional notions of Heaven and Hell, and deterred by Liza's coquettish anti-Semitism, Pnin thinks to himself: "If people are reunited in Heaven (I don't believe it, but suppose), then how shall I stop it from creeping upon me, over me, that shriveled, helpless, lame thing, her soul?" (*Pnin*, 58 [ch. 2]). At that very moment, when Pnin seems "on the verge of a simple solution of the universe" (*Pnin*, 58 [ch. 2]), a squirrel interrupts his thoughts. The squirrel communicates an "urgent request," and Pnin understands her perfectly. " 'She has fever, perhaps' " (*Pnin* 58), he thinks, pressing the contraption on a water fountain so the squirrel could quench her thirst. Possibly Mira's spectral presence[24] (Mira's last name, Belochkin, derives from the Russian *belochka* a diminiutive feminine noun meaning "little squirrel") – the Jewish squirrel surfaces in the novel to remind Pnin of his moral responsibility and direct his increasingly unorthodox metaphysical quest. As though sensing Pnin's departure from organized religion, a Russian friend warns him that one day he will lose the "Greek Catholic cross on a golden chainlet that Pnin removed from his neck and hung on a twig" before swimming. Pnin responds that "perhaps [he] would not mind losing it":

As you well know, I wear it merely from [*sic*] sentimental reasons. And the sentiment is becoming burdensome. After all, there is too much of the physical about this attempt to keep a particle of one's childhood in contact with one's breastbone. (*Pnin*, 128 [ch. 5])

The Jewish theme in the novel culminates in the episode where Pnin visits The Pines, a country estate of his Russian émigré acquaintance. At one point, just as previously, he is forced to sit down on a bench by an approaching "cardiac sensation," described as "an awful feeling of sinking and melting into one's physical surroundings" (*Pnin*, 131 [ch. 5]). At this very point, Pnin is accosted by Roza Shpolyanski, the wife of a Jewish liberal politician of the 1910s: "I don't think we ever met. But you knew well my cousins, Grisha and Mira Belochkin. They constantly spoke of you. He is living in Sweden, I think – and, of course, you have heard of his poor sister's terrible end …" (*Pnin*, 131 [ch. 5]).[25] Pnin resists a meeting with the past, but his memory perseveres. Thereafter follows a lengthy recollection, both tortuous and idyllic, of Pnin's first love, in part reminiscent of Nabokov's accounts of his own first love in *Speak, Memory* and elsewhere: summertime romance, oaths and kisses, gardens and kerosene lamps.

Why does Pnin resist remembering Mira? What does it mean that "in order to exist rationally, Pnin had taught himself, during the last ten years, never to remember Mira" (*Pnin*, 134 [ch. 5])? Pnin's *modus vivendi*, his prohibition against remembering his dead beloved, is a direct consequence of the Holocaust. How can Pnin, a moral and compassionate human being, continue living in a post-Holocaust void by denying himself the right to remember its victims: "if one were quite sincere with oneself, no conscience, and hence no consciousness, could be expected to subsist in a world where such things as Mira's death were possible" (*Pnin*, 135 [ch. 5])? Could it be that Nabokov's Russian protagonist has formulated a profound if grave truth that a human mind seeks to come to terms even with such incomprehensible disasters as the loss of six million Jewish lives?

The account of Pnin's intimations of Mira's death belongs to the finest pages of literature about the Holocaust:

One had to forget – because one could not live with the thought that this graceful, fragile, tender young woman with those eyes, that smile, those gardens and snows in the background, had been brought in a cattle car to an extermination camp and killed by an injection of phenol into the heart, into the gentle heart one had heard beating under one's lips in the dusk of the past. And since the exact form of her death had not been recorded, Mira kept dying a great number of deaths in one's mind, and undergoing a great number of resurrections, only to die again and again, led away by a trained nurse, inoculated with filth, tetanus bacilli, broken glass, gassed in a sham shower bath with prussic acid, burned alive in a pit on a gasoline-soaked pile of beechwood. According to the investigator Pnin had happened to talk to in Washington, the only certain thing was that being too weak to work (though still smiling, still able to help other Jewish women), she was selected to die and was cremated only a few days after her arrival in Buchenwald, in the beautifully wooded Grosses Ettersberg... an hour's stroll from Weimar, where walked Goethe, Herder, Schiller... and others. (*Pnin*, 135 [ch. 5])

Nabokov himself lost dear Jewish friends in the Holocaust. Nabokov's brother, Sergei, although he was not Jewish, "died of inanition" in a Hamburg concentration camp in 1945 (*SM*, 258 [ch. 13]). Right after the war, Nabokov wrote to Rozoff that Germany would have to be "reduced to ashes several times over in order to quench [his] hatred of it, whenever [he thought] of those who perished in Poland."[26] In the 1970s Nabokov spoke of making a further "statement" about the Nazi concentration camps: "There is a sense of responsibility about this theme which I think I will tackle one day. I will go to German camps and *look* at those places and write a *terrible* indictment..."[27]

Much of Judaic belief was subject to re-evaluation by the Holocaust and the spiritual emptiness that it created. Jobian questions were being asked by Jewish thinkers after World War II. How does one make sense of God's omnipotence and goodness in view of a collective catastrophe resulting in the deaths of six million Jews? How can suffering of the righteous be explained and furthermore justified? What was the collective destiny of the Holocaust martyrs following their physical annihilation by the Nazis? What were the individual destinies of the loved ones the Jews lost in gas chambers? The daunting task of contemporary Judaism has been to reconcile Jewish philosophy of the afterlife and the incomprehensible reality of the Holocaust. Just as many a Jewish thinker after World War II, Timofey Pnin is skeptical of the existence and authority of an omnipotent and beneficent God. How can he go on living after what was permitted to happen during the Holocaust? How can he hope for personal immortality when six million innocent people have disappeared, and no one seems to be able to explain their disappearance in either metaphysical or ethical terms?

And yet, however spasmodic, memories of Mira's death help Pnin intuit a model of post-mortem survival that validates his experience in a post-Holocaust world:

> Pnin slowly walked under the solemn pines. The sky was dying. He did not believe in an autocratic God. He did believe, dimly, in a democracy of ghosts. The souls of the dead, perhaps, formed committees, and these, in continuous session, attended to the destinies of the quick. (*Pnin*, 136 [ch. 5])

CODA

How strikingly and seamlessly biography dovetails with fiction when Nabokov thinks and writes about the Jews! This essay has only begun to raise and formulate some of the questions regarding the place of Jewish history and Judaic thought in his artistic career. In place of a conclusion – and to situate Nabokov further in the modern debates on the Jewish question – I would like to travel back in time to June 23, 1945, when the *New Yorker* ran its first in a long series of Nabokov's short stories. Titled "Double Talk" and later renamed "Conversation Piece, 1945," this American story owed much to Nabokov's feuilletonistic Russian stories of the early 1930s. The main character, a Russian émigré writer like Nabokov, is haunted by a double. He visualizes his "disreputable namesake, complete from nickname to surname," as a "very White émigré, of the automatically reactionary type" (*Stories*, 587). During the years both spend in European exile, his ubiquitous anti-self causes Nabokov's protagonist much chagrin. At one point, the writer receives a recall notice that "in exasperated tones" demands that he return a copy of *Protocols of the Elders of Zion* (*Stories*, 587). The horrible namesake represents everything that the protagonist is not – a vulgarian, an anti-Semite, a diehard reactionary – and he too ends up in the United States. Just as in a fairy-tale where a virtuous prince finds himself trapped in the domain of villainy, the protagonist mistakenly accepts an invitation, intended for his evil twin.

Set in a Boston apartment building with an elevator attendant "oddly resembling Richard Wagner," this abominable soirée showcases anti-Semitic types including a "Colonel Malikov or Melnikov," who complains of the way "the Jewish Bolsheviks used to treat the Russian people" and adores Stalin, as well as a Mrs. Mulberry who is shocked by an old Russian Jew prepared "to strangle with his own hands the very first German soldier he met" (*Stories*, 591, 593). The stellar guest is one Dr. Shoe, who calls himself "a German ... of pure Bavarian stock, though a loyal citizen of this country" (*Stories*, 590). Dr. Shoe's talk might have passed for a genuine plea to help the Germany of poets, philosophers, and musicians brought to destruction by mad Adolf – and help the Americans did! – had the speaker not focused on the origins and perceptions of the Holocaust. Do not be misled: this propagandist "with sleek, dark hair and a glistening brow" (*Stories*, 589) never uses the term "Holocaust." Rather, he speaks of "German boys proudly entering some Polish or Russian town," expecting a welcome reception by the local population but seeing instead streets "lined with silent and motionless crowds of Jews, who glared at them with hatred and who insulted each passing soldier" (*Stories*, 592–93). Dr. Shoe explains that

at first [the Germans] tried to fight that hatred with patient explanations and little tokens of kindness. But the wall of hatred surrounding them only got thicker. Finally they were forced to imprison the leaders of the vicious and arrogant coalition. What else could they do? (*Stories*, 593)

Dr. Shoe's malicious lies strike home among those present. A "stout woman who sat with her knees wide apart" exclaims that "any sensitive person will agree with what you say about [the Germans] not being responsible for those so-called atrocities, most of which have probably been invented by the Jews" (*Stories*, 593). Enchanted by the reception he receives among the Anglo-Saxon intelligentsia, Dr. Shoe attributes what the Americans heard about the Nazi concentration camps to "the workings of the vivid Semitic imagination which controls the American press," but also to what he labels "many purely sanitary measures which the orderly German troops had to adopt in dealing with the corpses" (*Stories*, 593). Dr. Shoe concludes his presentation by offering to play "The Star-Spangled Banner." At this point, the outnumbered and nauseated protagonist rushes out of the apartment. While this witty story continues to unravel, abundant as it is with metafictional delights, I would like to stop here in order to pay tribute to Nabokov's prophetic foresight. Writing brilliantly in an adopted language, Nabokov warns his postwar American readers, the Mrs. Halls and Mrs. Mulberries of the story, about current (and perhaps future) attempts to falsify the history of the Holocaust. In fact, this is one of the earliest statement on the Holocaust in all of American fiction, and it sums up the discussions of anti-Semitism in his Russian works, including those in *The Gift*. Nabokov alerts all of us to the dangers of anti-Semitism, often dressed up and disguised by rhetoric that appeals to the cultured and the patriotic. Nabokov's verdict hits the nail on the head: anti-Semitism is fueled not only by hatred, but also by complacency. Before slamming the door on his way out, stammering with indignation, the Russian writer tells his hostess: "You are either murderers or fools ... or both."

NOTES

I acknowledge the assistance of the Kennan Institute for Advanced Russian Studies and the Lucius N. Littauer Foundation. I am grateful to Stanley J. Rabinowitz, Director, Amherst Center for Russian Culture, for permission to accede to and quote from Z. Shakhovskoy's papers. The only overview I know on the subject of Nabokov's Jewish theme is L. Kosman's brief article, "Vladimir Nabokov i evreistvo," *New American* 1.12 (1988): 47–48. Where a source of an English translation is not given, the translation is mine. Leona Toker considers Nabokov's treatment of the Holocaust in "'Signs and Symbols' In and Out of Context," in *A Small Alpine Form: Studies in Nabokov's Short Fiction*, ed. Charles Nicol and Gennady Barabtarlo (New York: Garland, 1993), 167–80.

1. An incomplete catalogue of Jewish characters and topics includes: Klara in *Mary*; Dr. Weiner in "The Doorbell"; a decrepit Jewish chess genius in *The Defense*; Patkin and Iogolevich in *Glory*; a well-known member of the Black Hundreds in "Recruiting"; a mad old Jewish man in *Invitation to a Beheading*; Mr. Silbermann and Helene Grinstein in *The Real Life of Sebastian Knight*; "a swarthy Russian girl in New York who was so troubled by the possibility of being mistaken for her notion of a Jewess that she used to wear a cross under her throat" ("Conversation Piece, 1945"; *Stories*, 589); the elderly Russian-Jewish couple in "Signs and Symbols"; Charlotte's friend John Farlow, who wrongly suspects Humbert Humbert of being Jewish (*Lolita*), and Humbert himself who envisions the Holocaust in his phantasmagorical dreams.
2. Brian Boyd, *Vladimir Nabokov: The Russian Years* (Princeton University Press, 1990), 27, 55, 101, 435, 539 n. 5.
3. See also Andrew Field, *Nabokov: His Life in Part* (Harmondsworth: Penguin, 1978), 109–27.
4. Boyd, *The Russian Years*, 179; Field, *Nabokov*, 78.
5. Boyd, *The Russian Years*, 213.

6 See Zinaida Shakhovskaia [Shakhovskoy], *V poiskakh Nabokova* (Paris: La presse libre, 1979). See also Brian Boyd, *Vladimir Nabokov: The American Years* (Princeton University Press, 1991), 396–97; Dmitri Nabokov, "The *Lolita* Legacy: Life with Nabokov's Art," *The Nabokovian* 37 (Fall 1996): 14, 26–7.
7 N. Krivosheina to Zinaida Shakhovskaia, July 4 [n. d., approx. 1950s], letter in the Personal Papers of Zinaida and Dmitry Shakhovskoy at Amherst Center for Russian Culture, Amherst College, box 2, folder 14.
8 For a study of Nabokov's metaphysics, see Vladimir E. Alexandrov, *Nabokov's Otherworld* (Princeton University Press, 1990).
9 See, for instance, Boyd's account of Nabokov's conversation with a Cornell professor of fine arts, Peter Kahn, about the iconography of Christian saints (Boyd, *The American Years*, 291).
10 For a recent investigation of Judaic models of postmortem survival, see Simcha Paull Raphael, *Jewish Views of the Afterlife* (Northvale: Jason Aronson, Inc., 1994). See also "World To Come," Louis Jacobs, *The Jewish Religion: A Companion* (Oxford University Press, 1995), 599–601; "Afterlife," Geoffrey Wygoder (ed.), *The Encyclopedia of Judaism* (New York: Macmillan, 1989), 31–32; Louis Jacobs, *A Jewish Theology* (New York: Behrman House, 1973), 301–22. Useful observations are also found in Jack Riemer (ed.), *Jewish Insights on Death and Mourning* (New York: Schocken Books, 1995); see esp. ch. 11.
11 In a letter of January 21, 1942, Nabokov angrily ("ia tak zol") criticizes a novel by Aleksandra Tolstaia, published in *Novyi zhurnal* (The New Review), for its alleged anti-Semitism; see Andrei Chernyshev, "Kak redko teper' pishu po-russki...," *Oktiabr'* 1 (1996): 130–31.
12 Andrei Garf, "Literaturnye pelenki," *Novoe slovo*, March 20, 1938, 6–7.
13 Boyd, *The American Years*, 22.
14 Boyd, *The American Years*, 311, and Field, *Nabokov*, 20, 275. See also Andrew Field, *VN: The Life and Art of Vladimir Nabokov* (New York: Crown, 1986), 302–03.
15 Boyd, *The American Years*, 107.
16 Boyd, *The Russian Years*, 421, 521.
17 Boyd, *The American Years*, 528–83; Field, *Nabokov*, 226.
18 "To Sergei Rozoff," 1967, letter quoted by Yuri Zavyalov-Leving in "Samuel Izrailevich: *Pnin*'s Character, Nabokov's Friend," *The Nabokovian* 39 (Fall 1997): 16; see also Boyd, *The American Years*, 583, 650. For details about Nabokov's unrealized trip to Israel, see Yuri Zavyalov-Leving, "Phantom in Jerusalem, or the History of an Unrealized Visit," *The Nabokovian* 37 (Fall 1996): 30–43.
19 Svetlana Malysheva has recently discovered that one of Nabokov's great-grandfathers was a Jewish convert to Christianity; see Svetlana Malysheva, "Praded Nabokova, pochetnyi chlen Kazanskogo universiteta," *Ekho vekov* (Kazan), 1/2 (1997): 131–35. I am grateful to Yuri Zavyalov-Leving (Jerusalem) for providing this information.

20 Nabokov, *Sobranie sochinenii v chetyrekh tomakh* (Moscow: Pravda, 1990) III:381. (Hereafter *SSoch*.)
21 I am grateful to Olga Proskurina for pointing out that Pavel E. Shchyogolev (1877–1931) was a literary scholar and historian who attacked the Russian-Jewish literary historian Mikhail Gershenzon. Note also that in his capacity as the Russian Minister of Justice from 1906 to 1915, Ivan G. Shcheglovitov (1861–1918) was instrumental in introducing and implementing anti-Semitic policies; he was one of the architects of the Beilis trial.
22 My argument about the attitudes of Nabokov's non-Jewish characters to the Jews is based, here and elsewhere, on a psychological, anthropological and cultural model of the Self-Other dichotomy. I therefore deem it central to Pnin's experience with a Jewish beloved as well as with anti-Semitism that he is *not* Jewish; he is both a Slav and at least outwardly an Orthodox Christian. In her book, *Pniniad: Vladimir Nabokov and Marc Szeftel* (Seattle: University of Washington Press, 1997), Galya Diment explores the connections between Pnin's character and his alleged prototype, the émigré historian Marc Szeftel, who was Jewish.
23 Gennadi Barabtarlo, *Phantom of Fact: A Guide to Nabokov's Pnin* (Ann Arbor: Ardis, 1989), 188.
24 See W. W. Rowe, *Nabokov's Spectral Dimension* (Ann Arbor: Ardis, 1981), 62–67. Barabtarlo disagrees with Rowe's interpretations (see *Phantom of Fact*, 22). Incidentally, Nabokov's use of the squirrel image to evoke a soul or spirit might originate in *The Gift*, where Fyodor watches a squirrel climbing a park tree, experiences a heart sensation, then observes "a golden, stumpy little butterfly," another shadow of his father's psyche, and then realizes again that "his father was nonetheless dead" (*Gift*, 305 [ch. 5]).
25 Barabtarlo believes Mr. Shpolyanski is based on Rafail Abrámovich Abramóvich, a Menshevik leader (*Phantom of Fact*, 198). It is not unlikely that the name was suggested by the birth name of the émigré satirical poet Don-Aminado (1888–1957), Aminad Petrovich Shpolyanski.
26 "To Samuil Rozoff," 1945, letter quoted in Zavyalov-Leving, "Samuel Izrailevich."
27 Field, *VN*, 104.

CHAPTER 5

"The dead are good mixers": Nabokov's versions of individualism

Leona Toker

The ethical ideology that is evolved in the fictional works of Vladimir Nabokov can be described as an idealistic variety of rational individualism. I shall argue that this is a pervasive stance and that it is reflected in a compromise staged in Nabokov's texts, a middle way between the carnivalesque and the anti-carnivalesque narrative modes.

I

Individualism as ethical ideology means that moral values are derived not from a vision of a collective good but from a respect and concern for the rights of every single individual – so long as that individual's aims do not encroach on the rights of the individuals around him. One of the most basic rights of the individual is to preserve his or her identity; one of the most basic obligations is to recognize this right for others. Nabokov's characters fall into two groups: (1) those who respect the rights of others to an independent identity (Martin Edelweiss, Fyodor Godunov-Cherdyntsev, Timofey Pnin, John Shade), and (2) those who either solipsistically ignore that right (Ganin, Dreyer) or actively violate it (Hermann, Humbert, Kinbote). The former usually find themselves in a defensive position, repulsing the encroachments of others on their mind and soul, yet at times they embark on pursuits or perform actions that conflict with their self-interest, actions that are entirely selfless, altruistic or motivated by transcendent aims.

Which is what gives their individualism an idealistic coloration. Ethical idealists are not satisfied with the belief in doing as one would be done by; they respect the individual rights of others not because of a calculation that this conduct would boomerang but because it is (deontologically) right. They dispense with the expectation of reciprocity along with the basic assumption of philosophical egoism, namely, that all ethical motivation ultimately derives from considerations of self-interest. Instead, their ideal is that of supererogation, which one must be *prepared to appreciate* in others but which one does not have a right to *demand* from anyone but oneself.

Not expecting reciprocity, let alone supererogation, from another anchors idealistic individualists, not allowing them to drift into sweeping sentimental self-deceptions. The "high" view of human possibility which characterizes them also takes into account the photo-negative of supererogation, that is, profound, unmotivated evil. By contrast, the "low" view of human possibility characteristic of philosophical egoism explains away both the highest flights of the human spirit and the depths of iniquity.[1] By reducing all human motivation to narrow or extended personal interests, the "low" view interprets selflessness, self-sacrifice, or self-denial as the price paid in the pursuit of pleasurable states of mind, and perceives violence as a misguided trading of long-term well-being for short-term satisfactions.

Nabokov's characters do not excel in utilitarian ethical calculations. They play with high stakes, and without much hope of the jackpot. Martin risks his life in an attempt to overcome physical fear and, having won, risks – and evidently loses – his life in an attempt to commune with his lost homeland; his beloved Sonia rejects advantageous offers of marriage in order to remain close to her family and true to her ideal of love; Fyodor renounces mundane success and devotes his life to an ideal conception of artistic excellence; Pnin forfeits his heart to the exploitative Liza, does not waver in his generosity to her and risks his heart again in a surrogate father–child relationship with her son; John Shade risks madness in his active search for intimations of immortality after his daughter's suicide; Cincinnatus C. and Adam Krug, heroes of Nabokov's dystopian novels, risk, and lose, their lives in non-conformity to oppressive regimes. In all these cases, idealistic acts enter into complex relationships with self-interest or personal compulsions, yet the latter merely support rather than dictate the characters' choices. Nabokov's texts discourage skeptical interpretations of his characters' motives in frameworks such as psychological egoism, long-term interest, or neurosis.

II

The feature that accounts for this interpretive constraint in Nabokov's texts is their partial kinship to the carnivalesque mode. According to Bakhtin, the carnival, "a pageant without footlights and without a division into performers and spectators,"[2] has left cultural traces in the development of the novel. In fact, the relative intensity with which carnivalesque elements are articulated in works of prose fiction can well be used as a basis for a modal paradigm.[3] For Bakhtin, the clearest expression of the carnivalesque mode in fiction is Rabelais's *Gargantua and Pantagruel*, with Dostoevsky's novels being rather close to that pole. At the opposite pole one might, perhaps, find the novels of Jane Austen and Henry James. Nabokov's fiction would be located in about the middle of the spectrum.

Most of Nabokov's novels are set among exiles, people torn out of their hierarchical compartments and thrown into each other's company, so that the "distance between people is suspended, and a special carnival category goes into effect: free and familiar contact" among people formerly separated by social barriers.[4] The new circumstances lead to a defamiliarization of the characters' ways of looking at the world and at their neighbors,[5] and to "working out, in a concretely sensuous, half-real and half-play-acted form, a new mode of interrelationship between individuals,"[6] a mode characterized by disruptions of custom, midsummer-night reversals, and the lure, or threat, of a blending of identities with a concomitant loss of their integrity and discreteness.

It is owing to the latter phenomenon that Nabokov seems to have resisted the carnivalesque syndrome, while unable, and obviously unwilling, to cut off all of its inroads. The carnivalesque impulse tends to erase distinctions not only between social classes in a pageant and not only between the actors and observers of that pageant, but, more generally, between the individual and the environment. The need for maintaining a hold on one's identity and not letting it dissolve in the magma of the collective flow is among Nabokov's pervasive concerns; it is wittily formulated in the narrative comments on Pnin's heart attack in Whitchurch park:

I do not know if it has ever been noted before that one of the main characteristics of life is discreteness. Unless a film of flesh envelops us, we die. Man exists only insofar as he is separated from his surroundings. The cranium is the space-traveler's helmet. Stay inside or you perish. Death is

"The dead are good mixers": Nabokov's versions of individualism 95

divestment, death is communion. It may be wonderful to mix with the landscape, but to do so is the end of the tender ego. (*Pnin*, 20 [ch. 1])

This passage obviously deals not only with the inroads of physical disease, swooning, and death (the pores and other apertures of the body open up to the environment; wounds bleed; consciousness fades) but also, symbolically, with the possibility of the loss of a person's intellectual discreteness within a collective discourse. Indeed, the mixing of one's physical self with the "landscape" is an apt metaphor for a dissolution of identity in a crowd, in a collective emotional heightening, in a prevailing ideology, or in a mystical transport. It may be lethally irreversible: "the dead are good mixers."[7] Yet an entrenched resistance to the lure of these pools of power can lead to pettily self-interested emotional and intellectual sterility. Nabokov's texts enact the process of contact in which breaches of varying magnitude are allowed in the protective insulating layers of the individual self.

There are three main types of "the other" with whom a Nabokovian individual comes into an osmotic contact: the crowd, the mystery, and the partner.

III

The *crowd* is the most dangerously effective solvent of the individual human being. Its attractiveness for an individual is sometimes accounted for by the pleasurable sensation of the magnitude of the collective body[8] or else by a liberating loss of the fear of being touched, especially touched by the unknown.[9] Both effects are bound up with varieties of the so-called "oceanic feeling," the reassuring sense that "one's personality dissolv[es] as a grain of salt in the sea; but at the same time the infinite sea seem[s] to be contained in the grain of salt".[10]

Crowds are of little use to Nabokovian characters: the touch of the unfamiliar or of the alien, such as the kiss of the Toad in the darkness in *Bend Sinister*, does not so much frighten as disgust them. Time and again, however, they find themselves baited by crowds.[11] Young Luzhin, introduced by the teacher as the son of a celebrity, is immediately confronted with a concerted "hatred and derisive curiosity"[12] of his new classmates; Vasiliy Ivanovich of "Cloud, Castle, Lake" is enthusiastically tormented by the baiting pack of fellow sightseers; Cincinnatus C. is exposed to the vulgar feasting crowd and later to the voracious execution crowd; David Krug is tortured and killed by a pack of juvenile delinquents; Timofey Pnin is turned into a laughing stock by fellow academics; the paranoid Kinbote fancies himself physically pursued by assassins and emotionally baited by academic colleagues; and the deranged young man in "Signs and Symbols" perceives even the winds and trees as a maliciously conspiratorial baiting crowd.[13]

The hostility of the crowd, which loves to grow and resents desertions, is usually provoked by the stubbornness of a non-joiner, a dreamy Vasiliy Ivanovich who rejects vulgar games, a Cincinnatus who will not collaborate with tormentors and spies, an Adam Krug who will not join the media campaign for the legitimization of a totalitarian dictator, a Kinbote or a Pnin who will not subscribe to intellectual fashions. It was as a non-joiner that the Maenads tore to pieces the melancholy Orpheus. But difference, non-uniformity, may also provoke the wrath of the crowd since it is perceived as a potential for treason. The main feature of the members of the crowd is equality.[14] Hence the grimly carnivalesque "Shigalevshchina"[15] of the dystopian "Ekwilism" in *Bend Sinister*,[16] a theory, according to which an outstanding individual must be eliminated so that the quality that he possesses in abundance might be more equitably distributed among the others. The name Skotoma that Nabokov gives to the ideological proto-Ekwilist is associated both with the Greek for "darkness" and with the Russian for "cattle" (*skot*): his teachings, indeed, reduce society to a herd of cattle in which, as in the society ruled by Stalin, no one is unique or irreplaceable and, according to Paduk's speech in chapter 6, everyone is offered a chance of an ecstatic dissolution in the "virile oneness of the state" by "adjusting ideas and emotions to those of a harmonious majority," so that separate "groping individualities will become interchangeable and, instead of crouching in the prison cell of an illegal ego, the naked soul will be in contact with that of every other man in this land" (*BS*, 97 [ch. 6]).

A Nabokovian character has little chance of winning in a head-on confrontation with the crowd as crowd. Humbert dies a voodoo death in prison, David Krug is tortured to death, and Luzhin transfers his fear of the crowd to the fear of an invisible opponent from whom he escapes through suicide. In *Transparent Things*, Hugh Person, fearful of communal contempt, joins the schoolboy pack that he cannot beat and turns, together with it, against his headmaster father; later he attempts to join an athletic pack that he likewise cannot beat on their own grounds – Armande and her ski companions. At the end of the novel (and, in fact, at the very beginning, though on the first reading we do not know it), after his death in a hotel fire, this "Person" (the pun obviously intended) is in the process of joining another crowd that has prevailed upon him, the "invisible crowd" of ghosts.[17]

The way in which Nabokov imagines the death of some of his characters – not all (significantly, not that of Shade, and not that of women who die in childbirth, that is, in the process of impeded individual creation) – is associated with the symbolic transformations of the crowd. Hugh Person dies in a hotel fire – fire, if we believe Canetti,[18] is one of the most wide-spread and potent symbols of the crowd. When young Luzhin first encounters the hostility of his schoolmates, he feels "a burning mist" (*Def*, 29 [ch. 2]) in his eyes; the internalized symbol of the crowd returns at the peak of his chess career when, at the approach of a nervous breakdown, Luzhin gets hurt by a match which he has forgotten to extinguish. The forest into which Martin Edelweiss disappears at the end of *Glory* and the sea where the protagonist of "Perfection" drowns are also phenomenological symbols of the crowd.[19] The bulky, idiosyncratic Kurt Dreyer, totally free from crowd-related paranoia, remains unaware of the threat of death by drowning from which, at the last moment, he is saved.

Not surprisingly, Nabokov's characters are often shown engaged in different forms of defense against the crowd, the whole, the collective. Martin Edelweiss, like Nabokov himself, is a goalkeeper, a solitary figure, on a Cambridge soccer team, and much attention is paid to his putting on the insulating soccer gear (cf. the space-traveler's gear in *Pnin* – "stay inside or you perish"). Intellectual counterparts of this insulation can be seen in Pnin's and John Shade's spasmodic struggle for privacy, Luzhin's and Kinbote's escapes into the worlds of the mind, Smurov's fantasy of disembodiment in *The Eye*, and the moroseness of the French instructor in "The Vane Sisters."

Whereas self-insulation is a passive type of defense, an active defense consists in attempts to master the crowd, to win it over, turn it around, so that the victim of the baiting might turn into the champion of the crowd. At the end of *Despair* Hermann attempts to persuade the crowd of spectators to come to his side and protect him from the police; Humbert in *Lolita* makes a bid for the sympathies of the imaginary crowd in the courtroom, and Pnin attempts to charm his students by his impassioned tales; when the creaking of his chair breaks the spell, the "loud young laughter" in the classroom reminds him, with unstated implications, of a Berlin circus. By discovering and developing his capacity for chess Luzhin not merely escapes from the unstructured world of social realities but also manages to turn the baiting crowd of his classmates into an admiring audience in chess cafés. And the tormented protagonist of Nabokov's *Nikolai Gogol* first flees from and then starts preaching to an internalized audience which admires him for the wrong reasons and may start baiting him at any moment.

If defenses against a crowd-related paranoia crumble in Nabokov's novels, the idea that seems to pass the narrative tests is that of prophylactics: a crowd does not come into being if it is not treated as an assemblage – if, that is, the separate individuals in a grouping are not defaced. The protagonist-narrator of "The Vane Sisters" tends to regard Cynthia Vane's guests as a dull and somewhat vulgar crowd, but Cynthia teaches him to see them as separate icebergs, with only the tips visible on a social occasion. Their coats are left in an aggregate heap in the bedroom, according to what the narrator calls the "barbaric, unhygienic, and adulterous custom" (*Stories*, 627), but they themselves remain discrete, and circulate in each other's presence without need for artificial insulation. Only in the realms of the hosts of the dead do the discrete identities begin to blend ("the dead are good mixers"), since the memory of each person, Cynthia or Sibyl, Charlotte Haze or Luzhin's father, is made up of images – whether of raindrops, or eyelashes, or parking meters – which do not belong to that person alone.[20] Whatever success Pnin may have with his students lies in their being not a uniform gray mass but a convergence of discrete colorful personalities, such as Betty Bliss and Charles McBeth. Meaningful character names are, in fact, one of the ways in which the writer forces the reader to focus his or her attention on traces of individual "auras" (in the language of "The Vane Sisters") in potentially defacing lists. For Dolly Haze, her classmates are not a crowd; they are her rich social circle; this is one of the points suggested by the ample complexity of motifs created by the famous *Lolita* class list.[21] There is, apparently, some basis for hoping that a group of individuals will not congeal into a crowd if it is not treated like one, if each of its members is given some form of individual recognition.

IV

Nabokov's approaches to mysticism and the theme of the "otherworld" (*potustoronnost'*) running through his corpus have by now been well researched.[22] For the purpose of the present argument, attention must be called to a recurrent motif associated with that thematic concern – namely, the motif of an "aperture."[23] The pores of the body widening during Pnin's heart attack, the "red eye" on Hugh Person's toe where the shoe has scraped off the skin, "a hole in the hay" of Armande's slightly disturbed sleep (*TT,* 78 [ch. 20]), the window through which Armande climbs out in a fake rehearsal of a fire drill and the one through which Luzhin leaps to his death, doors that come ajar in *King, Queen, Knave* and in *Look at the Harlequins!,* the oblong puddle and the kidney-shaped lake which connect the different levels of reality in *Bend Sinister,* the hole in the ice of the lake where Hazel drowns in *Pale Fire* – these and similar somatic, architectural, and landscape images belong to the semantic field surrounding "a rift in the texture of space" (*TT,* 60 [ch. 16]). Life can begin to ooze out through these apertures; at the same time breezes from a world that transcends the self can ooze in, energizing the closed system of "average reality" and thus preventing it from running down, from beginning to "rot and stink" (*SO,* 118). In "Terra Incognita" scenes of an oneiric tropical adventure quite *literally* shine through the rifts in the wallpaper-like image of the hotel room where the protagonist is dying; in *Invitation to a Beheading,* a moth, an evanescent view from the window, the spark of genuine emotion in the mother's gaze, a sweet memory, a dream of escape, are *symbols* of the rift in the prison space, heralds from a world beyond the prison-house universe; and the young man in "Signs and Symbols" *literalizes the metaphor* of the rift by trying to tear a hole in his world and escape. Apertures are also responsible for "leakings and drafts" from another dimension (*SM,* 35 [ch. 2]), such as colored hearing, a psychological approximation of mystical experience. The motifs of "leaking" and of "a draft" are present in the scene of the evening before Armande's death in *Transparent Things*: the latter is evoked in the phrase "The windy March night found something to finger in the room" (*TT,* 77 [ch. 20]) and the former in "the pinking of waterdrops on the linoleum under a defective radiator" (*TT,* 78 [ch. 20]), an instance of "average reality" allowed to run to seed. In a sense, some of the author's personal signatures are self-reflexive textual enactments of the motif of aperture: the mind of the author beyond the "reality" of the fictional world may be glimpsed via the anagrams of "Vladimir Nabokov" such as Vivian Darkbloom in *Lolita* (*Lo*, 33 [pt. 1, ch. 9]) or Adam von Librikov in *Transparent Things* (*TT*, 75), via the fake-Freudian slipping in of Russian words into the discourse pertaining to non-Russian characters – "the crystalline crust heaving up with [Hugh Person's] heart from the bottom of an immemorial *more* (sea)" (*TT*, 89 [ch. 23]), via the disruption of the alphabetic order of examination papers by a misplaced V in "The Vane Sisters,"[24] or via other kinds of the more or the less overt auto-allusions.[25]

Nabokov's texts abound in beatific moments when the perception of scenes grants one an experience which could be described as aesthetic, spiritual, or plainly happy. A moment of happiness at the contemplation of a sunbathed cityscape is shared by the narrator and the protagonist of "Recruiting" and is given to the doomed young lover in "Details of a Sunset;" similar moments sustain Fyodor Godunov-Cherdyntsev in *The Gift* and brightly punctuate the experience of Martin Edelweiss and Cincinnatus C. In Nabokov's works it is difficult to distinguish between the moments of aesthetic bliss and those of the mystical heightening of the spirit; both are disinterested and both suspend a person's continuous struggle for the discreteness of his identity. Such an experience eludes a guilty Humbert, but can be available to Nabokov's "fellow dreamers, thousands of whom roam the earth" keeping to the same "irrational and divine standards during the darkest and most dazzling hours of physical danger, pain, dust, death" (*LL*, 373).[26]

According to the deranged Falter of "Ultima Thule" (the would-be adept who believes that the Mystery has been revealed to him), the knowledge of Mystery is tantamount and conducive to death or madness, and possibly available through them. Indeed, the hierophany of Nabokov's personages is not a matter of overwhelming revelation or mystical trance; rather, it is the experience of fleeting "drafts" which, however, suffice to promise that spots of intense happiness, aesthetic reveling, or lyrical dreaminess are but harbingers, prefaces, "pocket money," whereas "the real wealth, from which life should know how to get dividends in the shape of dreams, tears of happiness, distant mountains" (*Gift*, 164 [ch. 3]) is stocked elsewhere. In "Ultima Thule" the recently widowed Sineusov's eschatological interrogation of Falter, a mystic *malgré lui*, expresses a carnivalesque yearning for the transcendence of the borderlines of a living identity, while Falter's resistant response to them is the life-preserving anti-carnivalesque constraint. The tension between the two attitudes is, however, most often enacted within the same character, a Krug, a Godunov-Cherdyntsev, an Edelweiss, or a Pnin. Yet "Ultima Thule" does not merely separate the conflicting impulses of a Nabokovian character, a wavering "Doubtful Asphodel" (*RLSK*, 23 [ch. 3]); it does not merely distribute the two terms of the tension between two characters. It also suggests that the thirst for a mystical knowledge is, largely, a response to bereavement, a refusal to accept its finality.

v

The relationship between the self and the partner in Nabokov's novels is characterized by the same interplay of carnivalesque impulse and restraint. Here one will not find lengthy, Dostoevskian, on-stage debates and effusive confessions through which a Marmeladov might cast a spell over a Raskolnikov. Nabokov's direct-speech exchanges are relatively brief; even in *The Gift*, where they are longer than in the other novels, the melodrama which transforms itself into the tragedy of Yasha Chernyshevski's death is provided in a summary, and Fyodor's lengthy dialogues with Koncheyev take place only in Fyodor's imagination.

Nabokov's characters often wish to bind the others to themselves through speech, but in such cases they speak about things other than themselves, offering the loved ones gifts selected from the life of their own spirit.[27] In *Glory*, Martin's imaginative pictures of Horace in the "sprawling village" of Rome are an indirect language of his love for Sonia who would allow no direct outpourings ("To talk to her of love was useless"); the images he conjures up are a restrained-carnivalesque combination of the Apollonian marble edifices and Dionysian scenes of "people chasing after a mad dog".[28] In *The Gift*, Zina's narratives about her work in the office that she hates (*Gift*, 188–92 [ch. 3]) are her tribute to Fyodor, to the intermittent happiness that he offers her, and perhaps to his own talent as a satirist. By contrast, Fyodor's love poems to Zina ("To fiction be as to your country true"; *Gift*, 156 [ch. 3]) demand more of her than he himself might be prepared to give: the appeal "Oh swear to me that while the heart-blood stirs, you will be true to what we shall invent" (*Gift*, 157 [ch. 3]) places the lovers on the very threshold of a *folie à deux*. Yet Fyodor does not cross that threshold: his love for Zina does not generate an obtuseness to other people, as do the loves of Humbert or Van Veen – as if to signal this, Nabokov gives Fyodor a wave of pity for Marianna Nikolavna (whom he has never liked) during his parting from her in the closing chapter (*Gift*, 357 [ch. 5]). And if Dolly Haze declines to discuss God or Shakespeare with Humbert, it is not merely because he might soil them for her but also because a finely tuned intellectual discussion might hold her captive:[29] one may recollect how in Nabokov's story "Music" a piano performance at a party holds a woman, against her will, in her former husband's company.

The threat of capture that one's partner may represent thus pertains not only to the emotional but also to the intellectual sphere. Unlike Van Veen who imposes some of his preferences and values on Ada, Fyodor Godunov-Cherdyntsev appeals for Zina's faithfulness to "what *we* shall invent" (*Gift*, 157 [ch. 3], italics added). Indeed, the lovers' construction of a shared world, an overlap between the worlds in which each one lives, is about the only kind of collective creation that Nabokov accepts. In the story "The Admiralty Spire," however, he explores the possibility of such a collective effort going awry. The protagonist-narrator of this story is repelled by the way a novelist, in whom he recognizes his erstwhile beloved, belies the world that they had once seemed to create together; yet, in his struggle for "a state of aesthetic autonomy from the finalizing categorizations" of another,[30] he slips into similar categorizations himself; in his resentment over the blow struck against his sense of his own uniqueness, he thus reciprocates, and replicates, the offense.

There are few love relationships in Nabokov's fiction in which something is not held back or kept half-closed: the images of locked, closed, and half-open doors in *The Gift* carry the symbolism of relationships based on various degrees of respect for the privacy of the other. In *Ada* an unguarded blending of personalities in ecstatic love-making takes place in the early stage of Ada's and Van's love: here brother meets sister, like meets and loves like, in a reciprocal projection of narcissism, causing serious injury to everyone around, as egotism and narcissism are bound to do. The relationship is different after Van's and Ada's reunion in old age, when no one is left to be hurt by their love: by that time the elderly siblings have gone through dissimilar experience and developed divergent personalities. Significantly, their contact involves a remove in space (their rooms are at palatial distances from one another) as in time: Ada gives Van the symbolic signal of their new form of relationship by first pretending to abort their reunion after their long separation.

The mind of even one's closest partner is never completely annexed to one's own, and the success or failure in the continuous cultivation of the lovers' relationship is explored in most of Nabokov's works. Falling in love is akin to mystical experience, as if the door on the "hereafter" comes "slightly ajar in the dark."[31] The image of the door coming ajar is both a conduit (the light can shine through), a barrier (the passage is not wide open), and an option (one may slam the door shut or open it wide). The "hereafter," with which the narrator of *Look at the Harlequins!* translates the Russian *potustoronnost'* may be an attempt to convey the near-mystical coloring of the dreamy elevation of the spirit which overtakes one's soul in that rare and happy state, helping to distance it from the "average reality." Yet *potustoronnost'* may also suggest the mystery of the mind – the inner world – of the other, the world with which one is given a chance to connect, by opening the floodgate of one's own soul, with the attendant risk of exposure. Falling in love is a *gift* one receives – in keeping with the title of the novel where that experience is prominently present; yet it takes courage to accept the gift along with the responsibility that it brings.

Indeed, reciprocal love, beyond the initial *vlyublyonnost'*, is an active effort to keep the door in its half-opened state, a constant and conscious endeavor to maintain the qualities that are important for one's beloved. Hugh Person wins Armande's *ricochet* affections through a pathetic but determined emulation of her Swiss lover's athletic exploits: though at first he miserably fails to keep apace with Armande and her ski companions, he does better with every sally into the mountains, showing both a lover's perseverance and a potential for achievement in the sphere to which Armande attaches intrinsic value though he does not. After marriage he quietly gives up athletic exertions; and it is alone that Armande goes on the skiing vacations in search of her lost love. Having literally gone to school with the father who did not know how to maintain his son's affections, Hugh allows his personality to go to seed in other ways as well – mainly, by not striving to develop his quite promising literary talent and by settling for a humdrum editorial job instead. When addressing him on the telephone, Armande mispronounces his name as "You," unwittingly reproducing Nabokov's address to his wife in the last chapter of *Speak, Memory*: there is a potential of an I–Thou relationship in their case. But Hugh will not know how to keep the door ajar: he will either seek to open it wide by pseudo-Humbertian maudlin adorations, or let his wife shut it before him, leaving him no links to "another brain humming near his" (*TT*, 58 [ch. 16]) on the pillow.

The person addressed as "You" in *Speak, Memory* is not an indolent proofreader but, among other things, an ideal reader of the very text through which she is thus addressed. The text itself is a gift and a graceful courtship, like Martin's stories told to Sonia or Zina's to Fyodor, a courtship both of the beloved and of the reader, whom the beloved partly represents. In writing his autobiography Nabokov restrains the carnivalesque confessional impulse by, among other things, placing the reader in a complicated deictic situation, that of a witness, by invitation, to a monologue addressed to a third party, the speaker's partner, in a world adjacent to his own but at a remove from ours. The last chapter of *Speak, Memory* is a kind of an extended prose apostrophe which distances the audience before bidding it good-bye,[32] removing the vestiges of the carnivalesque "free and familiar contact" between the audience and the actors. This effect is parodied in the final episode of *Look at the Harlequins!* where the speaker's last wife is also addressed in the second person rather than described in the third, like his previous loves. Yet this unnamed woman is also the subject-matter of part six of *Look at the Harlequins!*, so that at times the use of the second-person "you" sounds like a somewhat artificial replacement of the third-person "she." By contrast, Vera Nabokov, named in the dedication of *Speak, Memory*, is never turned into the subject-matter of the autobiographical narrative; instead, in the last chapter she is invited to recollect the things seen, lived, and loved together. "Love only what is fanciful and rare," writes Fyodor in a poem to Zina (*Gift*, 156 [ch. 3]), meaning not that which is unavailable to the multitudes but that which has become particular, rare, because it has left a mark on the "subjectively perceived texture" animated by "the act of individual creation " (*SO*, 118) – not just any bird but the swift we have just seen flying over the old bridge (*Gift*, 94 [ch. 2]). What is referential for the person addressed as "You" in *Speak, Memory* is representative for the other readers; nevertheless, the images evoked for her sake resonate for all those of us who can also recollect the warmth of an infant's hand seeping through a mitten, or the "benches and park chairs, stone slabs and stone steps, terrace parapets and brims of fountain basins" (*SM*, 302 [ch. 15]) on which one has rested while watching one's child at play.

VI

Thus the author–reader relationship set by Nabokov's version of the individualist stance is likewise characterized by a restrained-carnivalesque oscillation between charm and detachment. As if inviting a friend to look at the same things with some of the same feelings, a Nabokovian text casts a spell on the reader by its crystalline style and the poignancy of what it tells us about Luzhin, Clare Bishop, Dolly Haze, Pnin, John Shade, Sonia Zilanov, or Sibyl Vane, as the case might be. At the same time, through an intricate patterning of motifs, witty paronomasia, Horatian satire, chesslike hermeneutic puzzles with multiple solutions,[33] and other kinds of the slightly agonistic intellectual play, the text also erects a partition, a screen which, though porous, restrains the emotional resonance between our world and its own "humming near."

NOTES

1 On the "high" and the "low" views of human possibilities, see Dorothea Krook, *Three Traditions of Moral Thought* (Cambridge University Press, 1959), 1–18.
2 Mikhail Bakhtin, *Problems of Dostoevsky's Poetics*, ed. and transl. Caryl Emerson (Minneapolis: University of Minnesota Press, 1984), 122.
3 This paradigm might supplement Northrop Frye's grouping of literary genres into "modes" (mythical, high mimetic, low mimetic, etc.) in accordance with the superiority, equality, or inferiority of their protagonists to the reader and to their own environment – see *The Anatomy of Criticism: Four Essays* (Princeton University Press, 1957), 3–69. In accordance with the purposes of genre analysis, one might also propose other bases for classification, such as, for instance, the ontological status of the *fabula* and its constituents – see L. Toker, "Towards a Poetics of Documentary Prose – From the Perspective of Gulag Testimonies," *Poetics Today* 18 (1997): 189–93.
4 Bakhtin, *Problems of Dostoevsky's Poetics*, 123.
5 I have dealt with this issue in the case of Nabokov's *Mary* in *Nabokov: The Mystery of Literary Structures* (Ithaca: Cornell University Press, 1989), 36–38.

6 Mikhail Bakhtin, *Rabelais and his World*, trans. Helene Iswolsky (Bloomington: Indiana University Press, 1984), 123.
7 *Transparent Things* (1972; New York: Vintage International, 1989), 93 (ch. 24). (Hereafter *TT*.)
8 See Bakhtin, *Rabelais and his World*, 255–56.
9 See Elias Canetti, *Crowds and Power*, trans. Carol Stewart (New York: The Seabury Press, 1978), 15. Canetti's cruelly demythologizing approach to mass psychology may be read as a counterweight to Bakhtin's theory of the carnivalesque.
10 Arthur Koestler, *Darkness at Noon*, trans. Daphne Hardy (New York: Macmillan, 1941), 256. The term "oceanic feeling" has been made popular by Freud – see *Civilization and its Discontents*, trans. and ed. James Strachey (New York: Norton, 1962), 8.
11 See Canetti (*Crowds* 49–63) on four types of crowds, including "baiting" and "feast" crowds.
12 *The Defense*, trans. Michael Scammell in collaboration with the author (1964; Vintage International, 1990), 29 (ch. 2). (Hereafter *Def*.)
13 The young man may, in fact, be literalizing a symbol: according to Canetti (*Crowds* 75–90), rain, rivers, forest, wind, the sea, and fire are among the most prominent symbols of the crowd.
14 Canetti, *Crowds*, 18.
15 Cf. Fedor Dostoevsky, *The Devils*, bk. 3, ch. 6. On Nabokov's reworking of other elements of this novel see John Burt Foster, Jr., *Nabokov's Art of Memory and European Modernism* (Princeton University Press, 1993), 100–04.
16 See Michael André Bernstein on "the viciousness that can be released by the carnival's dissolution of the accumulated prudential understanding of a culture" as a factor to be taken into account in our assessment of utopian theorizing – *Bitter Carnival: Ressentiment and the Abject Hero* (Princeton University Press, 1992), 8. On the grim para-utopian transformations of the carnival see also my article "Représentation de la crise dans l'oeuvre de Nathaniel Hawthorne: Le mode carnavalesque" in *Eclats de voix: Crises en représentation dans la littérature Nord-Américaine*, ed. Christine Raguet-Bouvart (La Rochelle: Rumeur des Ages, 1995), 97–109.
17 Canetti, the English translation of whose *Crowds and Power* was first published in 1962, talks of the "invisible crowds" of the dead (42–47); Nabokov's Timofey Pnin prefers to imagine more structured groups of ghosts: "The souls of the dead, perhaps, formed committees, and these, in continuous session, attended to the destinies of the quick" (*Pnin*, 136 [ch. 5]).
18 See Canetti, *Crowds*, 75–80.
19 *Ibid.*, 80–85.
20 This is the reason why studies of the ubiquitousness of ghosts in Nabokov's fiction, from W. W. Rowe's *Nabokov's Spectral Dimension* (Ann

Arbor: Ardis, 1981) to Brian Boyd's "The Problem of Pattern: Nabokov's *Defense*," *Modern Fiction Studies* 33 (1987): 575–604, strike me as undue literalizations of the persistence of a character's leitmotifs after the character's death in the *fabula*. Which is not to deny that in *Transparent Things* Nabokov does play with the idea of spectral presences; a case can be made, however, that even in this novel the "ghosts" serve as, for instance, the vehicle through which the device of "poetic justice" is self-consciously foregrounded. I tend to agree with Michael Wood that Cynthia's theory of the surviving "auras" of the dead is a strong response "to a need not to let go of the dead" (*The Magician's Doubts: Nabokov and the Risks of Fiction* [London: Pimlico, 1995], 79); Pnin's playfully formulated belief in "a democracy of ghosts" (*Pnin*, 136 [ch. 5]) is an expression of the same need.

21 See Gavriel Shapiro, "*Lolita* Class List," *Cahiers du Monde russe* 37 (1996): 317–36.

22 See, in particular, Julian Moynahan, "A Russian Preface for Nabokov's *Beheading*," *Novel* 1 (1967): 12–18; D. B. Johnson, *Worlds in Regression: Some Novels of Vladimir Nabokov* (Ann Arbor: Ardis, 1985), 185–223; and Vladimir E. Alexandrov, *Nabokov's Otherworld* (Princeton University Press, 1991).

23 Julian Moynahan, *Vladimir Nabokov* (Minneapolis: University of Minnesota Press, 1971), 13.

24 The Cyrillic letter "B," phonologically equivalent to the Latin "V," is the third letter of the Russian alphabet; the Russian-born author leaves his mark on the sequence of examination papers in the pile.

25 For a systematic study of Nabokov's auto-allusions, see Pekka Tammi, *Problems of Nabokov's Poetics: A Narratological Analysis* (Helsinki: Suomalainen Tiedeakatemia, 1985), 341–58 [and Gavriel Shapiro's essay in the present volume – ed.].

26 This statement from the lecture "The Art of Literature and Commonsense," is not overly optimistic, since the reference to the dreamers "roaming the earth" is a proviso: one can roam only when one is physically free. I was forcefully reminded of the truth of these words when reading the novels *The Keeper of Antiquities* and *The Faculty of Unnecessary Things* by Yury Dombrovsky, who was still in the Gulag when Nabokov's lecture was being delivered. Varlam Shalamov's short story "The Path," dealing with the author's ability to compose poems while walking on a self-made path in Kolyma woods, likewise resonates with Nabokov's lecture, in its own way. One day the authorial persona of the story notices someone else's footprints on his path: this intrusion of the world of Kolyma labor camps makes the path unsuitable for his poetry.

27 Even then, the content of the characters' monologues is usually rendered in a combination of summary and free-indirect speech, with very little or no use of direct speech utterances.

28 *Glory*, trans. Dmitri Nabokov in collaboration with the author (1971;

New York: Vintage International, 1989), 143–44 (ch. 34). (Hereafter *Glory*.)
29 Nabokov's allusions to the author of *La nouvelle Héloïse* ("I, Jean-Jacques Humbert"; *Lo*, 124 [pt. 1, ch. 28]) suggest a possible connection between mentorship and tyranny; see Christine Raguet-Bouvart, *Lolita: un royaume au-delà des mers* (Presses Universitaires de Bordeaux, 1996), 149–71.
30 Julian W. Connolly, *Nabokov's Early Fiction: Patterns of Self and Other* (Cambridge University Press, 1992), 143.
31 *Look at the Harlequins!* (1974; New York: Vintage International, 1990), 26 (pt. 1, ch. 5). (Hereafter *LATH*.)
32 Cf. Jonathan Culler, *The Pursuit of Signs: Semiotics, Literature, Deconstruction* (Ithaca: Cornell University Press, 1981), 135–36 on the embarrassing effect of apostrophe on the reader.
33 The eschatological significance of such puzzles is, unfortunately, beyond the scope of this paper. In *Aerial View: Essays on Nabokov's Art and Metaphysics* (New York: Peter Lang, 1993), 170–75, Gennady Barabtarlo gives an example of the possible use of a theological source (the religious philosopher Pavel Florensky) in a discussion of one of Nabokov's *aporiae*.

CHAPTER 6

Nabokov's trinity
(On the movement of Nabokov's themes)
Gennady Barabtarlo

> We give to Space an image, and to Time
> Our recollection, and to Matter – love.
>
> Dandelio

THE THEME

What single aspect makes Nabokov's polyhedral fiction so extraordinary? After all, few practiced readers will not agree with Martin Amis that Nabokov does "all the usual things" – creates characters, threads storyline, writes prose – "better than anybody else."[1]

The most striking difference between a casual reader of his writings, even an intelligent one experienced in good reading, and a seasoned student of Nabokov who has traversed his books many times, is that fine shades of meaning may escape the former, since it takes many successive readings of a Nabokov text to discover and then study higher planes of narrative strategies. Depending on the student's (the notorious Nabokovian "re-reader's") individual talents and experience, he will sooner or later make out the subtle recurrence of images and situations which weave, at a proper remove from the scene of action, thematic grids. The intricately beautiful meaning and function of these patterns – along with their aesthetic and even metaphysical implications – cut the most distinctive facet of Nabokov's work.

This essay considers the general subject of Nabokov's themes, in an attempt to single out and arrange several larger strains in them. In the last section, I take up the example of one of his earliest works, only recently published, to show that those strains were formed astonishingly early and ran a surprisingly long and stable course.

Before going any further, I should define the volume of meaning associated with the term *theme* inasmuch as it can be applied to

Nabokov. One excellent source for a clear-cut definition amidst the frightful confusion that reigns in this particular branch of terminology is chapter two of Richard Levin's classic book.[2] He distinguishes between two main definitions: the first has to do with the studies of themes that "trace the recurrences within a work (or among works) of various motifs or conceptions, embodied in the direct statements of the characters, the action and situation, the diction and imagery, and other components."[3] He sees in these mere tabulation that can be very useful but which admits of any number of interpretations, yet favors or even traces none in particular. The other, and in his view better, thematic reading entails an "approach to interpretation" which attempts to sort out recurrences and select among them "the real subject of the work" under examination. This allows the reader to interpret a work of imaginative literature "as the representation or expression of some abstract concept, which will therefore give the work its unity and its meaning." The latter part of this statement in particular strikes me as very fragile in its rigoristic simplicity – what is the "central idea" of any of Nabokov's novels? Besides, it is possible to argue that the generic distinction between "non-conceptual" and "conceptual" themes in Nabokov's instance is unclear because he treated the space of his fiction as if it were in principle completely and essentially ordered and cultivated by its maker and thus *any* recurrence within it is to be viewed as thematically, and thus conceptually, functional. Nabokov calls any such meaningful recurrence a "theme," whether referring to his own work or to that of a fellow writer, – and this is the meaning assigned to the term here.[4]

Brian Boyd, who publishes in unhurried increments an ongoing interpretation of *Ada*, counts over three-hundred themes of which he keeps record. He calls them *motifs*, and examples of these from a mere two pages of *Ada*'s chapter 10 enlist "generations," "sanatorium," "flowers," "black," and even "Ex" and "trans-."[5] It would appear that what we have here is a list of "themes" of the first subdivision in Levin's terminology. Yet this is scarcely so, because in Nabokov's mature fiction such recurrences are real and potent capacitors that carry thematic charge either across a local space (of a part or chapter) or in a submerged but periodically surfacing line stretching across the entire length of the book. Moreover, these numerous thematic threads are often connected and twined to form a complex pattern, an *anthemion* (one of the titles he toyed with for his autobiography), and sometimes missing one or two thematic nodes breaks the integrity of the chain severely – even though Nabokov as often as not builds in a possible detour.

THEMATIC CIRCULATION

No matter how true the above may be, or how many times this truth has been variously put to print, one can try to take a sharply different view, a "squinting" view as it were, and reduce the number of truly conceptual themes in Nabokov's fiction to a compact stock.

When one scans all that Nabokov has written in two languages chronologically, one can discern a gradual change from a motley, exuberant, omnivorous profusion of "themes" (in the first sense employed by Levin) to the more functional and concentrated ensemble of "informing themes," among which a few can be singled out as persistent. The global "Eye" – peeled, panoramic, unblinking (yet twinkling), insatiable – of his earlier experiments in fiction becomes, by the end of the 1920s, much more selective, sharper-sighted, and sometimes tearful.[6] Links among thematic points grow into an ever more intricate web, and their intricacy becomes more meaningful as Nabokov's art gains strength. Very soon the regular reader – that is, not an occasional guest of this or that book by Nabokov but one who revisits them all at certain intervals – notices that some of his themes migrate from book to book, evolving as the author's noosphere evolves. That regular reader may reach a stage of study from which Nabokov's novels, famous especially for their structural rigidity, lose much of their discreteness and gradually become entangled into a larger system, first engaging thematic links between adjacent works, then transmitting them to groups of books, and lastly seeing the entire complex of Nabokov's lifetime's work in two languages as an expanse of fiction divided into lots but irrigated by one furrow system of major themes.

The regal solitude and inescapable self-awareness (of mind, of the heart, of talent); nobility opposite vulgarity; bleak or disastrous marriage; carnal love; a warped perception of the world by one passionately obsessed; provisional authorial interference from beyond; spectral agency; death, usually violent; the translucent world of the hereafter. The string can no doubt be extended to double in length but at this level of generalization not much more. The resulting list allows not only obvious branching, with great amplification, but also further compaction under *fewer* headings. Naturally, subjects so lumped would be common to many authors; it is only at specific levels of "sub-headings" that a theme receives a patented Nabokovian treatment. It is, for example, specifically a peculiar mark of Nabokov's fiction that a child should exceedingly rarely have any siblings but very often be lost to its parents; that a maniac's thoroughly distorted view of the world should be made supremely plausible through an ingenious narrative technology; that a first-person narrator surviving the narration must have no verifiable surname;[7] that the author would often intensify and repeat "natural" phenomena (wind, rain, electric storm, a fire caused by lightning, swarms of mosquitoes, a patroling butterfly) at critical moments of the narration, or sometimes send a disguised plenipotentiary agent to inspect the scene; or that the world beyond the grave should be made pervious to light in one direction only, like in special interrogation rooms where those inside see but a mirror on the wall or a lethargic landscape, yet suspect that the glass is pellucid for the invisible, keen-eyed spectators outside.

GRINDING PERSONAL MATTER: "SPRING IN FIALTA"

A good student of Nabokov's life and art could not help noticing, even before the publication of Brian Boyd's analytical biography, and most certainly while reading that establishing work, that these and similar themes stood in a certain angular correspondence with the themes of Nabokov's life, his psychological circumstances and beliefs. Moreover, the artistic choice and treatment of a certain theme would go through a transformation that somehow agreed with the change in those circumstances and views. What is *Speak, Memory* if not a long and highly elaborate essay on precisely this sort of contrapuntal correspondence of art, life, and afterlife?

His father's sudden and violent death in 1922; his marriage in 1925 to a woman who influenced his views and his writing in a very profound, and not well understood, manner; the birth of his only child in 1934; the real possibility of losing both his wife (in 1934 and again in 1937) and son (then and any time thereafter); his mother's death in 1939 – these fateful events formed his Russian fiction and affected the English in a way that reflected them through a series of prisms and mirrors, often with the hidden object of staving off a possible catastrophe by describing it in depth and in advance.[8]

The most obvious examples of such personal studies can be seen in the various re-tellings of the calamity of losing a child (always the only one): to illness (*Camera Obscura* – a priori, as it were, *The Event*), to the imbecilic forces of a communistic evil empire (*Bend Sinister*), to madness ("Signs and Symbols"), to a catastrophic accident ("Lance"), to a maniac abductor (*Lolita*), to suicide (*Pale Fire*). For all his superabundant, bursting imagination, Nabokov was, in a sense, a surprisingly empirical writer.

Chunks of one's private life are to be pressed through the meatgrinder of a sharp imagination, blended with other ingredients, and only then made into shape suitable for use in fiction. The hero of *The Gift* explains to his fiancée that, for a future autobiographical novel (i.e. the one the reader is about to finish reading), he will "so shuffle, twist, mix, rechew and rebelch everything, add such spices of my own and impregnate things so much with myself that nothing remains of the autobiography but dust – the kind of dust, of course, that makes the most orange of skies" (*Gift*, 304 [ch. 5]).

As Timothy Henderson so aptly wrote in a recent exchange on the electronic forum NABOKV-L,

... there is a sense of autobiography everywhere in Nabokov, but in almost every case ([he] never lets you get away with sweeping statements) there is a tragic and purely fictitious flaw. He thinks he is perfect just as he is, or perhaps he loathes public introspection. So he invents problems he does not have, nightmare mutations of himself as paedophile, homosexual, fundamentalist, libertine, dimwit, Philistine, madman, criminal, American. He slings himself with misfortunes like poverty, alcoholism, the deaths of his wife and child, inescapable terror. Thus he stays on the solid ground – his heroes all share [by far the larger part] of his inner life, and there is no need for any journalistic immersion in other lifestyles and cultures – at the same time he has this tremendous patch of quicksand where he can let his imagination run wild.[9]

The truth of this latter proposition becomes especially evident in the novella "Spring in Fialta," stylistically and compositionally one of the best-crafted things Nabokov made. It stems from a very personal, and painful, patch of quicksand. Contemporaneous with the episode in his life that ignited the story and was still tender, "Spring in Fialta" is in some aspects oddly, and quite atypically of Nabokov, insistent on running, at times, very close to the guardrail of "real life," down to such details as a fiancé going away to a "tropical country" to work as an engineer while the heroine, her name plainly rhyming with the original, stays in Europe.[10] Incidentally, the name of the narrator, Vasily, is thoughtfully rendered "Victor" for the English version, so as not to change the initial letter in transit (which "Basil" would) and thus not to upset *its* "rhyme." But what is really astonishing about the novella's design is that the theme of the brief, poignant, fitful trysts of two strange lovers, notwithstanding its personal ring, is not, in the artistic sense, main here; nor is Nina's automotive death behind the scene, advertised by the intermittent reminders of the coming of a touring circus whose truck, advancing on Fialta, is on a collision assignment with her motorcar leaving the town. No, it is Fialta itself, and more specifically Fialta in springtime, that is the main theme of the story. Both its title and opening ("Spring in Fialta is cloudy and dull") bring that theme to the fore, and the narrative abandons at every opportunity the very simple, dotted storyline to break into rapturous, lavish, and startlingly vibrant descriptions of the minute and panoramic particulars of that particular time of year in that particular place. The somnolent, milky, damp, and fresh Fialta, that *italicized* Yalta with its quietly-agonizing Chekhovian implications,[11] is wholly invented yet almost wholly recognizable. We all have seen, or seem to have seen, sponges in the window of a seaside-town shop "dying a thirsty death," or entered such shops through the "streaming" bead curtain, or watched the "small swarm of gnats ... busy darning the air above a mimosa" – but Nabokov was there first, and deftly captured the image like a butterfly and affixed and described it, and the effect of his poetics depends on our effort to assimilate the image and recognize it as part of our own memory stock. His images are so vivid that sometimes Nabokov forces one to adopt them as belonging to one's own experience rather than to one's invaded and infected imagination.

In the original Russian the second paragraph of the story reads, interestingly, "raskryvaius', kak glaz, posredi goroda na krutoi ulitse, srazu vbiraia vsë ..." – "[I find myself] opening wide like an eye on a steep little street in the middle of town, taking in everything at once" (a list of beautiful minutiae follows). In his English version (which was a radical reworking of Peter Pertzoff's draft[12]), Nabokov replaces the image of an opening eye with "I found myself, *all my senses* wide open ..." And although all the narrator's senses are engaged in avid perception, it is, once again, his peeled eye focusing its loving attention on the world's things and situations, that makes "Spring in Fialta" so imaginable and so memorable. And this absorbent eye at the entrance of "Spring in Fialta" is not a one-time special device; Nabokov had used it before and would use later on, from *Sogliadatai* (*The Eye* in English) to "The Vane Sisters" ("it only sharpened my appetite for other tidbits of light and shade, and I walked in a state of raw awareness that seemed to transform the whole of my being into one big eyeball rolling in the world's socket" [*Stories*, 619]) to *Transparent Things*, where this eyeball rolls in the socket of a discarnate world from which it peers at ours.

It is worth noting that the narrator of a story so masterly written is himself apparently a non-writer – a highly cultivated man whom emigration had forced into commerce, but one who "never could understand what was the good of thinking up books, of penning things that had not really happened in some way or other ... were I a writer, I should allow only my heart to have imagination, and for the rest rely upon memory." And so the narrator who is a supreme craftsman of prose declares from within the very prose he is weaving that he is not a writer. This is a technical paradox of the story inherent in the first-person mode, extremely limiting on every hand; Nabokov had easily skirted that narrative bind in *Glory*, a third-person novel about another gifted non-writer. But in the Russian original of "Spring in Fialta" he makes an odd attempt to imply that somehow V. is perhaps a writer after all. Recollecting one of Nina's past visits, he mentions that he was busy writing when she rang the bell, and then lets us in on what went on between the two by saying that he "never finished whatever [he] was writing." Translating the story, Nabokov saw a glaring contradiction with the "non-writer" clause above, which could baffle a good reader (that V. might be scribbling office notes would be a dreadfully lame explanation), and he completely erased all mention of the narrator's writing in that episode and instead made him point, after Nina had left, at her dropped hairpin as *un objet compris à demi-mot*.

The second and very peculiar thematic paradox of this story, noted earlier, is that the recurrences of its romantic and tragic theme punctuate the recurrences of the "Spring in Fialta" theme, and not the other way round, as one would expect. It is gracile Nina – generous and casual in love, light-hearted and heart-rending – who resembles and points up hyaline Fialta at every turn of the two themes' pulsating parallel course through the story, and not the other way round. Here is one excellent illustration of this seeming paradox.

Segur complained to me about the weather, and at first I did not understand what he was talking about; even if the moist, gray, green-house essence of Fialta might be called "weather," it was just as much outside of anything that could serve us as a topic of conversation as was, for instance, Nina's slender elbow, which I was holding between finger and thumb, or a bit of tinfoil someone had dropped, shining in the middle of the cobbled street in the distance. (*Stories*, 423)

Not only is Nina's "slender elbow" made merely an instance of linear analogy with Fialta's ambience and moreover "essence" – the main subject of the story – but it is not even the only such instance, for next comes the bit of tinfoil, which is given the same weight in that amorous tribute to Fialta. Of course, the implication of *Nina*'s essence being "moist, gray, and green-house" is too subtle for words and is supported elsewhere in the story; and, of course, one should be able to link that tinfoil wrapping to Ferdinand, Nina's equine husband, who appears in the preceding paragraph nibbling on a "moonstone candy" (which, however, is said to be a "specialty of *Fialta*"); but both these subtleties reroute us back to the head of the analogy. In the very last, tremendous sentence of Nabokov's famous congested type[13] (its closing function and cadence and sheer winding length are matched in the cascading finale of *The Enchanter*) which sums up the novella, revisits and resolves its main theme, Fialta in spring, and relates the news of Nina's death, we learn at last why the tinfoil was shining: the hygroscopic skies over Fialta, dull and gray in the opening sentences, had imperceptibly become soaked with sunlight that in the last sentence burst through immediately before the announcement of the automobile crash survived by Nina's repulsive husband and his queer companion but not by Nina herself.

In short, it is doubtless a love story, but of a very special, Nabokovian sort, in which love for a body and a place is consummated in the ecstasy of an unprecedented description that immortalizes love's object, be it animate or inanimate. The verbal expression of that love subjugates, throws up in high relief, and ultimately commands the romantic theme of the story. One way to define that theme would be to say that in a world well-described – in a penman's imitation of a world well-created – or, to use John Shade's phrase, in a "universe scanned right," even a tragic love, even death is accounted for and resolved, either on the plane of narration, or more often on another, higher plane, where the radii of love drawn from the artist's "personal matter" converge in the unfathomable beyond.

In his first collection of short stories, *The Return of Chorb*, Nabokov placed two key stories, "Beatitude" and "Terror" (the latter comes last in the book), in close proximity to one another, separated only by "The Potato Elf." The first is about an overwhelming love for fellow creatures which overcomes a personal misfortune and laves and fills all the cracks of life; the latter, about the sore, abraded matter of existence when it is stripped of the protective coating of sympathy and appears literally beyond recognition. And the one in the middle – a structured tale, longer than the other two combined – deftly twists together both adjacent theses, the beneficence of love and the terror of unlove.

THREE PLANES

Love moves everything, and it quickens Nabokov's art in three staggered stages.

In every work, even in the shortest stories, he tries to capture and depict the "outer world," driven by an insatiable love for material detail accessible to any of the five senses. In most, he also explores the "inner world" of man's mind and heart by placing his character in a sharply critical situation. Love for the created natural world, in its immense variety and beauty, infuses and frames Nabokov's compassionate (or antipathetic) presentation of the psychological condition of a human creature, no less varied, pulsating between the beautiful and the ghastly.

And in many works, he sets out to examine the limits of both the outer and the inner spheres and projects his thought from the border of either into the (imagined) "other world," knowing and admiring its absolute resistance to advance probing yet finding repeated probing irresistible, because, as Dmitri Sineusov and John Shade have discovered, the very blunders in this pursuit can be, if not revealing, then rewarding.

All three stages have been put to intense study in the past thirty years; the trends have followed the natural order set above – from the more obvious to the more difficult and to the impalpable. Waves of scholarship rolled over one another in a relatively quick succession. Brian Boyd was the first to try and integrate all three in his study of *Ada* and in Nabokov's biography.[14]

Composing his mother's intimate portrait in *Speak, Memory*, Nabokov reveals a causal link essential for the understanding of his aesthetics, the link between love and a memory stocked with lovingly selected and collected gifts.

To love with all one's soul and leave the rest to fate, was the simple rule she heeded. "*Vot zapomni* [now remember]," she would say in conspiratorial tones as she drew my attention to this or that loved thing in Vyra – a lark ascending the curds-and-whey sky of a dull spring day, heat lightning taking pictures of a distant line of trees in the night, the palette of maple leaves on brown sand, a small bird's cuneate footprints on new snow. (*SM*, 40 [ch. 2])

This aetiological step from the premise of "loving with all one's soul" to storing in one's memory "things loved" is of much significance for our topic. Nabokov sometimes engages this device in the very process of describing its effect, and in the passage quoted he uses the very words with which his mother would urge him to commit something to memory precisely because it was the love for his mother that led him to store her words in the innermost vault of his mind and now to retrieve them, along with her diction, her intonation, and the expression of her face. Upon some modification, he put to good artistic use the dear things here listed as examples, and the attentive reader who follows his mother's advice will greet them with a salute of sudden recognition in an alley of his novel or in a line of his verse.[15]

That attractive love, which is always transitive, which has, that is, a direct object for its application, motivates Nabokov's exploration of the world given to our senses as well as the world imperceptible. That motive cannot be easily gathered from among Nabokov's published words. On one pressing occasion, however, he let his guard drop momentarily because an especially tense lyrical passage in his most personal work, the carefully engineered memoir, required that tremulous note of an unusual private admission. Just as he recalls, at the beginning of the book, his mother's instruction to preserve "loved things," so in its last chapter Nabokov invokes the second person, the "you" of the memoirist's beloved, to whom this book, as well as his other books, owes more than even his famous one-word dedication, omnipresent and omniloquent, can express. The first-person narrator is returning home from a hospital, around five o'clock in the morning; the second-person of his narration is about to give birth to the "third," and this event will complete the circular composition of the book and make its universe "scan right":

In the purity and vacuity of the less familiar hour, the shadows were on the wrong side of the street, investing it with a sense of not inelegant inversion, as when one sees reflected in the mirror of a barbershop the window toward which the melancholy barber, while stropping his razor, turns his gaze (as they all do at such times), and, framed in that reflected window, a stretch of sidewalk shunting a procession of unconcerned pedestrians in the wrong direction, into an abstract world that all at once stops being droll and loosens a torrent of terror.

Whenever I start thinking of my love for a person, I am in the habit of immediately drawing radii from my love – from my heart, from the tender nucleus of a personal matter – to monstrously remote [Russian: "monstrously evanescent"] points of the universe. Something impels me to measure the consciousness of my love against such unimaginable and incalculable things [Russian: "personal love against impersonal and immeasurable things"] as the behavior of nebulae (whose very remoteness seems a form of insanity), the dreadful pitfalls of eternity, the unknowledgeable beyond the unknown, the helplessness, the cold, the sickening involutions and interpenetrations of space and time.... When that slow-motion, silent explosion of love takes place in me, unfolding its melting fringes and overwhelming me with the sense of something much vaster, much more endurable and powerful than the accumulation of matter or energy in any imaginable cosmos, then my mind cannot but pinch itself to see if it is really awake. I have to make a rapid inventory of the universe, just as a man in a dream tries to condone the absurdity of his position by making sure he is dreaming. I have to have all space and all time participate in my emotion, in my mortal love, so that the edge of its mortality is taken off, thus helping me to fight the utter degradation, ridicule, and horror of having developed an infinity of sensation and thought within a finite existence. (*SM*, 296–97 [ch. 15])

Nabokov's autobiography is born of his intense love for the two tight innermost circles of two families, one revolving round Vyra, the other round Véra. In the first, at the onset of the memoirs, he is "the third person" walking between his parents down an alley on their estate; in the second, the "I" and the "You" lead their six-year-old son between them towards the sunset, and the book closes. The narrator himself is the planimetric intersection set within the double-arc of these two overlapping family circles.

All the above-noted main components of Nabokov's depictive, exploratory, and contemplative art reach their most intricate coordination and concinnity in *Speak, Memory*. Their relative presence is typical for his system: the most noticeable is the profusion of marvelously fresh details found in the world which the narrator shares with his readers, treated against decay by literary means; a partly submerged yet rich emotional psychological description of human relations and reactions; and a dotted thematic line touching on the mystery of death and the world to come. Even in the shortest possible space of the passage quoted one can see all three components in the action of their timed sequential combustion: the street is rendered unfamiliar by the lighting of a very early morning and the ingenious comparison with the outside world reflected in a barber's mirror (at this exact moment the narrator must be strolling past a closed barbershop); then comes a rapt hymn to mortal love, i.e., love limited by its duration yet keenly felt to be aimed at infinity and charged for eternity – for the "unknowledgeable and unknown" immortality.

This principle of graduated ascent from "outer" to "inner" to "other" is also clearly evident in *The Defense*, with its copious reproduction of precious facets of the material world, its tragic theme of the destructive power of consumptive passion and the healing one of selfless compassion, and its secret over-plot of the titanic struggle of spirits, with Luzhin's heart and mind as their battlefield – all three planes intersect in the most well-ordered and complex manner imaginable, which makes this novel one of the very few rigorously three-dimensional works of fiction known.

In the space of two or three opening pages Nabokov quickly engages, and pegs for future back-reference, all our senses, one after another, appealing above all to our ability to recognize an image as both familiar and yet never registered before – certainly not the way the image is captured and fixed by his art. This double requirement almost always underlies Nabokov's choice of a detail and its description. The smells of "lilac, new-mown hay, and dry leaves" that summarized a summer for a Russian boy (*Def*, 15), the "inky taste of the sticks of licorice" under one's tongue (16), the "crisp, crackling sounds" of the wicker chair (16), the tactile vision of "the mosquito fastening onto [Luzhin's] skinned knee and blissfully raising its rubescent abdomen" (16), the wool of his cloak irritating his neck (19) – every perceptive nuance is vivid and true in its singular beauty, and at the same time it will be revisited as Luzhin revisits his childhood later in the book.

All Nabokov's best books are written in accordance with this system. Indeed, it can be said that his very drive to write fiction originates in his desire to discharge, or express, his love at these three scaled levels. This of course holds true for every creative effort, but Nabokov, let me repeat, evolved a *system* in which precise description of the outward reality not only leads to higher and more complex phases of exploration by artistic means but is a required precondition for any philosophical or theosophical experiment. In this system, an unobservant or indifferent man cannot be an original thinker, and a professor Bolotov or even a professor Pnin (despite his strange, trance-induced intuitions) are much farther from the ultimate frontiers of the knowable than a professor Krug or for that matter the poets Koncheyev or Shade. I think that much of Nabokov's dismissal of Dostoevsky as an original thinker (let alone writer) derives from the fact that the latter was incapable of noticing the outside world in its specificity and was oblivious of such basic distinct characteristics, lovingly sought out and depicted by both major and weak artists, as scenery, weather, seasons, the floral landscape, or the chromatic variegation of the world, particulars in the appearance of the earth and of man. In some of his writer-characters, such as Ivan Luzhin or Shirin (*The Gift*), Nabokov points up this handicap as decidedly crippling in a prose writer, and in his Cornell lectures he cleverly proposes that Dostoevsky had crashed into the wrong genre, because his dialogue-crammed books are not properly novels whose specific art is the art of description, but rather oversized tragedies that twist and maul (but do not discard altogether) the dramatic conventions.[16] To Nabokov's eye, Dostoevsky's novels, reduced to mere dramatic explorations of rankled human psyche, are badly flawed because they are raw, unprepared, artistically uncultivated. Nabokov firmly believed that a psychological experiment in fiction cannot be fruitful without that admiring attention which the world open to man's perception is due. In other words, one cannot very well see through a perversion inside man's mind when one is incapable of seeing perfection outside one's own, as gross mistakes and incongruities will inevitably result (of the sort Nabokov impatiently points out to his Cornell students). A fictional world so poorly constructed comes apart at the first deft poke by an expert who knows its weak spots.

AN EARLY PROOF: *THE TRAGEDY OF MR. MORN*

Since the congenital limitations and generic conventions of the dramatic genre principally exclude description, with its loving gravitation to detail – the very matter of prose – in favor of dialogical characterization and spastic development by stages, it is an unsuitable vehicle for the sort of depictive-constructive, rhematic-thematic art of which Nabokov was champion. This is why, in part, he chastised Dostoevsky for turning his novels into exorbitant dramas and was known to remark that he at once put aside contemporary novels without further ado when, on rifling through them, he saw a vast preponderance of dialogue over description. His own attempts at dramaturgy (all Russian) show most obviously how discomforted he was by the lack of a narrative option. "For Nabokov writing for the stage was like playing chess without his queen."[17] He tried to overcome stock conventions with bold inventions, but as often as not he would simply lapse into a third-person narration (lengthy stage remarks, lengthy asides, stage description, preliminaries), which, however, sharply differs from the regular prosaic mode by virtue of its present tense, minced syntax, and an oddly subterranean narrative voice. This technical ingenuity blossomed in *The Event*, Nabokov's last and best play, but so did the purely prosaic elements in it.

It is the more astounding to discover that in one of his earliest works – indeed, in his very first major work, only now published – Nabokov displays an artistic command of all the stages noted above: verbal, thematic, compositional, psychological, and even metaphysical, a complexity that we had not expected to see until *The Defense*. Nabokov worked on *The Tragedy of Mr. Morn* in late 1923 and finished it in January of 1924. The play is a quick-paced, full-fledged, five-act lyrical tragedy in blank iambic pentameter, of incredibly high dramatic and poetical quality. In sheer expressive power it greatly surpasses anything that Nabokov had composed in verse before, and in the sense of total artistic worth it stands above most of his contemporary prose, excluding perhaps only "The Potato Elf" written later that year. The Russian original was published, in an imperfect and possibly unfinished state, only in 1997.[18] No English version exists yet, and the poetic ebullience of the thing, with its condensed metaphorical language, make translation quite difficult; it may well be quite some time before readers not versed in Russian will have access to it. For the present, they have no place to go but to Brian Boyd's account of the play, which is thorough but insufficient in some important spots.[19]

A few years ago I published a study of "Revenge," an uncollected, and at the time untranslated short story written almost concurrently with *Tragedy*, in an attempt to trace a number of themes deeply notched and developed in Nabokov's later writing to that pale yet interesting piece.[20] My straight argument was that Nabokov, even as a beginning prosaist, had collected a remarkably stable store of certain favorite themes and situations, as well as means to play them out, but still lacked stylistic dexterity and especially compositional sophistication, though he went on to gain both and bring these to perfection in short order. In light of the discovery of *Tragedy* this thesis must be, if not discarded, then completely worked over, for the play gives extraordinary evidence of technically mature and poetically brilliant expression and a well-built structure of what now appears to be Nabokov's first large, multi-partite work (it is made up of more words than many of his longer "tales" – more than, for example, "Spring in Fialta"). The peculiar feature of this unexpected masterpiece is its genre: Nabokov shows here a super-precocious command of high-level craftsmanship, not in prose but in drama, and in dramatic verse to boot. And yet in *Tragedy* he sets out to prove that a number of the depictive resources available to a true master of prose can be placed at a playwright's disposal if his model is, paradoxically, a *poet* (such as Shakespeare, or Lermontov, or Rostand, to name those closest in dramatic spirit to *Tragedy*) and not a prose writer who dabbles in drama either deliberately, like Chekhov, or unwittingly, like Dostoevsky. A steady supply of rich metaphors; puns and sound-clusters sparkling here and there; brisk velocity; an excellent coordination of the three main parts of the plot (Morn's dilemma; Ganus's torment; Tremens's delirium); a complication in the form of a super-agency (the Stranger) and an all-embracing and all-resolving theology (Dandelio) – Nabokov transferred these and other special features and thematic lines of *Tragedy* to his prose fiction where they underwent an evolution and reached the level of sophistication and beauty for which it is famous.

Boyd's account underestimates one most interesting singularity of this play. What he took for a "detailed plan" of the play is really a prosaic script, or rather a corollary exposition, of equal size (about eight-thousand words) and of immense value for the understanding of the work's concept and many particulars.[21] In content, it is a ringful of keys to the play's riddles; generically, it is one huge stage-direction that has become a detachable and independent work of strong prose. In fact, every other sentence betrays Nabokov's itching desire to yield to prosaic description, for every now and then he sinks into the historical past tense from the dramatic present and indulges in marvelous sketching of a physical or psychological landscape, and then only the plain syntax of short sentences reminds one that this is a script and not a novel.

My purpose here is far from offering even a cursory analysis of *Tragedy* although I firmly hold that a serious study should not be delayed until a translation comes along, both because it may be a long wait and because any translation will inevitably dull its brilliance and thus may diminish the scope of the study. For this article, I only want to extract from *Tragedy* a few remarkable examples of the three-fold thematic system of artistic treatment outlined above as instance or proof that Nabokov's thematic devices, main routes, and even ideas can be found in his earliest works – yet found much easier and in a much clearer-cut shape in the large and magnificent *Tragedy* than in the short and anaemic "Revenge." Moreover, at the end of the play the reader receives an amazing definition of that trinitarian system, or principle, in a concise formula fashioned by the strangely well-informed Dandelio,[22] one of the two most important characters; such open proclamations, and on such authority, are of course exceedingly rare in Nabokov's fiction.

Since the formal mold in which the play is cast is responsible for the way the images and thoughts are delivered, I have preserved the meter in the examples that follow; the accuracy is sufficient for my purpose, but one should remember that these renditions are mere illustrations.

a) Nabokov's typical inclination for a metaphoric and alliterative device finds a more natural environment in verse than in prose. Clusters such as "*i grezoi stanet griaz'*" ("and muck will be a dream") or "*ia ne iashcher – ne otrashchu*" ("Love's clasped my heart, and holds, and won't let go, / I pull at it – it only squeezes tighter / As death draws nearer... How can I tear off / Myself from my own heart? *I am no lizard – / I can't regenerate it...*"), are very frequent. A slightly more complex instance:

> ... yet in my glass of wine
> A bee's wings float, and so in every joy
> I see a hyaline sadness.
> [*krylyshki pchelinyia – prozrachnaia pechal'*]

One step up, at the level of phono-semantic associations, we can register, for example, the "crunching" sound which serves to allegorize a particularly difficult description of carnal desire, a Nabokovian demonstrative effect familiar to the reader of *Lolita* and *Ada*, and especially of *The Enchanter* where it crops up several times in the course of the story and bursts at the end into a veritable croaker-choir.[23] Insofar as I can determine, it originates in *Tragedy* where at the beginning Ella tells of her dream in which she is a "new white bridge" crunching "under the blind hooves" of her horse-mounted lover Clian, while at the play's close it is Clian (he is a bombastic but not giftless poet) who resorts to a similar sound effect:

> my hungry genie
> Is spinning in the dust, longing for you,
> Crackling his wings, beseeching...

In one of his very last Russian pieces, Nabokov reproduces this Lermontovian image in order to drape a nondescript state of mind or body (the "enchanter" is riding on a train to take possession of his prize): "The throbbing of the car's partitions was like the crackle of mightily bulging wings" (*En*, 53–54; that this simile is not an innocent poetic exercise becomes clear when the woman sitting next to him gets up and at once leaves the compartment).

Swooning in the first chapter, Pnin sees himself as a sick boy, his torso bared, and the doctor "press[ing] the icy nudity of his ear and sandpapery side of his head" to it. In *Tragedy* we see the first attempt at recapturing that childhood memory (Nabokov inserts here a monaural stethoscope between the "icy nudity" of the ear and the fever-hot one of the body):

[*Morn puts a revolver to his chest*]
> ... The barrel's cool,
> As was that polished, horn-like instrument
> My doctor used to fit [to my bared chest]:
> He huffed and listened ... his bald head and tool
> Heaved with my heaving breast.

In "That in Aleppo Once," when the nebulous wife of V.'s correspondent leaves him, he finds the room empty of any trace of her except for "a rose in a glass on the table ... nothing at all in the room to enlighten me, for of course the rose was merely what French rhymesters call *une cheville*" (*Stories*, 566). That detail had to wait at least twenty years to be published; here is Morn, in the very same situation:

>   ... She's taken everything,
> And I am left with nothing but these roses,
> Like in that song ... Their slightly crumpled edges
> Are barely touched by gentle fringe of rust,
> And water in the elongated vase
> Reeks of decay and death, like underneath
> Some ancient bridges ...

One can moreover find in *Tragedy* entire strata of plot material lifted like a large patch of sod and transplanted to Nabokov's late fiction. Who, for example, will not recognize in the following passage about the discovery of the King's underground passageway to his mistress's house (Ganus's wife Medea) a key episode in *Pale Fire* (with *Solus Rex* as an intermediary)?

> CLIAN   ... the rabble pressed
> Against the palace ... we were doomed; but five
> Horrific days we stayed the hurricane
> Of popular belief ... And then one night
> They burst in, and they hounded us all over
> The palace, me and Tremens, and the rest ...
> I ran, carrying Ella, through the chambers,
> Through inner galleries, and back, and forth,
> And up, and down, and heard around me shots
> And shouts, and rumble, and, twice, Tremens' cold
> Laughter ... And Ella moaned so horribly,
> So ... [*Pause*] Suddenly I see a swatch of drapery
> And silk behind it – off with it – and lo!
> A passage! Don't you see? A secret passage!
>
> DANDELIO   Of course I see ... The King made use of it
> To fly away unnoticed ... to return
> After his wing'd adventures to his labors ...

As if to make the family resemblance between the two plot-lines more striking, the King's bejewelled crown gets lost and found several times under unusual circumstances: during a single-self-combat which Morn wins at the cost of his honor, self-assurance, and the crown; during a revolt accompanied by the obligatory ransacking and looting; and during the counter-revolt, when Dandelio has it last.

At the higher level of thematic arrangement (so-called "patterns"), we see that Nabokov's beloved "magic carpet," whose pattern reveals its meaningful mapping when it is specially folded, has a regular part even in that early play. In a fist-fight with Ganus, Morn, a good boxer, is dancing round his clumsy and raging adversary, baiting him before knocking him down: "Right, rip the carpet, go ahead! Don't snuffle, / Don't haw! Make sharp, make sharp! Here comes a comma, / And now – a full-stop!" In the "script," however, Nabokov clearly marks this detail as thematically significant (clearly, that is, for the seasoned readers of his future works): "A table is knocked off. One corner of the carpet got folded over" ("zavernulsia krai kovra"). This will become Nabokov's code phrase for a secret aetiological coincidence of thematic lines in a number of works, worded in surprisingly like formulas. Here are a few between 1934 and 1949: "And, as often happened with him ... Fyodor suddenly felt ... the strangeness of life, the strangeness of its magic, as if a corner of it had been turned back for an instant and he had glimpsed its unusual lining" (*Gift*, 183 [ch. 3], and then again in chapter 5); "... to fold its magnificent carpet in such a fashion as to make the design of today coincide with the past, with a former pattern";[24] "I like to fold my magic carpet, after use, in such a way as to superimpose one part of the pattern upon the other. Let visitors trip" (*SM*, 139 [ch. 6]). In *Tragedy* Nabokov seems to fold it this way for the first time, and indeed the careful reader receives a *special* invitation to trip. The carpet reappears in the King's study, ripped by the rebels in several places, and then again in the last act, after the counter-coup, when Tremens says "they cleaned the royal chambers, beat the rugs, / Shook out my cigarette-stubs, Ella's hairpins." Thus the "carpet-pattern": Morn's easy, teasing victory over the doubly humiliated Ganus turns into his own humiliation and fleeing, through the agency of Tremens who, as witnessed by Dandelio, rigged the drawing of the lots ("of the two / That heart to me was dearer which was fiercer / In passion," he explains later); in consequence Morn loses Medea, over whom the two men fought in the first place, but Ganus does not get his wife back, etc., etc. – the line runs through very many dots and thus covers much of the ground "without lifting the pencil." As Tremens sums it up in the end,

> ... with cold curiosity
> I study convolute designs of patterns –
> The causes and effects – on that bright sword
> Which tips against my chest ...

In fact, one of the most amazing features of *Tragedy* is this total reciprocal engagement of all dramatic gears, so that every slightest turn of a larger cogwheel causes various revolutions in the smaller ones elsewhere in the mechanism of the plot, – and the other way round. Nothing spins uselessly in the void, nothing seems expendable, which is a wondrous feat for a first try and which, in some way, prefigures the perfectly smooth propulsion of Nabokov's later prosaic plots.

b) Why does Nabokov, in so many of his books, stress the utmost importance of the careful folding of the fiction's fabric so that the lines on the backside correspond with the face pattern? It is because this trope hints at the possibility of a third and a fourth dimension, a depth, a *lining*, which is placed in a harmonized relation with what his pencraft and compositional cunning have charted on the face of it. The volume of Nabokov's composition is often intersected by two or three planes, as he takes pains to explain in an extraordinarily outspoken letter to Katharine White of *The New Yorker*, who failed to see the lining in "The Vane Sisters" and rejected the story as a gimcrack (see *SL*, 115–18). Even though the eye has so much to feast on in his best fiction, there is always more in it than meets the eye. These other, invisible planes appeal to the reader's moral and metaphysical perception, in ascending order, expecting full like-mindedness on the former and offering the latter only as a thrilling option to the specially attuned.

The ethical tier of *Tragedy* rests on one main dilemma, but it is a complex one – and, once again, one that we see in Nabokov's fiction thenceforth through at least the mid-1960s. The King whose mask-name is Morn is the first in the long series of Nabokov's focal heroes endowed with nobility of lineage and heart and all the distinctive traits that come with this happy combination brightened by the presence of a strong mind. Each of these excellent qualities, however, has a shadow counterpart, with a latent tendency to take over under a special condition of intense passion, usually erotic. If Van Veen is a prime late example of this sort of psycho-ethical disaccord, "Rex X" of *Tragedy* is the first. His character combines personal honor and haughty pride; selfless service to his people and the vainglory underlying it; the advantages of a superior upbringing, intellect, and talent displayed in Morn's generosity, humor, and general brilliance – and a ruthless use of these advantages to an egotistic end and at the expense of the doubly disadvantaged Ganus, the enraged husband of the King's mistress, who was allowed by the King's unadvertised magnanimity to escape from the penal servitude to which he had been sentenced for his part in the uprising stirred by Tremens. The admirable becomes reprehensible when the centrifugal forces of love – the "radii" in that remarkable passage from *Speak, Memory*, streaming forth from one's heart – reverse direction and become ego-petal, as it were. The specific application of this difficult but well-known ethical condition takes in *Tragedy* the form of a rather original dilemma. The tragedy of Mr. Morn is that he is a *noble coward*. Love of self dictates self-preservation above all other considerations, and Morn, after much struggle, succumbs to it. In that sense, and in a classical sense, practically all Nabokov's fictions are tragedies, and with very few exceptions (all arguable), his novels escalate to a tragedy in the end, resolving the plot by a staged, reported, or implied death, usually violent.

Nabokov makes this early "solus Rex" face the dreadful dilemma as he faces the barrel of a pistol, alone in his study, obliged by the rule and word of honor to kill himself. His bravado a moment ago, in Tremens's house, when he seemed ready to do it there and then, has given place to mortal fear. He invents an abject but telling excuse of being unable to abandon Medea; it follows that he must sacrifice his throne and his honor for the sake of love. He knows perfectly well, however, that this romantic ploy is but shameful veneer covering a terrible flaw underneath, the flaw that will lead him to suicide, which is also a regicide, at the curtain.

In his "script," which, as I said earlier, wants to be descriptive in the prosaic sense, Nabokov names that flaw as "noble cowardice." He went on to treat it in several other works, playing with the "nobility" ingredient, for example, in *Glory* and "An Affair of Honor," whose original Russian titles, *Podvig* and "Podlets," render the opposition clearer; the first designates a noble effort to overcome fear, the second, the exact opposite of "noble," ignoble and opprobrious – the hero of the short story flees from the duel site after having challenged, quite out of keeping with his cowardly character, the lover of his wife to a "single combat." In the "script" Nabokov reminds himself to "make clear the difference between Clian's [base] cowardice and Morn's [noble one]."[25] And in Nabokov's last play, *The Event*, we see the selfsame theme of a particularly base variety of cowardice (with complications), explored against the terribly painful void of a dead child as a backdrop.

The direct plainness of the following summation of *Tragedy*'s ethical concept is very unusual for Nabokov, whose style usually becomes more ornate the closer he moves to moral matters: "Every spiritual trait in a man, even if it is fiercely protected, will come to the fore sooner or later, in this or that action, which will be base if the trait is base, or good, if the opposite is true."

His fatal flaw, once fully realized, irreversibly turns the King into Mr. Morn. The mask can no longer be removed because now it covers the grimace of common shame rather than the gleam of royal glory. "Fooled rabble does not know how dark and sweating / The torso of a knight is, clenched by th'armour / Of legendary make" he says in his final monologue-confession, filled with anguished contempt for himself and remorse, claiming that "everything" – his happy reign, his love, his honor, and in a sense his life – has been a dream, "and dream, once interrupted, can't continue." His death is cast in a somewhat Empedoclesque ecstatic "night radiance," and Edmin's words at curtain are a marvel of compact summation:

> ... nikto ne dolzhen videt'
> Kak moi korol' iavliaet nebesam
> Smert' Gospodina Morna.
>
> [... No man
> Should see my King as he presents to Heavens
> The death of Mr. Morn.]

c) The words about an interrupted dream and life are not a stale homage to Calderon. They carry a thematic load of much significance for the play's architecture and philosophy. *Tragedy* is chock-full of surprises; it is with much surprise, for instance, that we discover Nabokov's intermediary agent at work so early. Called "Stranger" (or foreigner, "inostranets"), he visits the stage at the beginning, at Medea's soirée, where the plot's knot is tied, and again in the end, the moment before it is cut. He shows up and vanishes like an apparition, and Morn cleverly calls him "somnitel'nyi somnambula," a dubious sleepwalker, because he drifts in and out of thin air and also because his mutter often sounds like a somniloquy. He makes it known that he is from twentieth-century Russia, "the northern land of children's fairy tales," to the best of Dandelio's knowledge – and Dandelio knows more than anybody else in *Tragedy*. During both the first and last visit the Stranger seems troubled by the direction and resolution of the plot, and we soon see why; the whole thing is but his dream, an intricate hallucination of a creative mind, a "dream of a drunken poet"! "Ia khorosho vas vydumal" ["Well did I make you up"], matter-of-factly he tells the amiably receptive King-Morn. This explains his vanishing trick: when the poet dozes off, he slides into the scene that his imagination has charted and peopled, but disappears from it when he wakes up:

DANDELIO ... Where did you hide yourself?

STRANGER I was aroused from sleep. The wind awoke me;
The sash banged. Took me quite a while
To fall asleep again ...

We had assumed that this agency does not appear until at least *King, Queen, Knave*, where it takes a form at once blunt and blurred. We see now that from the very outset Nabokov experimented with a contrivance that he would employ and perfect throughout his writing life. Why was he so devoted to it, trying hard – and usually in vain – to find similar "representatives" in great works of fiction, for example, in the macintoshed man traversing the pages of *Ulysses?* If I may be allowed to quote myself, "Nabokov always produces a medium: a true or specious vicar ... a narrative agent, often of questionable integrity or even identity, – because [a constructed] world cannot in principle withstand a direct touch of the [constructor's] hand."[26] Nabokov has often encoded and twisted his name, inserting various Vs, and VVs, and VVNs, and Bokes, and anagrams into his fiction, most laboriously in his last published book where both his penname and real name, not to mention the titles of his books, are cleverly jumbled and incrusted. But "the name's the thing," and to alter it in any way does not, as some suppose, mean to hide one's identity; it means to clone it, producing one's serial representative, a middleman required for the sort of artistic experimentation that was Nabokov's favorite undertaking. "Pseudonym" is the *mot juste*. I was stunned to discover, after many years of reading Nabokov, what surely is the only instance of his using his real name in fiction. Translating his 1939 story "Vasiliy Shishkov" – an earnest, well-rigged hoax[27] – for the 1975 collection, Nabokov inserted the following addition (italicized here): "and to you, *Gospodin Nabokov,* I must show this" (*Stories*, 495), which is doubly amazing, and not merely because this is entirely unexampled in his works but also because it is rather gratuitous in that particular story (a Russian poet, even at self-introduction, would scarcely address a fellow-artist in this buttoned-up fashion, instead of the usual name-and-patronymic formula), to say nothing of that "Mr." left untranslated! But this odd instance serves only to underscore Nabokov's principle which reigns everywhere else in his fiction, namely that "v zale avtora net, gospoda" ("the author is not in the house, gentlemen," "The Paris Poem" [1943], 120–21) – or rather, that one cannot see him.

It is interesting to note that the entire Stranger line is clean absent from the "script," which differs from the play in verse in a few other important ways, providing in most instances clarifying or enlarging commentary. And in regard to the baffling character of Dandelio, a saintly wiseman with a cat, then with a "holy parrot," the sketch found in the earlier prosaic version is both rudimentary and complementary. In the "script," he is said to have "a calm and in a sense radiant disposition towards all things. Everything in the world is a game for him, always equally amusing, always equally chance." This goes well with the following lines which endow Dandelio with the eye of an artist in love with detail:

> ... to incidental trifles
> My eye is well accustomed – I have studied
> Burrows of beetles, scratches on the body
> Of ancient furniture, fragments of pigments,
> Dust-specks on paintings unattributed.

In the key episode, the sharp-eyed Dandelio notices Tremens's switching the lots which settled whether Ganus or Morn must kill himself, but did not interfere, for the reason cited above. When both he and Tremens face certain death at the play's end – a fate set in motion, in a labyrinthine way, by Tremens's tampering with fate earlier and Dandelio's silence – Dandelio calmly, artistically, admiringly states his view, in response to Tremens's "Are you afraid of death?":

> I like it all: light, shadow, specks of dust
> Whirling in conical sunbeams, these puddles
> Of light splashed on the floor, and these big tomes
> Which smell of time. Death, I admit, is curious.

Suddenly interested, Tremens comes out of his strange soporific shivering and asks, "Do you accept death?" and Dandelio gives an unexpectedly clean-cut, dogmatic answer, confessing a creed of an unorthodox and non-Orthodox doctrine which, however, is more Christian than gnostic in essence:

> Yes. To resurrect,
> Matter must decompose. I see quite clear
> The Trinity. What Trinity? This: space
> Is God, matter is Christ, and time
> Is Spirit. Hence we posit that a world
> Composed of these three – that this world of ours –
> Is but Divine [bozhestven].[28]

Tremens, who, like all anarchists, is a flat thinker despite the grandeur of the Miltonian metaphors generously supplied him by Nabokov, and who is very unhappy and secretly yearns to be cured of the delirious tremor of his chronic nihilism, is fascinated by these words. Following his habit, yet almost wishing to be gainsaid, he tries feebly to interject a skeptical remark, but is at once cut short by Dandelio who reaffirms his credo and takes it further.

TREMENS   ... And yet our world ...

DANDELIO   ... is but Divine. And all is happiness,
> And therefore we must sing ev'n as we toil,
> For living on this Earth means working for
> That Master in three persons: space, and matter,
> And time. But time is up, the work is done,
> And we depart hence for the feast eternal,
> *Committing time to memory, and space*
> *To form, and love – to matter.*
> [*Dav vremeni – vospominan'e, oblik –*
> *prostranstvu, veshchestvu – liubov'* – emphasis added]

One cannot be certain that the parable of laborers in a vineyard (Matthew 20) is the allusion here – just as in the earlier lines about de- and re-composition of "matter" one can see a paraphrase of John 12:24 without being sure of it. What is clear, however, is that quite suddenly Dandelio's trinitarian principle takes on the artistic dimension so dear to Nabokov and so remarkably immutable throughout his life and literary labors. Memory was for him the only, yet conclusive, evidence of one's own place in time, and thus a necessary but sufficient means of feeding the imagination that informs the space of consciousness, prodding, steering, and improving one's memory. If we invest the word "imagination" with the artificial sense of "creating images," we can arrive at a familiar Nabokovian postulate that the grafting of memory onto imagination and the infusion of imagination into memory is not only a condition of art but perhaps also its cryptic essence, if art is to be understood as man's attempt to imitate the creative force of his Creator. "Time and space, the colors of the seasons, the movements of muscles and minds, all these are for writers of genius" (*LL*, 2). What follows "time and space" in this statement is, of course, the matter of the "outer" and "inner" worlds, for which time and space are formative, disciplining, and above all loving conditions.

This brings our long illustration back to its departure point. This cooperative transformation cannot occur without an enveloping and inspiring love for "matter." Nabokov, as said before, has installed and expressed that love in his art as yet another triad:

- the "eye-thirsty" love for the created world, in all its micro- and macro-forms, for things small and large, unnoticed or unworded before and thus begging to be brought to life by precise and fresh description;
- the love of the "first person" for the "second" and the "third" (the grand scheme of *Speak, Memory*), and its extension to others mostly by means of (quiet, unobvious) compassion and gentleness;
- a mysterious love for the invisible and the incomprehensible, based on an inarticulate but insuperable faith in the principal Divinity of the world, or the worlds – outside, inside, and beyond us; external, internal, and eternal.

The first kind drove and nourished Nabokov the craftsman, the surpassing master of words and cadences and architectonics – and, as the most conspicuous side of his art, it also drove and fed an early wave of his critics. The second kind took longer to recognize because its signs are much more withdrawn and also because it necessarily brings forth the sort of moral psychology that at the time (late 1970s) was shunned by all but the bravest or the most self-confident. Trained experts in Nabokov's verbal virtuosity were embarrassed by attempts to apply moral dialectics to a synthesized fictional world of Nabokov's high standard, while naive outsiders assumed that Nabokov was a self-engrossed logolept, at best indifferent to morality, at worst given to immorality, and in any event supremely arrogant. To quote a most recent summation of this sad situation,

Some readers still read Nabokov only as far as his negative irony, his trenchant ability to deflate, to register disappointments, humiliations and horrors, the kind of thing that they think demonstrates his scorn and *Schadenfreude*. As his Hermanns and his Humberts and his Paduks and his Graduses indicate, Nabokov is anything but blind to the darkness of life. But readers who stop there, and think that *he* stops there, in modernist irony or in a post-modernist *abîme*, miss altogether his positive irony, his attempt to encompass all the negatives, as he suspects life itself does, and reverse their direction in the mirror of death. The search for that possibility is what makes Nabokov different, and what makes him write.[29]

The search for the possibility of life after death can be fueled by the love for life *before* death, in all its diverse wealth and secret harmony. But even Nabokov's ghosts, on the most well-concealed plane of his system, make their imperceptible appearances in his novels precisely because of their protective love for the living who were and remain dear to them. Nabokov seems to return them to earth on the same rays of special charity that he says he feels issuing from his heart towards the "monstrously evanescent points of the universe" where he believed some of the dead who were and remain dear to him might somehow be reached.

Space, time, and matter are viewed in young Nabokov's speculative ontology as God (the Father), Spirit, and Christ, and to that Trinity human laborers devote their imagination ("image-making"), memory, and love. Not much later this ontology appears to have changed to a specialized form of gnosticism, although Nabokov was very reticent with regard to his private theology and one should tread warily there. However, it can be said with great certainty based on the good authority of his books, that space, time, and matter in his art are – not defined as (for definitions delimit), and are not understood as (for these notions surpass understanding), but *given* to us as, respectively, infinity, eternity, and immortality, and it is to these three, and to their alliance, that Nabokov devoted his art, often describing instances of their semantic opposites in conditional earthly life – yet sometimes also pointing up the irresistible pull this ternal principle has for the mortals.

Naturally, this level of difficulty was attained last of all, and only after Nabokov (and later his widow) had hinted at certain possibilities lurking there, which caused the plainer minds to engage in crude attempts to take full inventory of these possibilities, while the subtler ones became given to much throat-clearing on the sides. If it was hard enough to consider the moral aspect of Nabokov's work without chipping one's scholarly bonnet, then accepting Nabokov also as a mystic could well damage a strong reputation and ruin weaker ones. But even though these days it is much safer, easier, and pleasanter to bring new texts by Nabokov to light from a rather accessible trove,[30] the most, perhaps the only, fruitful method of future research will require, I am convinced, a synthetic consideration of the three overlapping planes, loosely defined here as artistic (or perceptive, or rhematic, or "outer"), psychological (or moral, or "inner"), and metaphysical (religious, mystical, or "other"). Each plane is backstitched by "themes," and these themes, as well as the planes they compose, are in a prodigiously complex but coordinated relation to one another, and that relation is mobile, and that mobility is of the kind that closes, yet "does not terminate," Dante's ternary, divine world.

NOTES

1 Martin Amis, *The Sublime and the Ridiculous. Nabokov's Black Farces* (London: Weidenfeld and Nicolson, 1979), 73.
2 Richard Levin, *New Readings vs. Old Plays* (The University of Chicago Press, 1979).
3 *Ibid.*, 11ff.
4 In fact, Levin notes that the terms "the central theme" or simply "the theme" are used indiscriminately to mean the same thing as the work's "informing motif" or even "governing idea"! (*ibid.*, 11). See *LL*, 91, 139, 283, and *passim*, for Nabokov's regular use of the term.
5 *The Nabokovian* 39 (1997): 52–55.
6 More on this in D. Barton Johnson, "'Terror': Pre-texts and Post-texts," in *A Small Alpine Form: Studies in Nabokov's Short Fiction*, ed. Charles Nicol and Gennady Barabtarlo (New York: Garland, 1993), 63 n.
7 See especially *Despair*, *The Real Life of Sebastian Knight*, *Pnin*, "The Vane Sisters," "Spring in Fialta." In *Look at the Harlequins!* this particular treatment becomes very prominent. *Lolita* and *Pale Fire* present special cases of dead narrators (death reported) whose surnames however cannot be verified within the book. *The Enchanter* is an even more special instance in Nabokov's onomastics: in it, he deliberately avoids mentioning *any* names (with one notable exception). On this see Gennady Barabtarlo, "Those Who Favor Fire," *Russian Literature Triquarterly* 24 (1991): 91.
8 See Charles Nicol, "Nabokov and Science Fiction: 'Lance'," *Science-Fiction Studies*, 14.1 (1987): 9–20; and *The Garland Companion to Vladimir Nabokov*, ed. Vladimir Alexandrov (New York: Garland, 1995), 103 and 114.

9 NABOKV-L@ucsbvm.ucsb.edu; directed by Donald Barton Johnson. October 4, 1997.
10 See Brian Boyd, *Vladimir Nabokov: The Russian Years* (Princeton University Press, 1990), 433.
11 Cf. a similar allusion to "The Lady with a Lapdog" at the end of "That in Aleppo Once," a story with a like setting (seashore town, a heart-rending love story, even though more or less quietly told).
12 New material on their collaboration on this and other stories can be found in Maxim Shrayer's article "After Rapture and Recapture: Transformations in the Drafts of Nabokov's Stories," to be published in *Russian Review*, vol. 58 (1999).
13 Of the greatly improved Dickens's patent: see *LL*, 21, and Gennady Barabtarlo, *Phantom of Fact* (Ann Arbor: Ardis, 1989), 106–07.
14 Brian Boyd, *Nabokov's Ada: The Place of Consciousness* (Ann Arbor: Ardis, 1985), and Boyd, *Vladimir Nabokov: The Russian Years* and *Vladimir Nabokov: The American Years*.
15 For example, "bird's cuneate footprints on new snow" can be spotted at the beginning of the poem "Pale Fire."
16 A similar observation had been made by at least two fellow émigré writers in the 1930s – see Alexander Dolinin, "Plata za proezd (Beglye zametki o genezise nekotorykh literaturnykh otsenok Nabokova)" (Fares for the Ride: Sundry Notes on the Origin of Nabokov's Literary Evaluations), *Nabokovskii Vestnik* 1 (St. Petersburg: Dorn, 1998). See also his "Tri zametki o romane Vladimira Nabokova 'Dar'" in *V. V. Nabokov: Pro et Contra*, ed. B. Averin et al. (St. Petersburg: Izdatel'stvo Russkogo Khristianskogo gumanitarnogo instituta, 1997), 697–740.
17 Boyd, *The Russian Years*, 482.
18 *Zvezda* 4 (1997): 10–98.
19 Boyd, *The Russian Years*, 222–26. Galya Diment's short paragraph on the play in *The Garland Companion* (588–89) derives from Boyd's description, as *Tragedy* was not yet published at the time.
20 Gennady Barabtarlo, "A Skeleton in Nabokov's Closet: 'Mest′,'" in *A Small Alpine Form*, 15–24.
21 It is published in the same issue of *Zvezda*, after the text of the play.
22 One weak point of the play is the profusion of more or less transparent *noms parlants*: Morn/Mourn, Tremens (delirium), Midia/Medea, Edmin/Admin, Ganus/Ganos (bright; also possibly Janus or even Jason). Old Dandelio may owe his stage name either to his sunny nature, or perhaps to the Russian phrase "Bozhii oduvanchik," heavenly dandelion, said of angelic-looking old men whose bald pate fringed by white hair may resemble at once a dandelion's flower-head gone to downy seed (and ready to be breezed away) and a nimbus. In the prosaic "script" he is once referred to as "an old man resembling a dandelion" (*Zvezda* 4 [1997]: 90). His name is spelled "Dandilio" in Russian, to

account for the English pronunciation of the flower (just as Medea is spelled "Midia"), but it is "Dandelio" in the "script."
23 See Barabtarlo, "Those Who Favor Fire," 93-94.
24 "The Paris Poem," *Poems and Problems* (New York: McGraw-Hill, 1970), 122-23. (Hereafter *PP*.)
25 *Zvezda* 4 (1997): 92.
26 Gennady Barabtarlo, *Aerial View: Essays on Nabokov's Art and Metaphysics* (New York: Peter Lang, 1993), 177.
27 For a brief account of this story's origin see Boyd, *The Russian Years*, 509-10.
28 This adjective in Russian has exactly the same secondary secular currency as "divine" does in English, e.g. "it's a *divine* poem" and the like.
29 Brian Boyd, *Nabokov's Pale Fire* (forthcoming), pt. 3, ch. 9.
30 Mostly, in one main depository of the Berg Collection in New York Public Library.

PART 2

Literary and cultural contexts

CHAPTER 7

Nabokov's (re)visions of Dostoevsky
Julian W. Connolly

A writer's relationship to the literary legacy of the past finds expression in a multitude of forms. Theoretical works by Yury Tynianov, Harold Bloom, and Gérard Genette, among others, have outlined some of the ways in which writers may articulate their attitudes toward the work of their predecessors. Vladimir Nabokov's attitude toward writers of the past was itself multi-faceted. When examining his approach toward the legacy of the past, readers need to distinguish between the declarations he made in interviews and lectures, and the more subtle reminiscences or allusions he incorporated into his literary texts. This is especially true in the case of Nabokov's treatment of Fedor Dostoevsky. While there were enormous differences in artistic temperament, stylistic technique, and philosophical world view, and Nabokov's professed antipathy for Dostoevsky's excesses was both highly critical and highly public, the evidence of his prose fiction reveals a more complex relationship. When one looks at the entire body of Nabokov's fiction, one must conclude that Dostoevsky was not just a "figure of fun" to Nabokov the writer. On the contrary, it is apparent that Nabokov's views on Dostoevsky underwent a complex evolution.[1] Most important to Nabokov, perhaps, were Dostoevsky's remarkable explorations of human consciousness. As we shall see, the young Nabokov found in Dostoevsky's work a stimulating set of ideas and techniques that helped shape his own unique portraits of human imagination and obsession. Dostoevsky's fiction provided Nabokov with provocative models of human imagination, both in terms of the kinds of visions attributed to his fictional characters and in terms of the way these visions are conveyed to the reader (that is, through particular kinds of first-person, confessional narratives). This article attempts to chart the dimensions of Nabokov's evolving relationship to the work of Fedor Dostoevsky.[2]

We may perhaps discern echoes of Dostoevsky in Nabokov's first novel *Mary* (*Mashen'ka*, 1926). Lev Ganin, Nabokov's protagonist, may be a distant relative of a figure represented in Dostoevsky's early writings, the character known as the "dreamer." Dostoevsky wrote about the dreamer both in a feuilleton, "The Petersburg Chronicle" ("Peterburgskaia letopis'," published on June 15, 1847), and in his short story "White Nights"("Belye nochi," 1848). According to Dostoevsky, the dreamer is one who loses touch with the everyday environment because of his intoxication with the alluring visions created in his imagination. For such a person, the world apprehended in one's dreams has more substance and appeal than the world in which one eats, sleeps, and moves. The young narrator of "White Nights" confesses to being such a dreamer, and he describes one radiant dream involving a romance between two young lovers in a gloomy, deserted garden, "with its paths overgrown with weeds, dark and secluded, where they used to hope, grieve, love, love each other so tenderly and so well."[3] The story of the romance continues with complications involving the young woman's old husband, the separation of the lovers, and their ultimate reunion "far from his native shores" in an "alien land" (WN, 168). Immersed in such dreams, the dreamer acknowledges how startling it is to be interrupted by "a dear old lady" who stops him in the middle of the street and "politely asks him the way" (WN, 165).

Ganin too becomes caught up in a series of reveries about a romance that unfolded in the dark paths of an old estate in Russia and culminated in the separation of the lovers. The woman he loved is now married to an older man, and Ganin too imagines a reunion with his beloved in an alien land, Germany. Like the dreamer, he is immersed in his reveries as he roams the city streets until he is "politely stopped by a foot passenger" who asks him "how to get to such and such a street."[4] Also like the dreamer, Ganin feels that the scenes created in his mental reverie have more substance than the world in which his body moves (see, e.g., *Mary*, 55 [ch. 8]). Is it coincidence that Ganin's immersion in his recollection of romance lasts four days and comes to an end on the morning of the fifth day, and this happens to be almost the precise amount of time covered by the dreamer's infatuation with a woman he meets in "White Nights"?[5]

Of course, one could point out that Ganin's reverie is the recollection and recreation of an actual romance that took place over a much longer period of time than the romance which forms the main plot of "White Nights." Yet it is also worth noting that the dreamer's experience of infatuation and loss is recounted from memory as well. What is more, Dostoevsky's dreamer characterizes himself as a poet, and it is possible that his account may have been subject to a process of artistic rearrangement and revision. Indeed, at one point, the woman he is talking with reproaches him for his style of narration: "You see, you talk as if you were reading from a book" (WN, 163).[6]

A more important difference, however, between Dostoevsky's and Nabokov's portraits of the dreamer lies in the way the two writers *conclude* their works. Both texts end with a scene of "awakening," and these scenes have some striking elements in common. Not only are both scenes set in the morning, they both contain an experience of seeing the world with a fresh vision, as we shall see below. Yet here is where the two authors' visions diverge. Crushed by the collapse of his romantic hopes, Dostoevsky's dreamer awakens to see the world grown older and darker ("The walls and the floors looked discoloured, everything was dark and grimy"; WN, 200). Ganin, in contrast, awakens to see a world flooded with bright light and new hopes. As if to underscore the disparity between *his* character's new state of mind and that of Dostoevsky's dreamer, Nabokov follows Dostoevsky in including a passage in which his hero looks at a nearby building. The difference in what the two men see is telling. First, the dreamer's observation: "I don't know why, but when I looked out of the window the house opposite, too, looked dilapidated and dingy, the plaster on its columns peeling and crumbling, its cornices blackened and full of cracks, and its bright brown walls disfigured by large white and yellow patches" (WN, 200). Ganin, however, looks at a new house that is still under construction. The description reads, in part: "The wooden frame shone like gold in the sun ... the yellow sheen of fresh timber was more alive than the most lifelike dream of the past" (*Mary*, 114 [ch. 16]). While Dostoevsky leaves his dreamer motionless in his room, passively contemplating the crumbling remnants of his unfulfilled dreams, Nabokov has Ganin abandon his room, and confidently stride off to undertake new experiences and new adventures. In ending this novel as he does, Nabokov suggests that Ganin has achieved a kind of *balanced* view of dreams and reality. While appreciating the richness of mental reverie, Ganin also discovers a new alertness to the potential richness of "real" life. Dostoevsky's dreamer, on the other hand, has become so dependent on his insular dreams that he is shattered by his contact with "real" life. In this, perhaps, he anticipates the anxiety experienced by the narrator of Nabokov's novel, *The Eye* (*Sogliadatai*, 1930). While both "White Nights" and *Mary* hint at the potential dangers of intoxication with dreams, only *Mary* illuminates a path out of that entrancing yet enervating realm.[7]

Whatever impact the image of Dostoevsky's dreamer may have had on Nabokov, there can be no doubt that Dostoevsky's early novel *The Double* (*Dvoinik*, 1846) represents a crucial text for Nabokov in his investigation of certain dimensions of human consciousness. Much of the fiction that Nabokov created during the years in which he became a writer of the first rank (the late 1920s and early 1930s) revolves around themes presented in that novel. Nabokov scholars have commented on numerous motifs that connect *The Double* and works such as *The Eye* and *Despair* (*Otchaianie*, 1934).[8] It is my intention to delineate a few fundamental thematic patterns that will underpin Nabokov's major fiction from this point on in his career.

In *The Double* Dostoevsky focuses on a man who is desperately insecure about his place in the world. Alternating between postures of self-affirmation and self-effacement, Yakov Goliadkin feels such stress at his vulnerability before others that he undergoes a strange bifurcation of identity: he sees in his world an identical double, and he alternately tries to make friends with this double and to expose him as a fraud. Ultimately, though, Goliadkin becomes overwhelmed with fear that his double will squeeze him out of his position in the world and take his place altogether. Nabokov found this tale to be a fertile source of personal inspiration. In an uncharacteristically warm assessment of Dostoevsky's writing, he told his Cornell students that the story is "a perfect work of art."[9] Yet in the same series of lectures on Dostoevsky, while commenting on books that one might dislike, he noted that one "may still derive artistic delight from imagining other and better ways of looking at things, or what is the same, expressing things, than the author you hate does" (*LRL*, 105). When one studies Nabokov's fiction of the early 1930s, one senses that he examined Dostoevsky's achievements in *The Double* with great care, and then went on to imagine "other and better ways" of expressing these achievements in works such as *The Eye* and *Despair*.

One of the most distinctive features of *The Double* is a basic hesitation it creates in the reader's mind. When Goliadkin imagines that his identical double has occupied a desk directly opposite his own, or that the double steals a document from under his nose and takes it into the director's office, or that the double makes jokes about Goliadkin with the other clerks, the reader cannot be sure whether Goliadkin is *imagining* the entire episode, or whether there actually is another person in Goliadkin's office upon whom Goliadkin projects his sense of physical identity. One critic has even argued that almost *all* the incidents described in *The Double* are nothing but a hallucination, and that they take place entirely within Goliadkin's fevered consciousness.[10]

Imagining other and better ways of manipulating this situation, Nabokov created a series of fascinating variations on its basic themes. In *The Eye*, for example, the narrator's claim that he is observing an independent "other" – the character Smurov – turns out to be false. There is no "double"; there is only the narrator who has come up with the idea of viewing himself from the outside as a kind of defense against public opinion. While the initial creation of the other self in *The Eye* stems from conditions remarkably similar to those described in *The Double* (the insecure narrator's fragile ego receives a crushing blow when he is humiliated in front of others, and he begins to see his "other" after he undergoes a kind of psychic death),[11] Nabokov provides an entirely different resolution to the initial dilemma. Dostoevsky's Goliadkin is desperately afraid of losing his place in the world, and he has a terrifying nightmare in which he sees hordes of Goliadkins springing up behind him to fill the entire city of Petersburg. Nabokov's narrator, in contrast, claims to welcome the fact of his own "non-existence," and he seemingly relishes the task of collecting the numerous images of Smurov circulating around him. This, then, is one of the major distinctions between Dostoevsky's narrative and Nabokov's text: where Dostoevsky's text is saturated with tones of anxiety, dread, and horror, the story narrated by Nabokov's protagonist is conveyed in a spirit of relentless bravado. Also important is the impact of the story on the *reader*. Whereas Dostoevsky weaves a tale that leaves the reader utterly confused over what is really going on in the work, Nabokov fashions a small puzzle that he invites his readers to solve as they savor the work. Indeed, Nabokov asserts in the preface to the English translation of the work that "only that reader who catches on at once will derive genuine satisfaction from *The Eye*."[12] The lucidity of Nabokov's narrative contrasts vividly with the confusion generated by Dostoevsky's uneven narrative tone.

In *The Eye*, Nabokov fashioned one variant of the initial situation created in *The Double*. His hero claims to be observing an individual who serves as his rival in certain situations (such as wooing a woman named Vanya), but the claim turns out to be illusory: Smurov and the narrator are *not* separate individuals; they are one and the same. In *Despair*, Nabokov fashions a new variant of the situation found in *The Double*, this time *reversing* the resolution he offered in *The Eye*. Here, the narrator Hermann Karlovich claims to have found an identical double in the person of a tramp named Felix. Yet this time, the resolution of the initial situation is not that Hermann and Felix are one and the same. In fact, they *are* separate individuals. The trick here, however, is that Hermann and Felix do not look at all like each other.

Thus, Nabokov has appropriated the fundamental ambiguity created by Dostoevsky in *The Double* and resolved it in two different directions in two different works. Reading *The Double*, one does not know whether Goliadkin actually sees another person in his office who looks like him, or whether he is entirely imagining the existence of another person. In *The Eye*, Nabokov explores the second alternative, and in *Despair*, he explores a variant of the first. Moreover, in each novel Nabokov introduces a playful rebuttal to one of the central concerns haunting Dostoevsky's protagonist. The narrator of *The Eye* not only does not *fear* the existence of a multitude of mirror reflections, he *welcomes* them, for they open up the possibility for him to resist definition by others. The narrator of *Despair* introduces an alternate response to the issue of multiplication of the basic self: he too welcomes it, but for a different reason. In his words, he looks forward to a time when "all men will resemble one another as Hermann and Felix did; a world of Helixes and Fermanns; a world where the worker fallen dead at the feet of his machine will be at once replaced by his perfect double smiling the serene smile of perfect socialism."[13] Here Nabokov revises Goliadkin's horror of multiple doubles to satirize the Soviet dream of a world of mass equality, a faith in "the impending sameness of us all" (*Des*, 20 [ch. 2]).[14]

When composing *Despair*, Nabokov also drew on distinctive elements found in other Dostoevsky works to add to the basic theme of bifurcation of identity raised in *The Double*. These include the morally repugnant notion of committing murder to fulfill an abstract, self-serving scheme (from *Crime and Punishment*), and the anxious, wheedling tone of a personal confession (derived from *Notes from the Underground*). In a very real sense *Despair* may be the single work by Nabokov that displays the most prominent array of Dostoevsky intertexts. What is one to make of this? Several critics have noted that Nabokov's novel parodies narrative and compositional features that are broadly recognized as Dostoevskian.[15] Yet as Alexander Dolinin has shown, the target of Nabokov's parodic jabs in the original Russian version of *Despair* was not so much Dostoevsky himself as "a strong Dostoevskian strain in the contemporary Russian literature from Symbolists to the post-revolutionary modernists."[16] This is a distinction that Nabokov himself apparently made in a speech delivered in Berlin on March 20, 1931, and it is indicated in the title of the talk: "Dostoevsky without Dostoevskianism" ("Dostoevskii bez dostoevshchiny"). As we shall see, when Nabokov revisited the novel in preparing its translated version, he shifted the sights of his parody to target Dostoevsky himself more directly.

Nonetheless, the central theme found in *The Double* and developed by Nabokov in *The Eye* and *Despair* – the preoccupation of a character with an apparent alter ego and a concern over a possible mingling or exchange of identity – became an essential theme in Nabokov's work from this point onwards. Over the course of his career, he would produce several other dazzling variations on it. Thus, while traces of the theme can be found in such works as *Invitation to a Beheading* (*Priglashenie na kazn'*, 1935–36) and *The Gift* (*Dar*, 1937–38),[17] it emerges with full force as a core concern of his first English-language novel, *The Real Life of Sebastian Knight* (written 1938–39, published 1941). The narrator of the novel, identified only by the initial V., claims to be working on a biography of his late half-brother, a writer named Sebastian Knight. What makes the novel particularly distinctive is the way Nabokov creates a curious blending of "reality" and "fiction" in V.'s quest. That is, V. encounters people who seem to have come to life from the pages of Sebastian Knight's fiction, and V. discovers that his own research draws him perilously near to the central emotional experiences of Sebastian's own life. By the end of his narrative, V. proclaims: "I am Sebastian, or Sebastian is I, or perhaps we both are someone whom neither of us knows."[18] Readers of the novel have vigorously debated the issue of whether V. and Sebastian were indeed separate, autonomous figures or whether one "created" the other.[19] We must note, though, that the ambiguity raised by Nabokov in *The Real Life of Sebastian Knight* is of an entirely different order than the atmosphere of mystery and confusion permeating *The Double*. The apparent overlapping of identity is not a source of terror for Nabokov's protagonist, nor does it produce a sense of bewilderment for Nabokov's reader. Again, as in *The Eye*, Nabokov has created an intricate pattern that challenges the reader to ponder the relationship between "reality" and fiction, and to realize that any narrative about a life inevitably tends to fictionalize that very life. What is more, Nabokov's novel suggests that the "real" life of any writer rests in the writer's fiction, not in a mechanical recitation of names, dates, and locations.

Nabokov would return to this theme again in *Pale Fire*, but once more he produces a new variation on the basic theme. In this novel, a college professor named Charles Kinbote claims that an autobiographical poem written by John Shade contains veiled allusions to Kinbote's former life as King Charles II of the land of Zembla. Even more than in *The Real Life of Sebastian Knight*, Nabokov constructs his novel in such a way that the reader discerns an intriguing pattern of interlacing themes, details, and concerns between the lives and works of John Shade and Charles Kinbote. Once again, readers and scholars have engaged in a vigorous debate about whether Shade and Kinbote are truly separate beings, or whether one is the creation of the other, or whether they are both the creation of a third figure in the novel, such as a professor named Botkin.[20] Yet Nabokov has not merely retraced his own steps here. As a commentator on the life of another, Charles Kinbote does not seek merely to "find and follow" the patterns of his subject's life, as did V. in *The Real Life of Sebastian Knight* (see *RLSK*, 202 [ch. 20]). The worlds evoked both through Shade's poem and through Kinbote's commentary breathe with an energy and independent life of their own. Their relationship is less one of imitation or replication than of counterpoint and complement.

Once again, it is clear in this novel how far Nabokov had moved beyond the theme of multiplication of identity found in *The Double*. Although Charles Kinbote evinces a spirit of paranoia that may recall Goliadkin's anxieties in *The Double*, he tries to suppress his distress and instead reaches out to his audience, calling upon them to contemplate the mystery and beauty of patterns of recurrence in the world. What the reader finds both in *The Real Life of Sebastian Knight* and in *Pale Fire* is an attitude that constrasts sharply with the pervasive tension informing *The Double*. Unlike Goliadkin, who is terrified at the thought that there exist in his environment other beings who may be so like him that they can even take up his place in the world, Nabokov's protagonists seem to welcome the idea that the cosmos contains other "beings akin to them" (to paraphrase the final phrase of *Invitation to a Beheading*). Where does this attitude come from?

In part, it reflects Nabokov's own predilection for imagining other identities. He once told an interviewer that people "tend to underestimate the power of my imagination and my capacity of evolving serial selves in my writings" (*SO*, 24). He often created fictional alter egos who crop up in his work in various guises, sometimes bearing anagrammatic variations of his name. He even made a most un-Goliadkin-like pronouncement when he responded to an interviewer's inquiry about his "social circle" in Montreux. After mentioning the ducks and grebes of Lake Geneva, his sister Elena, Van Veen (he was finishing *Ada*), he asks: "Who else? A Mr. Vivian Badlook" (*SO*, 110).[21] Beyond the humor, however, one perhaps detects a deeper wish – the impulse to transcend the confines of the solipsistic prison of the self. In this regard, one thinks of Nabokov's analysis of the relationship of a writer and his audience: "I am all for the ivory tower, and for writing to please one reader alone – one's own self. But one also needs some reverberation, if not response, and a *moderate multiplication of one's self* through a country or countries; and if there be nothing but a void around one's desk, one would expect it to be at least a sonorous void, and not circumscribed by the walls of a padded cell" (*SO*, 37; emphasis added).

Yet beneath this desire for a "moderate multiplication of one's self" in the audience there perhaps lies an even more profound impulse. For this, we should consider Nabokov's description in *Speak, Memory* of the powerful effect that the feeling of love has on his sense of self: "Whenever I start thinking of my love for a person, I am in the habit of immediately drawing radii from my love – from my heart, from the tender nucleus of personal matter – to monstrously remote points of the universe" (*SM*, 297 [ch. 15]). He continues: "I have to have all space and all time participate in my emotion, in my mortal love, so that the edge of mortality is taken off, thus helping me to fight the utter degradation, ridicule, and horror of having developed an infinity of sensation and thought within a finite existence" (*SM*, 297 [ch. 15]). It is through intimate connections with other beings that one steps out of the "horror" of the solitary soul.

By the time he wrote *Pale Fire*, the complexity of Nabokov's fictions had developed far beyond the cunning variations on issues of identity and doubling found in *The Eye* and *Despair*. What is more, Nabokov's attitude toward Dostoevsky's legacy had undergone a considerable evolution as well. In the mid-1940s, as he began to teach works of Russian literature, first at Wellesley College, and later at Cornell, he re-examined many works by the major Russian authors. Now looking at these works with the probing eye of a teacher as well as a writer, he developed a more critical attitude toward Dostoevsky. In September 1946, Nabokov wrote to Edmund Wilson that he had been re-reading Tolstoy and Dostoevsky: "The latter is a third rate writer and his fame is incomprehensible."[22] He told his Wellesley students that we would give Dostoevsky the grade of C– as a writer (Tolstoy received A+).[23] The lecture notes preserved from his teaching at Cornell offer more detailed insight into the specific flaws Nabokov detected in Dostoevsky's writing (see *LRL*, 97–135). Perhaps most important was Nabokov's perception of Dostoevsky as a disturbing blend of journalist and prophet. In Dostoevsky's work, Nabokov perceived a deplorable tendency toward didacticism at the expense of art. In addition, Nabokov decried Dostoevsky's lack of attention to concrete detail, his weakness for sentimental clichés, and his reliance on melodramatic stage effects. A pithy remark he prepared for an interview in 1963 sums up his negative appraisal of Dostoevsky: "He was a prophet, a claptrap journalist and a slapdash comedian ... [H]is sensitive murderers and soulful prostitutes are not to be endured for one moment – by this reader anyway" (*SO*, 42).

This last comment about "sensitive murderers and soulful prostitutes" is, of course, a reference to *Crime and Punishment*, and it echoes a more discursive analysis in Nabokov's Cornell lectures of a sentence from *Crime and Punishment* that Nabokov characterizes as follows: "But then comes this singular sentence that for sheer stupidity has hardly the equal in world-famous literature" (*LRL*, 110). He then quotes the sentence – "The candle was flickering out, dimly lighting up in the poverty-stricken room the murderer and the harlot who had been reading together the eternal book" – and he subjects it to a scathing critique. What he finds most objectionable about the sentence is its linkage of a "filthy murderer" and an "unfortunate girl" (*LRL*, 110). He sees in this "a shoddy literary trick" and "a gust of false eloquence" (*LRL*, 110). Not only does he find it reprehensible that Dostoevsky would link the "inhuman and idiotic crime" of Raskolnikov with the "plight of a girl who impairs human dignity by selling her body" (*LRL*, 110), he accurately notes that while Dostoevsky describes in great detail Raskolnikov's crime, his muddled motives, etc., the novelist tells the reader almost nothing about Sonia's acts as a prostitute. He sums up this elision as "a glorified cliché": "The harlot's sin is taken for granted. Now I submit that the true artist is the person who never takes anything for granted" (*LRL*, 113).

I would argue that Nabokov's indignation over Dostoevsky's handling of the Raskolnikov–Sonia relationship played a role in the design of his most famous novel *Lolita*, which was written during his years at Cornell. The novel contains several threads of an anti-Dostoevsky polemic, and these are primarily centered on the relationship between Humbert Humbert and Dolores Haze, and on the way Humbert as narrator treats Dolly as the subject of his narration. Several critics have noted that the theme of sexual child abuse in *Lolita* recalls a series of parallel situations depicted in Dostoevsky's work: Svidrigailov has a reputation for child abuse in *Crime and Punishment*, and Nikolay Stavrogin in *The Devils* writes a document implicating himself in the abuse of a child who, at twelve, was the same age as Dolly Haze when Humbert first saw her. Humbert himself writes that he felt a "Dostoevskian grin dawning" as he contemplated the fact that by marrying Dolly's mother he would be able to have ready access to the child (*Lo*, 70 [pt. 1, ch. 17]). Yet Nabokov's handling of this theme engages in a subtle, though forceful, polemic with Dostoevsky. Just as Nabokov noted with indignation the relative lack of authorial attention given to Sonia and her plight, so too Katherine O'Connor has pointed out that the little girl mentioned in Stavrogin's confession hardly exists "as a living personality"; she is, in fact, "virtually expendable as a truly individualized character."[24] In *Lolita*, Nabokov set out to remedy this recurrent disregard for the living personality of the child, and he did so in a particularly subtle way. First, he created a narrator who initially seems to reproduce Dostoevsky's fundamental error: Humbert focuses almost exclusively on *his* suffering, his "crime," and he allows the reader almost no direct access into his victim's inner world. Indeed, he confesses near the end of the novel that he "did not know a thing about [his] darling's mind, and that quite possibly... there was in her a garden and a twilight, and a palace gate..." (*Lo*, 284 [pt. 2, ch. 32]). Nevertheless, he provides enough glimpses of Dolly's personality for the reader to recognize that behind the image of "this Lolita, my Lolita" exists a valiant, spirited child who struggles to find her independence much like a distant hill Humbert observes "scrambling out – scarred but still untamed – from the wilderness of agriculture that was trying to swallow it" (*Lo*, 153 [pt. 2, ch. 1]).

In addition to the theme of child abuse, Nabokov parodies other elements from Dostoevsky's work. Thus, Humbert's confession, with its clear awareness of the reactions of its intended audience, resonates with the self-conscious confessions written by the narrator in *Notes from the Underground* and by Stavrogin in *The Devils*. In each case, the narrator-confessor is acutely aware of the potential response of his anonymous audience, and he seeks to manipulate that response. Yet while all three confessions are pre-eminently self-centered and self-serving, the two confessions in Dostoevsky's work never break out of that mode.[25] Humbert's confession, in contrast, ultimately does serve another purpose. Most readers find in the final stages of Humbert's narrative a broader desire not merely to explain his behavior, but to atone or compensate in some small way for the damage he has inflicted upon Dolly. Unlike the suffering of Sonia Marmeladov or the 12-year-old Matresha, Dolly's suffering transcends the clichés of sentimentalism, and it merits both a serious exposure and a belated expression of remorse.

While Nabokov's *Lolita* displays other traces of the writer's new polemic with Dostoevsky,[26] it was when he revised his translation of *Despair* for the 1966 edition that Nabokov took full advantage of the opportunity to castigate his famed predecessor for his handling of the "inhuman and idiotic crime" of Raskolnikov's murder. Insightful readings by Davydov ("The Shattered Mirror"), Dolinin ("Caning of Modernist Profaners"), and Foster (*Nabokov's Art of Memory*) have delineated many of the specific ways in which Nabokov's novel responds to and rejects essential elements of Dostoevsky's art, and it would be superfluous to retrace those readings here. We should note with Dolinin, though, the primary effect of Nabokov's revisions. After dissecting the flaws of Dostoevsky's work in his Cornell lectures, Nabokov retargeted the aim of his parody of *dostoevshchina* ("Dostoevsky stuff") away from such epigones as Leonid Andreev and Il'ia Ehrenburg, and he directed his parody squarely at Dostoevsky himself.[27] Not only did he introduce new, derogatory references to Dostoevsky into his English translation (see, e.g., such phrases as "the *Dusty-and-Dusky* charm of hysterics" [*Des*, 188 [ch. 10]; emphasis added] and "Crime and Pun" [*Des*, 201 [ch. 11]]), but he also reshaped some earlier references to give them a more pointed edge. Thus, the original Russian phrase that read "in spite of a grotesque resemblance to Raskolnikov" becomes in English the more caustic "in spite of a grotesque resemblance to Rascalnikov" (*Des*, 189 [ch. 10]).

When we recall the specific criticisms leveled by Nabokov at *Crime and Punishment* in his Cornell lectures, we should take special note of the vehemence with which he disparaged Dostoevsky's treatment of Raskolnikov as a "sensitive" murderer. Not only did Nabokov find Dostoevsky's exposition of the reasons for Raskolnikov's crime "extremely muddled" (*LRL*, 113), but he also faulted Dostoevsky for failing to show any true development within the character. As he argues: "we see a man go from a premeditated murder to the promise of an achievement of some kind of harmony with the outer world, but all this happens from without" (*LRL*, 109). Having chided Dostoevsky for putting his characters in the position of "sinning their way to Jesus" (*LRL*, 104), Nabokov would have frowned upon Raskolnikov's sudden conversion at the end of the novel, when for some inexplicable reason the character suddenly experiences true love for Sonia and is ready to begin a new life of repentance and regeneration.

Indeed, in his foreword to the English version of *Despair* Nabokov refers to the issue of development and change within his own literary characters. Comparing Humbert Humbert with Hermann Karlovich, Nabokov suggests a significant difference between Humbert (whose sense of remorse we noted above) and Hermann, who steadfastly refuses to acknowledge the error of his ways: "Both are neurotic scoundrels, yet there is a green lane in Paradise where Humbert is permitted to wander at dusk once a year; but Hell shall never parole Hermann" (*Des*, xiii ["Foreword"]). Through these two characters, Nabokov offers two different responses to the kind of character created by Dostoevsky in Raskolnikov. Having castigated Dostoevsky for failing to show any development in Raskolnikov's personality, Nabokov offers Humbert as an example of a character who *does* undergo inner changes, with moving results. In the character of Hermann, on the other hand, he provides an alternative rebuttal to the Raskolnikov model: his murderer does not undergo *any* internal change, and never acknowledges his true culpability. At the same time, he is not offered any sudden transformation or redemption at the end of the novel. In this way, perhaps, Hermann's assertion that the "grotesque resemblance to Rascalnikov" is "canceled" (*Des*, 189 [ch. 10]) carries some validity. While he in many respects is a sterile follower of Raskolnikov, he does not succumb to any miraculous religious conversion. He remains a "filthy murderer" to the very end.

Nabokov would continue his efforts to debunk the mystique of Dostoevsky at various points in his career after the publication of the English-language version of *Despair*. One of the most strident of these occurs in his last novel, *Look at the Harlequins!* (1974). There, in a parody of his last Russian novel, *The Gift*, his narrator Vadim Vadimovich describes his own novel, *The Dare* (from *Dar*, the Russian title of *The Gift*). Whereas Nabokov's novel included a parodic biography of Nikolai Chernyshevsky, Vadim's novel includes a parodic biography of Dostoevsky, "whose politics my author finds hateful and whose novels he condemns as absurd with their black-bearded killers presented as mere negatives of Jesus Christ's conventional image, and weepy whores borrowed from maudlin romances of an earlier age."[28] Nabokov's "strong" opinions had clearly not weakened with the passage of time.

Over the course of his career, Nabokov's attitudes toward Dostoevsky's work underwent considerable evolution. From his obvious interest in Dostoevsky's treatment of issues of identity, delusion, multiplication of selves, etc., he became increasingly critical of what he saw as the author's basic flaws as an artist, and he was dismayed by the degree to which Dostoevsky's achievements were lauded in the West. Ultimately, he narrowed his critique to concentrate on Dostoevsky's treatment of the "sensitive murderer" and the "soulful prostitute." Detecting the privileging of allegory and ideology over aesthetics, he sought to parody and debunk the most famous figure in Dostoevsky's fictive universe. Through a series of media – interviews, lectures, and, of course, fiction – Nabokov sought to rewrite and reshape the classic Dostoevskian character. Seen as a whole, Nabokov's relationship to Dostoevsky forms an intricate design marked by points of striking engagement and recoil.

NOTES

1 Nabokov's own account of his repeated exposure to *Crime and Punishment* indicates some evolution in his views on Dostoevsky: "I must have been twelve when forty-five years ago I read *Crime and Punishment* for the first time and thought it a wonderfully powerful and exciting book. I read it again at nineteen, during the awful years of civil war in Russia, and thought it long-winded, terribly sentimental, and badly written. I read it at twenty-eight when discussing Dostoevski in one of my own books. I read the thing again when preparing to speak about him in American universities. And only recently did I discover what is so wrong about the book," Vladimir Nabokov, *Lectures on Russian Literature*, ed. Fredson Bowers (New York: Harcourt Brace Jovanovich / Bruccoli Clark, 1981), 110. (Hereafter *LRL*.)

2 We will focus on Nabokov's prose, not on poetry or drama. For commentary on Nabokov's poetic references to Dostoevsky, see Nora Buhks, "Nabokov and Dostoevskii: Aesthetic Demystification," *Russian Writers on Russian Writers*, ed. Faith Wigzell (Oxford: Berg Publishers, 1994), 132–33.

3 Fyodor Dostoevsky, "White Nights," trans. David Magarshack, in *Great Short Works of Fyodor Dostoevsky* (New York: Harper and Row, 1968), 168. (Hereafter WN.)

4 Vladimir Nabokov, *Mary*, trans. Michael Glenny in collaboration with the author (New York: Vintage International, 1989), 27 (ch. 3). (Hereafter *Mary*.)

5 The narrator's account of his romance is divided into four sections entitled "First Night," "Second Night," and so on, and it ends with a section entitled "Morning." A close examination of the narrative reveals, however, that an additional night passes without any description, and thus the events described in the story actually span six days, which happens to be the amount of time devoted to Ganin's activities in Berlin.

6 This comment oddly anticipates Dolly Haze's comment to Humbert Humbert: "You talk like a book, *Dad*" (*Lo*, 114 [pt. 1, ch. 27]).

7 Dostoevsky's dreamer speaks of the allure and the danger of the dreamer's life: "what can he find so attractive in the life which you and I desire so much? He thinks it a poor, miserable sort of life, and little does he know that some day perhaps the unhappy hour will strike for him too, when he will gladly give up all his fantastical years for one day of that miserable life" (WN, 167). This prediction seems to be borne out when Nabokov's character Podtyagin laments to Ganin: "I don't know, don't ask me, my dear chap. I put everything into my poetry that I should have put into my life" (*Mary*, 42 [ch. 5]).

8 See, *inter alia*, Julian W. Connolly, "Madness and Doubling: From Dostoevsky's *The Double* to Nabokov's *The Eye*," *Russian Literature*

Triquarterly 24 (1990): 129–39; Connolly, "The Function of Literary Allusion in Nabokov's *Despair*," *Slavic and East European Journal* 26 (1982): 302–13; Sergej Davydov, "Dostoevsky and Nabokov: The Morality of Structure in *Crime and Punishment* and *Despair*," *Dostoevsky Studies* 3 (1982): 157–70; and John Burt Foster, Jr., *Nabokov's Art of Memory and European Modernism* (Princeton University Press, 1993), 97–109.

9 *LRL*, 104.
10 See David Gasparetti, "*The Double*: Dostoevsky's Self-Effacing Narrative," *Slavic and East European Journal* 33 (1989): 217–34.
11 See Connolly, "Madness and Doubling," for the details of this process. On the other hand, the narrator's thoughts while contemplating suicide in *The Eye* have closer affinities with similar moments in Dostoevsky's "The Dream of a Ridiculous Man" and *The Devils* (also known as *The Possessed*) than with anything in *The Double*.
12 Vladimir Nabokov, *The Eye*, trans. Dmitri Nabokov in collaboration with the author (New York: Vintage International, 1990), xiv. (Hereafter *Eye*.)
13 Vladimir Nabokov, *Despair* (New York: Vintage International, 1989), 159 (ch. 9). (Hereafter *Des*.)
14 Dostoevsky, of course, was not the only writer whose treatment of the double would have come to Nabokov's attention. Others include E. T. A. Hoffman, Edgar Allan Poe, and Robert Louis Stevenson, about whom Nabokov lectured at Cornell. Yet it was not the double theme as often found in nineteenth-century literature (where doubling reflects a critical split in the human psyche, as, for example, between good and evil impulses) that attracted Nabokov's attention. As he told an interviewer: "The *Doppelgänger* subject is a frightful bore" (*SO*, 83). Rather, he was intrigued with the kind of imaginative freedom opened up by the concept of creating multiple alter egos and living in other identities.
15 See, for example, the discussions by Davydov ("Dostoevsky and Nabokov"), Connolly ("The Function of Literary Allusion"), and Foster (*Nabokov's Art of Memory*), as well as the comments of Liudmila Saraskina in "Nabokov, kotoryi branitsia . . ." in *V. V. Nabokov: Pro et contra*, ed. B. Averin, M. Malikova, and A. Dolinin (St. Petersburg: Izdatel'stvo Russkogo Khristianskogo gumanitarnogo instituta, 1997), 542–70.
16 Alexander Dolinin, "Caning of Modernist Profaners: Parody in *Despair*," *Cycnos* 12.2 (1995): 44.
17 In *Invitation to a Beheading*, Nabokov utilizes the theme of the double to illustrate Cincinnatus's struggle to cast off the constraints of enforced conformity he has accepted throughout his life. In *The Gift*, Nabokov creates an intricate pattern of doubling that is rooted in the very structure of the narrative point of view: the oscillations between the first-person and third-person modes of narration imply a complex relationship between the figure who narrates the action and that aspect

of the same figure who fulfills the role of a character *within* the narrated action. Incidentally, it is worth noting that the hero of the novel, Fyodor Godunov-Cherdyntsev, imagines a conversation in which his interlocutor, the poet Koncheyev, calls himself an "ardent admirer of the author of *The Double* and *The Possessed*"; see *Gift*, 341 (ch. 5).

18 *RLSK*, 203 (ch. 20).
19 For a discussion of some of these opinions, see Shlomith Rimmon, "Problems of Voice in Vladimir Nabokov's *The Real Life of Sebastian Knight*," *PTL* 1 (1976): 506–11.
20 For a summary of the early critical debate on the topic, see Pekka Tammi, *Problems of Nabokov's Poetics: A Narratological Analysis* (Helsinki: Suomalainen Tiedeakatemia, 1985), 201–04.
21 Note also Nabokov's admission of his interest in the writer "Sirin" in *SM*, 287–88 (ch. 14).
22 *NWL*, 172.
23 Hannah Green, "Mister Nabokov," in *Vladimir Nabokov: A Tribute*, ed. Peter Quennell (New York: William Morrow, 1980), 37.
24 Katherine Tiernan O'Connor, "Rereading *Lolita*, Reconsidering Nabokov's Relationship with Dostoevskij," *Slavic and East European Journal* 33 (1989): 68.
25 Those who make such confessions orally in Dostoevsky's work are sometimes more successful in reaching out to their intended audience; Raskolnikov's confession to Sonia is one such example.
26 See O'Connor, "Rereading *Lolita*," for a discussion of the parallels between Humbert's final meeting with Dolly Schiller and Svidrigailov's last encounter with Dunya in *Crime and Punishment*. For a discussion of parallels between *Lolita* and another Dostoevsky work – "The Gentle Creature" ("Krotkaia"), see Julian W. Connolly, "Nabokov's Dialogue with Dostoevsky: *Lolita* and 'The Gentle Creature'," *Nabokov Studies* 4 (1997): 15–36.
27 Dolinin points out that the "reorientation of the English *Despair* toward Dostoevsky" was prompted by the Western cultural context of the 1960s. He argues: "The main aim of Nabokov's individual crusade against Dostoevsky was not so much to dethrone his mighty predecessor as to undermine his critical cult in America, which tended to reduce all Russian cultural heritage to the soul-searching of *Notes from the Underground*, *Crime and Punishment* and *The Brothers Karamazov*." Dolinin, "The Caning of Modernist Profaners: Parody in *Despair*," *Zembla*, online, available at: http://www.libraries.psu.edu/iasweb/nabokov/doli1.htm, 2–3; this is a revised version of the article cited in n. 16 above.
28 *LATH*, 100 (pt. 2, ch. 5).

CHAPTER 8

Her monster, his nymphet: Nabokov and Mary Shelley
Ellen Pifer

Knowledge of Nabokov's privileged background has tended to confirm, for many readers over the past half-century, their wary impression of his fiction: that it is crafted by a "virtuoso stylist" coolly presiding over his universe and serenely, even cruelly indifferent to the plight of his characters.[1] To this familiar stereotype has been added, in recent years, the stigma of male chauvinism: Nabokov, we often hear it said, was a patriarch *par excellence*. The novelist's most widely read novel, *Lolita*, has only intensified the charges against him – inciting more than a few critics to label its author not just a sexist but a sexual pervert. The man who invented Humbert Humbert proved himself capable, after all, of fantasizing the most salacious, brutally oppressive conduct known to the male gender. For nearly three hundred pages the author lays out in rich, provocative detail the protracted sexual and social exploitation of a female – a helpless child, at that – by a pedophile who pretends to be her father. How far can the novelist's own perspective (and proclivities) lie, these critics ask, from his scurrilous narrator's?

Convinced that "most of the sympathies in the story" lie with Humbert Humbert, Naomi Wolf objects to the fact that in *Lolita*, "great art" makes the child's sexual exploitation seem, "if not good, then at least completely understandable."[2] Most troubling of all, it appears, is the way that the novelist extends his guilt-by-association-with-Humbert to *Lolita*'s readers. Invited to imagine (and thus to "understand") the nature of Humbert's desire, we come dangerously close, Wolf implies, to approving his actions: to regarding them as "good." The suspicion with which critics treat Nabokov's motives for writing *Lolita* may well raise questions about their own motivations as readers. Andrew Brink, for example, is wary of an author who could dream up "so perverse a theme" but does not, apparently, feel obliged to justify his detailed fascination with that theme.

Finding fault with Nabokov – for granting *Lolita*'s readers "permission to fantasize sexuality with very young girls" – Brink may be saying more about himself than he realizes.[3]

Recent commentary on *Lolita* has also made much of Nabokov's allegedly masculine "authorial narcissism." Voicing her antipathy, "specifically as a woman reader," to the novelist's penchant for narrative reflexivity, Virginia Blum detects in Nabokov's strategies a desire for "mastery" over his readers – the desire to "assimilate us in his solipsism" and "swallow us whole."[4] Several decades ago Alfred Appel, Jr., convincingly demonstrated, in his introduction to *The Annotated Lolita*, that by creating a sense of "the novel-as-gameboard," Nabokov distances *Lolita*'s readers from Humbert's narcissistic vision and undermines his claims.[5] More recently, Julia Kristeva has lauded Nabokov's reflexive strategies for exposing "the essential polymorphism of writing," which she defines – with a phrase familiar to students of Nabokov's style – as a process of "ongoing metamorphosis."[6] In an essay comparing Kristeva's linguistic theories to Nabokov's artistic practices, Elizabeth Ermarth similarly argues that Nabokov's emphasis on "parody" and "reflexive play" constitutes "an act of restoration of full power to a language" that realist narrative had reduced to "static forms."[7] But many readers are not convinced. For all its "linguistic and literary sophistication," Trevor McNeely contends, *Lolita* is a "world" in which "the concepts of purpose and value lose all meaning." While few critics would go along with McNeely's startling conclusion – that both Nabokov and his admirers are "Hitlerian nihilists" – a substantial number assume that no serious or sympathetic rendering of the child's plight can result from *Lolita*'s verbal highjinks.[8] In "a text that parodies all literary conventions," Blum maintains in *Hide and Seek*, the subject of child abuse becomes just another "literary convention" to be played with, another clever move or maneuver in "the author's delirious game" (214, 224).

Conflating *Lolita*'s author with its narrator, Blum ignores the novelist's strategies for undermining his protagonist's statements.[9] In a similar vein, Brink detects in Nabokov's "parody" a series of "clever disguises" by which he seeks to "camouflage" the essential identity of "Nabokov-Humbert" and the "hidden disreputable themes" at work in his "creative consciousness."[10] Others in the psychoanalytic camp likewise regard *Lolita*'s parodic structure as a "protective shield" against a "psychological interpretation" of the novel and its author.[11] Pressing the argument to an extreme is Brandon Centerwall, whose conflation of author and narrator leads him to declare in no uncertain terms that Nabokov was "a closet pedophile."[12]

Nearly fifty years ago, as though anticipating some of the cultural stereotypes he was to inherit, Nabokov made a candid confession in writing of his male bias. In a letter to Edmund Wilson (dated May 5, 1950) he stated, "I dislike Jane [Austen], and am prejudiced, in fact, against all women writers. They are in another class." Vexed by Nabokov's summary dismissal of Austen – whom he had identified in an earlier letter to Nabokov (dated April 7, 1950) as one of "the two incomparably greatest" English novelists – Wilson fired back on May 9, 1950: "You are mistaken about Jane Austen. I think you ought to read *Mansfield Park* . . . She is, in my opinion, one of the half dozen greatest English writers" (*NWL*, 241, 238, 243).

This exchange between two famous men of letters does not in the least suggest that Wilson was the more "liberated" male. To the contrary, while Nabokov admits to having a "prejudice" against women writers, Wilson elevates his personal bias to the level of an objective standard. In that same letter of May 9, 1950, his defense of Austen turns on "the fact," as he calls it, "that her attitude toward her work is like that of a man, that is, of an artist, and quite unlike that of the typical woman novelist, who exploits her feminine daydreams. Jane Austen approaches her material in a very objective way . . . She wants, not to express her longings, but to make something perfect that will stand" (*NWL*, 243).

More surprising than Wilson's rather typical pronouncements is the abrupt change of heart evinced by Nabokov only a week after Wilson advised him "to read *Mansfield Park*." Having consulted the novel in question, he quickly – and most "uncharacteristically," as John Updike observes – "capitulated" to Wilson's point of view.[13] "I have obtained *Mansfield Park*," Nabokov wrote to Wilson on May 15, 1950, "and I think I shall use it too in my course" (*NWL*, 246). That course, scholars know, was Literature 311–312, "Masters of European Fiction," which Nabokov inaugurated at Cornell University in the autumn of 1950. Under its auspices, he continued to lecture on Austen's novel – alongside works by Dickens, Flaubert, Proust, and Kafka – for nearly a decade, until *Lolita*'s *succès de scandale* allowed him to retire from teaching.

Two salient facts of Nabokov's life and career at mid-century undermine any facile assumptions about his presumed chauvinism – even those for which he is directly responsible. First, as his correspondence with Wilson makes clear, Nabokov's own confessed prejudice against women writers was set aside with remarkable alacrity – a mere week – after he opened the cover of Austen's novel. The second, far more telling fact concerns the composition of *Lolita*, which Nabokov began in earnest during the same period, 1950–51, that he inaugurated his course on European Fiction.[14] It is here, at the heart of Nabokov's most scandalous and suspect novel, that the stigma of sexism is definitively challenged.

Indelibly inscribed in *Lolita*'s ludic structure, I shall demonstrate, is the tribute it pays to two important female figures: one, the fictional child depicted in its pages; the other, a woman writer who composed her own literary "classic" when scarcely more than a child herself.[15] At the tender age of eighteen, Mary Shelley began work on her first and most famous novel, *Frankenstein, or the Modern Prometheus*, published in 1818.[16] Since then, her tragic "monster," like Nabokov's much younger "nymphet," has become a cultural icon and popular, if frequently misconstrued, figure of speech. (Just as Victor Frankenstein's name is often mistakenly attributed to the monster he creates, so the American kid, Dolly Haze, is repeatedly confused with the mythic creature, or seductive "nymphet," who takes life in Humbert's imagination.)

In recent decades, Shelley's novel has been regarded as a quintessentially "female" text, one that reflects at every level its author's painful experience of childbirth and child-loss. This characterization has held fast despite the fact that *Frankenstein* is even more exclusively focused on the male point of view than *Lolita*. (This exclusivity is yet another charge leveled in support of Nabokov's allegedly sexist preoccupations.) Just as Humbert's narrative is introduced by the Foreword ostensibly authored by John Ray, Jr., Ph.D., Dr. Frankenstein's narrative is framed by that of Captain Robert Walton, whose letters to his sister, Margaret Saville, precede his crew's rescue of Frankenstein from the Arctic's icy waters and prepare for Walton's ultimate task as a secondary narrator: to recount the story Victor Frankenstein tells him before he dies on board Walton's ship. Contained within this overarching frame is the creature's own narrated history: the account he gives Frankenstein, in volume 2 of the novel, of his solitary growth, development, and self-education.

Frankenstein, Ellen Moers points out in "Female Gothic," is "without a heroine, without even an important female victim. Paradoxically, however, no other Gothic work by a woman writer, perhaps no literary work of any kind by a woman, better repays examination in the light of the sex of its author."[17] Writing two decades after Moers, critics like Elisabeth Bronfen analyze the various ways in which Shelley's "personal experiences of birth" are reflected throughout the novel. In *Over Her Dead Body*, Bronfen points out that "by the time [Mary Shelley] wrote *Frankenstein*," her experiences of birth were "hideously and inextricably intermixed with death"; the text of Shelley's novel mirrors her "fear, guilt, depression and anxiety in relation to maternity."[18]

As numerous commentators have remarked, *Frankenstein*'s central theme reflects not only female but feminist concerns. The novel critiques male pride and ambition in its most lethal form: Dr. Frankenstein's overweening ambition to usurp the female's creative prerogative and engender, on his own, new life. In Anne Mellor's view, *Frankenstein* is "our culture's most penetrating literary analysis of the psychology of modern 'scientific' man ... and of the exploitation of nature and of the female implicit in a technological society." In *Mary Shelley: Her Life, Her Fiction, Her Monsters*, Mellor summarizes the femininist perspective that informs *Frankenstein*: "So long as human beings see nature as a loving mother, the source of life itself, they will ... protect and nurture all the products of nature – the old, the sick, the handicapped, the freaks – with love and compassion."[19]

If, in the letter he wrote Wilson on May 5, 1950, Nabokov appears to confirm his sexist label by voicing a "prejudice against all women writers," Mary Shelley likewise appears to condemn herself in her own words, which invite comparison with Wilson's stereotype of the "typical woman novelist." In her introduction to the revised (1831) edition of *Frankenstein*, Shelley openly identifies herself as a writer who, to recall Wilson's condescending phrase, "exploits her feminine day-dreams." The composition of *Frankenstein*, Shelley points out, was inspired by a "waking dream," whose "successive images" arose in her mind "with a vividness far beyond the usual bounds of reverie."[20] That Shelley's novel was born of reverie and inspired by "day-dreams" obviously constitutes grounds for Wilson to dismiss it; the same cannot be said of Nabokov. It was Wilson, not Nabokov, who defined the male writer's (superior) approach to his material as "objective." The Russian-born novelist had little faith and less interest in putative objectivity, particularly where aesthetic and literary matters are concerned.

A more likely explanation for Nabokov's stated "prejudice" against women writers was his relative indifference to the social and domestic world of manners and mores – the matrix in which most women's lives have for centuries been embedded and about which they have tended to write. When, therefore, Nabokov sends Wilson, in a letter dated November 18, 1950, a "mid-term report" on his course – and on "the two books," *Bleak House* and *Mansfield Park*, that Wilson had recommended to him – he categorically states: "In discussing *Bleak House*, I completely ignored all sociological and historical implications, and unravelled a number of fascinating thematic lines" (*NWL*, 253). (Here one wonders whether Nabokov may be playfully tweaking the nose of his American friend, whose weighty engagement with "sociological" issues was obvious to all who knew him and his work.)

The real proof, in any case, lies in the pudding – or, in the words of Nabokov himself, in the specific "fruit" of artistic inspiration, not the synthetic "jam" of general ideas (*SO*, 7). It is to *Lolita*'s narrative and thematic structure, and the homage it pays to *Frankenstein*'s, that we must turn. Let us note, to begin with, the striking resemblance between Shelley's famous protagonist and Nabokov's infamous one – a literary kinship that has thus far gone unnoticed. Perhaps the oversight is due to the obvious difference between the two characters. Victor Frankenstein, who endlessly delays marriage to the woman he says he loves, is almost comically indifferent to the force of sexual passion that consumes ardent Humbert. (From the vantage outlined by Brink in *Obsession and Culture*, however, Frankenstein's sexual indifference to Elizabeth would tend to suggest another basis for comparison with Humbert. In Brink's view, Humbert's nympholepsy betrays both "homoerotic" tendencies and a profound "ambivalence toward women."[21] Tellingly, Brink's conclusions correspond rather precisely to those of Humbert's own befuddled psychotherapists, who describe him, absurdly, as "potentially homosexual" and "totally impotent" (*Lo*, 34 [pt. 1, ch. 9]).

Once readers look beyond the disparity evinced by Humbert's sexual ardor and Frankenstein's sexual indifference, they will discover telling similarities between the two obsessed characters. The Promethean protagonist of Shelley's novel conceives in the bowels of his scientific laboratory the monster he comes to hate; Humbert conjures in the depths of his feverish imagination the nymphet he blames for bewitching him. Both of these solipsists engage in acts of creation that have disastrous consequences. The special poignancy of *Lolita*, like that of *Frankenstein*, derives from a vision of the child's sacred innocence, which both Shelley and Nabokov inherited from Rousseau and the Romantics.[22] But each of their male protagonists proves radically estranged from this resonant vision. That the offspring featured in each novel either lacks or loses a mother highlights the absence of a nurturing presence in their lives. What U. C. Knoepflmacher observes of *Frankenstein* is also true of *Lolita*: each is a "novel of omnipresent fathers and absent mothers."[23] In both novels, moreover, the protagonist is an accomplished liar, to himself as well as to others; he sustains his morally suspect project by means of elaborate and self-serving rationalizations.

Humbert's claim to have the "utmost respect" for "ordinary children" allows him to level ludicrous charges against the nymphet. To the "purity and vulnerability" of most little girls he contrasts her magical allure (*Lo*, 19 [pt. 1, ch. 5]). The nymphet, he argues, is not really a child at all: her true nature "is not human but nymphic (that is, demoniac)." Among the "innocent throng" of "wholesome children," he explains, the eager nympholept spies the "deadly demon" – the cruel enchantress disguised as a mere little girl (*Lo*, 16–20). Mythologizing the child as a juvenile *belle dame sans merci*, the pedophile transports himself, on wings of imagination, to that "enchanted island" where the "laws of humanity" conveniently do not obtain (*Lo*, 306 [pt. 2, ch. 6]). Taking refuge in fancy's "mossy garden" or "pubescent park," as he puts it, Humbert feels free to dally and disport at will (*Lo*, 16, 21 [pt. 1, ch. 5]).

The terms in which Humbert tries to justify his conduct expose the dark underside of his professed reverence for the child: "Humbert Humbert tried hard to be good. Really and truly, he did. He had the utmost respect for ordinary children, with their purity and vulnerability, and under no circumstances would he have interfered with the innocence of a child, if there was the least risk of a row" (*Lo*, 19–20 [pt. 1, ch. 5]). Here, unable to bear the weight of its own false logic, Humbert's argument instantaneously collapses. In one swift aside, the speaker bares his true motives, admitting that he would "interfere" with a child's "innocence" – that is to say (when the euphemism is decoded), he would tamper with her body – *only* if he could get away with it!

Giving him away at every turn, Humbert's rationalizations are as intriguing in their unwitting self-exposure as those of Victor Frankenstein. The linguistic parallels are also remarkable: the analogy, for example, between Humbert's self-styled "deadly demon," the alluring nymphet, and the dreaded "daemon," in Dr. Frankenstein's words, who haunts his creator (*Lo*, 17, 20 [pt. 1, ch. 5]; *F*, 39, 40, 56, 78, and *passim*). Monster and nymphet: each of these marvels of creation, the offspring of Promethean imagination, provokes torments in its creator. The true disaster, however, is one to which Frankenstein wholly, and Humbert partially, remains blind: the tragic betrayal of the child's original innocence. Just as Frankenstein's creature is trapped in the monstrous shape his maker conceives for him – a shape that alienates him from all humanity – so the child, Dolores Haze, is trapped in the nymphic guise conjured by Humbert's imagination.

"No creature," Frankenstein avows at the outset, "could have more tender parents than mine. My improvement and health were their constant care" (*F*, 19). In stark contrast to his own parents, the scientist assumes that, in Patricia McKee's words, he "ow[es] nothing to his offspring."[24] No sooner does Frankenstein bring his creature to life than he rejects him in horrified disgust. The misshapen monster is not the "beautiful" being his progenitor had dreamed of creating (*F*, 39). Frankenstein refuses to accept responsibility for the "filthy mass" of flesh-and-bone that he alone has brought into the world (*F*, 121). Blinded by disappointment as he formerly was by ambition, he does not recognize what his author, Mary Shelley, makes clear to her readers: ugly as the creature appears, he begins life as an innocent child in a benign state of nature. With a grotesque "grin" wrinkling his yellow cheeks, the trusting newborn instantly "stretches out" a "hand" to his parent – as Frankenstein, overcome by repulsion, rushes out of the room (*F*, 40).

As Shelley demonstrates later on in the novel, when the creature recounts his early history, Frankenstein's offspring began life as a "benevolent" being. As he tells the parent who abandoned him, "my soul glowed with love and humanity" (*F*, 78). Frankenstein's creature, Knoepflmacher observes, is a "genuine Wordsworthian child," one who delights as much "as any Romantic child" in the wonders of "feminine Nature." The creature's ugly, "contorted visage," Knoepflmacher adds, is but a "monstrous mask," beneath which "lurks a timorous yet determined female face."[25] Gendering as female the metaphorical face concealed beneath the creature's "monstrous mask," Knoepflmacher draws a parallel between the male monster and his female victims – particularly Frankenstein's innocent bride, Elizabeth Lavenza, whom the creature vengefully murders on her wedding-night. What Shelley invites us to see is that the murderer's original nature, his true "face," is not monstrous but benign. His humanity and vitality spring from that same idealized life-source, "feminine Nature," which animates Elizabeth's beautiful features. Ultimately, however, the monster grows ugly and twisted inside: psychologically speaking, he grows *into* the "monstrous mask" that once concealed an innocent nature. Yet as Shelley's readers well know, this *internal* distortion does not take place until the creature has suffered the most vicious blows from both strangers and the only parent he knows.

Like Frankenstein, who spurns the offspring he creates, Humbert betrays the covenant between parent and child while exploiting, at the same time, his role as her self-styled guardian. When, therefore, Humbert adopts an absurdly paternalistic note, lamenting the "definite drop" in young Dolly's "morals," readers are invited to consider the monstrous irony of his pretense. The perverse logic of Humbert's moral stance as *pater familias* is worthy of his literary precursor. Giving voice to his own brand of solipsistic fervor, Victor Frankenstein conceives of himself as "creator" not only of a single offspring but of a noble "new species" to follow in the wake of his initial experiment. Casting himself in the role of divine patriarch, he gloats over the "gratitude" he anticipates receiving from this new race of mortals (*F,* 36). His sudden *volte-face*, once the supposed paragon of this brilliant "new species" actually comes into being, is brutally comic in its reversal.[26] Cursing the "demoniacal corpse" that he brought to life, Frankenstein condemns his unfortunate offspring to an existence of isolation, misery, and finally rage against humanity (*F,* 39). The process by which Frankenstein projects his own "daemonic" energies onto his creature exposes in a sharper light Humbert's hazy references to demonic enchantment. Take, for example, the scene in which Humbert, having consummated his desire for the nymphet, stands at the hotel desk waiting to check out with his "little mistress." His "every nerve," Humbert comments, is alive "with the feel of her body – the body," he adds, "of some immortal daemon disguised as a female child" (*Lo,* 139 [pt. 1, ch. 32]). Here, as in Frankenstein's case, the narrator's rhetoric is more revealing than he knows. Humbert's evocation of the nymphet's mortal "disguise" draws attention to his own constant need to disguise his actions and bury his guilt.

Standing in the lobby of The Enchanted Hunters, Humbert strains to conceal what just took place in the hotel room upstairs, where he and the "female child" had "strenuous intercourse three times that very morning." As if that weren't enough, Humbert has other dreadful secrets to hide. Not until he has safely removed Lolita from the hotel and its onlookers will he dare to tell her the truth: that he has lied to the child about their destination as he has lied to her about her mother. The fact is, Charlotte Haze is not eagerly awaiting her daughter's arrival in some "hypothetical hospital" in a nearby town (*Lo*, 139–40 [pt. 1, ch. 32]). She is dead. Lolita is a hapless and helpless orphan.

As Humbert and the "lone child" drive away from the hotel, he is suddenly gripped by a feeling of "oppressive hideous constraint as if I were sitting with the small ghost of somebody I had just killed." Temporarily awaking to the fact that the little "waif" seated next to him is no "immortal daemon," Humbert reluctantly voices his guilt. In contrast to Frankenstein, whose little brother, William, is eventually murdered by the creature, Humbert has no hideous monster to blame for the violence perpetrated against a helpless child. There is only the "heavy-limbed, foul-smelling adult" seated next to her in the car (*Lo*, 140 [pt. 1, ch. 32]). No wonder Humbert feels haunted by a "small ghost": only a shade, or shadow, remains of Dolly Haze's brief childhood. The true "daemon" is the "pentapod monster," as Humbert later describes himself, who has defiled the offspring in his charge (*Lo*, 284 [pt. 2, ch. 32]).

The psychological process by which Humbert successfully blots out the image of the hapless child is identified, early on in the novel, as solipsistic. Recounting how he achieved, surreptitiously and onanistically, his first sexual ecstasy with the nymphet – as the child, munching an apple, lay sprawled on his lap – Humbert declares, "Lolita had been safely solipsized" (*Lo*, 58 [pt. 1, ch. 13]).[27] Humbert's vision of the "small ghost" takes on this added significance: to him, the child's reality is as fleeting and insubstantial as an apparition. Soon enough, the image of the nymphet reasserts its power over his imagination, blotting out the child's presence. To his dismay, says Humbert, he feels "the writhing of desire again, so *monstrous* was my appetite for that *miserable* nymphet" (*Lo*, 140 [pt. 1, ch. 32], italics added). Here the narrator's language offers a direct parody of Frankenstein's, as the scientist blames the "miserable monster" for what he himself has wrought (*F,* 39). In those moments, however, when Humbert's "monstrous" appetite temporarily abates, he again suffers "pangs of guilt." In realizing his "lifelong dream" by having sexual intercourse with a child, he has, he admits, "plunged" them both "into nightmare" (*Lo,* 140 [pt. 1, ch. 32]).

A similar descent into nightmare is traced by Shelley's narrator. Like Humbert, Frankenstein pursues his lifelong dream with solipsistic fervor – having "desired it," as he says, "with an ardour that far exceeded moderation." He too observes "the beauty of the dream" plunge into nightmare: a living hell that "even Dante could not have conceived" (*F,* 39–40). (In a similar allusion to Dante's *Inferno,* Humbert describes the strange admixture of guilt and rapture, heaven and hell in nymphet-love as the "first circle of paradise" [*Lo,* 283 (pt. 2, ch. 32)].) Seized by the Promethean ambition to create life, Frankenstein did not pause to consider the disastrous consequences that might follow. Blindly he assumed that the gigantic creature he was patching together out of bits and pieces – the flesh and "bones" collected in "charnel houses" – would be "beautiful"! Only after he assembles the severed "limbs" and body parts, stitches them together and jolts them into life, can he perceive what a dreadful "thing" he has done (*F,* 36, 39–40). Even so, Frankenstein does not accept responsibility for the "nightmare" that follows. Only after his infant brother and old father, his best friend and his bride have all died, does he fathom the extent of the destruction he has wrought.

The parallels that emerge between Frankenstein's "miserable monster" and Humbert's "miserable nymphet" help to clarify, as we have seen, the relationship of each protagonist to the child he victimizes (*F,* 39; *Lo,* 140 [pt. 1, ch. 32]). In addition, both of the protagonists suffer tremendous feelings of guilt, which they project upon others. Frankenstein curses the creature for the murderous actions he has set in motion; Humbert, on the other hand, reserves his purest hatred for the "fiend" who steals Lolita from him (*Lo,* 252, 259 [pt. 2, ch. 23, 26]). At a deeper level, however, both characters recognize in their hated adversaries a mirror-image of themselves. Frankenstein's hideous monster mirrors, first as a physical shape and then in his vicious actions, the scientist's monstrous disregard for moral and natural law. By the same token, Quilty, the pervert and pedophile, serves as a nasty, even more brutish reflection of Humbert's "monstrous" lust (*Lo*, 140 [pt. 1, ch. 32]). The passion enflaming both protagonists – one to usurp Nature and create life, the other to usurp a child's life for his own pleasure – is "monstrous" in the most fundamental sense: a transgression, as Humbert ultimately admits, of "all laws of humanity" (*Lo*, 306 [pt. 2, ch. 36]).

Like Frankenstein, Humbert eventually comes face-to-face with his hated reflection, or alter ego. Quilty, in collusion with Lolita, sets out to follow Humbert and his ward across the United States – until Dolly finds the chance to give her former "guardian" the slip. Relishing the game he has set in motion, Quilty adopts a series of playful guises and disguises. His object is not to avoid but rather to *attract* Humbert's attention, to taunt and bedevil him. Gradually it dawns on Humbert that he is enmeshed in a "demoniacal game" with a diabolically clever opponent: a creature who appears to know a great deal about him (*Lo*, 249 [pt. 2, ch. 22]).

As the hide-and-seek game between Humbert and Quilty intensifies, so do the intertextual echoes. After Lolita manages to disappear with Quilty, Humbert attempts to uncover the identity of his rival. Doubling back on the thousand-mile course that he, Lolita, and their tenacious "shadow" have traced across America, Humbert finds to his dismay that his secret sharer has once again anticipated his moves. Perusing the registers of countless hotels and motels, Humbert discovers a series of inciting clues and punning signatures, all pointing to his pursuer's grinning presence. Terrified and enraged, Humbert begins to regard his shadow as a "fiend" – employing the very epithet that Frankenstein repeatedly uses for the monster. Within the space of six short pages, Humbert calls his rival a "fiend" seven times: the series begins with the "red fiend" signifying Quilty's red convertible and progresses to "fiend's spoor," suggesting the trail left by an animal. It then proceeds to "shadow of the fiend," "loitering fiend," and "fiendish conundrum" – ending with two final references to "the fiend" (*Lo*, 247–52 [pt. 2, ch. 23]).

Caught up in a "cryptogrammic paper chase" with an adversary he loathes, Humbert has the uncanny sensation, nonetheless, of gazing into a mirror: his tormentor's "personality," "his type of humor," the very "tone of his brain," Humbert confesses, "had affinities with my own" (*Lo*, 249–50 [pt. 2, ch. 23]). Like Frankenstein, Humbert cannot deny the profound ties that bind him to his monstrous double, the despised creature who is at the same time, in an allusion to Baudelaire, his "brother" (*Lo*, 247 [pt. 2, ch. 22]). It takes years for Humbert to solve the riddle of Quilty's identity; and when he does, he vows to have his revenge. With the same fury that impels Frankenstein to destroy his creature, Humbert sets out to murder Quilty. For both protagonists, vengeance becomes the driving force of existence, the only reason to live. Each devotes his remaining years to pursuing his former pursuer, the creature who has robbed him of all that he loves. Stripped of friends and family, Frankenstein is reduced to the same state of isolation, despair, and hatred that has long since turned his creature into a murderer. Like the monster he created, Frankenstein now declares that "revenge" alone will keep him "alive": he will "pursue [the] daemon" until one of them "perish[es] in mortal conflict" (*F*, 171).

Spurred on by murderous rage, Frankenstein pursues the creature, as the creature has earlier trailed him, over the terrain of Europe, across the Mediterranean Sea, and through the "wilds of Tartary and Russia." Aware that he is being followed and, like Quilty, enjoying the game, the creature leaves taunting signs and symbols of his grinning presence. Even when Frankenstein pauses to rest in the "stillness of night," he is bedeviled by the sound of the creature's "loud and fiendish laugh ... I felt," he says, "as if all hell surrounded me with mockery and laughter" (*F*, 172). Taunting Frankenstein with the very epithets his creator has hurled at him, the monster now whispers "miserable wretch" in his maker's ear before vanishing into the shadowy night.

Staging an early version of the "cryptogrammic chase" that Quilty arranges for Humbert, Frankenstein's creature often leaves "a slight clue" or "some mark to guide" and goad his dazed pursuer. At one point in the game, as the two adversaries travel north into the snow, Frankenstein spies "the print of [the creature's] huge step on the white plain." At another stage, the scientist finds "a repast" mysteriously "prepared for [him] in the desert" (*F*, 172–73). "Sometimes," Frankenstein notes, the fiend "left marks in writing on the barks of the trees, or cut in stone." One day he finds the following inscription: "Follow me ... You will find near this place, if you follow not too tardily, a dead hare; eat, and be refreshed. Come on, my enemy; we have yet to wrestle for our lives" (*F*, 174).

As though taking their cue from Shelley's novel, Humbert and Quilty literally "wrestle for [their] lives" at the end of *Lolita*. After tracking Quilty down at long last, drunken Humbert proposes to kill his drug-dazed rival. A farcical chase-scene ends in a clumsy struggle for Humbert's "pistol," sent "hurtling under a chest of drawers." As the two men grapple for the gun, they literally "fall to wrestling," rolling over each other "like two helpless children." As their separate identities begin to merge in Humbert's gin-befuddled mind, their ludicrous tussle becomes a muddle of personal pronouns: "he rolled over me. I rolled over him. We rolled over me. They rolled over him. We rolled over us" (*Lo*, 299 [pt. 2, ch. 35]). Here the narrator's language parodies the theme of merging identities revealed in Frankenstein's tortured bond with his creature.

So similar are the phrases in which Shelley's creature and his creator ultimately express their woe, that readers are sometimes hard-pressed to differentiate between the two speakers. At one point in the narrative, Frankenstein, having reluctantly agreed to fashion a female companion for the lonely monster, recoils from the "filthy process" – saying how "sickened" he is by "the work of [his] hands" (*F*, 137). At the end of the novel, his lament is echoed by the creature. Gazing "on [his] hands," which have "murdered the lovely and the helpless," Frankenstein's monster is filled with self-loathing: the "abhorrence" of others, he declares, "cannot equal that with which I regard myself" (*F*, 190). Echoing Shelley's language and theme, Nabokov has Humbert similarly confess near the end of *Lolita*, "I have hurt too much too many bodies with my twisted poor hands" (*Lo*, 274 [pt. 2, ch. 29]). When, at the close of Shelley's novel, the "miserable monster" describes himself as "polluted by crimes, and torn by the bitterest remorse," he might well be speaking for both Frankenstein *and* Humbert Humbert (*F*, 190).

No matter how sharply the "fangs of remorse" tear at each novel's protagonist, neither Humbert nor Frankenstein overcomes his obsessive desire. Awareness of guilt does not quell the Promethean longing for immortality (*F*, 64). Frankenstein's narration, like Humbert's, is riddled with oscillations in emotional tone and moral register that signal each character's ambivalence. Even on his deathbed, in the midst of warning his friend Walton against the temptations of ambition and the desire for glory, Frankenstein's penitence gives way to pride: "Seek happiness in tranquility," he begins by telling Walton: "avoid ambition, even if it be only the apparently innocent one of distinguishing yourself in science and discoveries." But then Frankenstein abruptly breaks this train of thought: "Yet why do I say this?" he asks. "I have myself been blasted in these hopes, yet another may succeed" (*F,* 186). Humbert's own oscillations in tone – his alternating expressions of pride and repentance, remorse and romantic fervor – shed an equally ambivalent light on his declarations of remorse. To the frustration of many readers, Humbert's statements, like Frankenstein's, are grounded in nothing more stable than the shifting sands of his own contradictory perceptions.

Referring, near the end of Shelley's novel, to the "hideous narration" he is about to complete, Frankenstein appears, at least temporarily, to take full measure of his guilt. Repeating one of the epithets he has used to deplore the creature, Frankenstein now claims this epithet – "hideous" – for the story he has set in motion (*F,* 42, 56, 166, and *passim*). With a similar sense of the hideousness he has wrought, Humbert draws his tale to a close in this way: "This then is my story. I have reread it. It has bits of marrow sticking to it, and blood, and beautiful bright-green flies" (*Lo,* 308 [pt. 2, ch. 36]). Humbert's narration, like Frankenstein's, issues from the ruins of death and decay; it resembles, metaphorically, the monster Frankenstein created – a kind of living corpse.

The "public birth of the text," Bronfen observes of *Lolita,* "is grounded on the death of its author [that is, Humbert] and its privileged object of representation [Lolita]."[28] Unwilling to "parade living Lolita" in the pages of his memoir, Humbert vows to defer publication until they are both "no longer alive." His understandable, though incorrect, assumption is that young Mrs. Richard Schiller will "survive [him] by many years."[29] It is "in the minds of later generations," therefore, that Humbert ultimately hopes to achieve immortality – by making Lolita "live" there forever (*Lo,* 309 [pt. 2, ch. 36]). At the novel's end, he acknowledges the "local," or limited, nature of his creative efforts. No longer does he seek, like Frankenstein, to usurp Nature and transform human flesh and blood – the body of that "North American girl-child named Dolores Haze" – into his Promethean creation, the mythic nymphet (*Lo,* 283 [pt. 2, ch. 31]). Instead, he will rely on the only medium to which mortals can rightfully lay claim: the "durable pigments" of art. Chastened by knowledge of the misery he has wrought, Humbert as narrator attempts to realize a more qualified dream: to revive with the "local" magic of "articulate art" the nymphic image of a child whose "life," as he says, he "broke" (*Lo,* 283 [pt. 2, ch. 3], 308–09, [ch. 36], 279 [ch. 29]).

Although Frankenstein does not achieve even the partial recognition evinced by Humbert, Shelley's "modern Prometheus" is also a creator in this qualified, or "local," sense. Like Humbert, he wants his story to live on "in the minds of future generations." To Robert Walton, captain of the crew that rescues Frankenstein from the Arctic Ocean, he expresses his dying wish: that the body of his "narration" be preserved. He adds, "I would not that a mutilated one should go down to posterity" (*F,* 179). On the brink of death, Frankenstein ironically evokes the image of that "mutilated" corpse he brought to life. This telling adjective alerts Shelley's readers to the truth Frankenstein would yet ignore. His misshapen creature was only the first of many bodies and lives to be mangled and "mutilated" by his unholy experiment.

In both *Frankenstein* and *Lolita,* the monstrous nature of the narrative testifies to the destructive as well as creative power of imagination and the terrible beauty it engenders. Each text invites its readers to enter into the "controlled play with the daemonic" that is one definition, says Peter Brooks, of a work of art.[30] In both novels we discover the profound extent to which imagination and will can wreak havoc with nature and human nature. Entering into a relationship with the daemonic that is wildly *out of control,* each narrator produces his "hideous" story: hideous not because his desires are grotesquely thwarted, but because human hope and innocence – embodied for both Nabokov and Shelley in the image of childhood – are monstrously abused.

Both novels suggest, moreover, that the text itself is an offspring – a body that each writer, like a modern-day Frankenstein, constructs and brings to life for the first time. Like the creature that Frankenstein "piece[s] together out of disparate parts," Shelley's text, Nancy Fredricks observes, is similarly composed of "discontinuous" and "disjointed" elements – including "letters, first-person narratives, and frames within frames."[31] To an even greater extent, *Lolita* comprises a "patchwork of fragmentary" forms. As Linda Kauffman points out, not only letters but "poems, jingles, advertisements, plays and filmscripts, literary criticism, newspaper articles, psychiatric and legal reports are mixed with vestiges of the diary, confessional, journal, and memoir."[32]

Unlike their solipsistic narrators, both novelists are acutely aware of the profound responsibilities incurred by their acts of (literary) creation. "And now, once again," Shelley says in her introduction to the 1831 edition of *Frankenstein,* "I bid my hideous progeny to go forth and prosper. I have affection for it, for it was the offspring of happy days."[33] Here Shelley embraces the relationship that her creature, Victor Frankenstein, spurns. She avows her parental "affection" for the "hideous" offspring she has delivered into the world. Like a maternal expression of unconditional love, Shelley's stated affection for her "hideous progeny" implicitly comments on her protagonist's outright rejection of his: Frankenstein's failure to recognize, in Brooks's phrase, "the destructive potential of the creative drive."[34] Nabokov closely echoes Shelley's sentiments when he reflects, years after his novel's initial publication, on his own literary labors. *Lolita*, the author states, was "a painful birth, a difficult baby, but a kind daughter."[35] Delivering his "difficult" offspring into the world proved, Nabokov suggests, an excruciating literary task; but for him as for Shelley, it was clearly a labor of love.

Separated from Mary Shelley by gender, 150 years of history and culture, and vast differences in personal experience and artistic accomplishment, Nabokov both parodies and pays tribute to his female precursor. The changes that *Lolita* rings on Shelley's novel do not undermine so much as underscore *Frankenstein*'s celebrated themes. Today it has become a commonplace, in academic circles at least, to credit the collective forces of gender, race, class, and culture with near-absolute authority over individual thought and art. These are the ruling powers, we often hear it said, that dictate the nature of discourse and the shape of every text. Flying in the face of such deterministic assumptions, *Lolita* – Nabokov's "difficult baby" – honors Shelley's "hideous progeny" in profound and unexpected ways. For creating and then abandoning his offspring, Frankenstein stands eternally condemned; for having "broken" a child's life, Humbert suffers a similar sentence (*Lo*, 279 [pt. 2, ch. 29]). In each case, betrayal of the child's innocence signifies the greatest evil known to man or woman. For Nabokov as for Shelley, it constitutes nothing less than a crime against the cosmos.

NOTES

1 Gene H. Bell-Villada, *Art for Art's Sake and Literary Life* (Lincoln: University of Nebraska Press, 1996), 7; see also 194, 258–59. For a brief overview of a half-century's critical commentary, see Ellen Pifer, *Nabokov and the Novel* (Cambridge, MA: Harvard University Press, 1980), 11–13 and attending notes.

2 Naomi Wolf, *Promiscuities: The Secret Struggle for Womanhood* (New York: Random House, 1997), 193.
3 Andrew Brink, *Obsession and Culture: A Study of Sexual Obsession in Modern Fiction* (Madison, NJ: Fairleigh Dickinson University Press, 1996), 98.
4 Virginia L. Blum, *Hide and Seek: The Child between Psychoanalysis and Fiction* (Urbana: University of Illinois Press, 1995), 205, 230, 232.
5 Alfred Appel, Jr., "Introduction," *The Annotated Lolita* (New York: McGraw-Hill, 1970), lxix and *passim*.
6 Julia Kristeva, *Strangers to Ourselves*, trans. Leon S. Roudriez (New York: Columbia University Press, 1991), 33, 37. In her later work, *Maladies of the Soul*, trans. Ross Guberman (New York: Columbia University Press, 1995), 220–21, Kristeva critiques the notion of a "female language" distinct from its allegedly "male chauvinist" counterpart.
7 Elizabeth Deeds Ermarth, "Conspicuous Construction; or, Kristeva, Nabokov, and The Anti-Realist Critique," *Novel* 21 (1988), 335, 331.
8 Trevor McNeely, "'Lo' and Behold: Solving the *Lolita* Riddle," *Studies in the Novel* 21 (1989), 182–99; rpt. Harold Bloom (ed.), *Lolita* (New York: Chelsea House, 1992), 184, 187, 193.
9 Blum, *Hide and Seek*, 176.
10 Brink, *Obsession and Culture*, 137, 103, 124, 115.
11 Jeffrey Berman, "Nabokov and the Viennese Witch Doctor," *The Talking Cure: Literary Representations of Psychoanalysis* (New York University Press, 1985); rpt. Bloom (ed.), *Lolita*, 110.
12 Brandon S. Centerwall, "Hiding in Plain Sight: Nabokov and Pedophilia," *Texas Studies in Literature and Language* 32 (1990): 468 and *passim*.
13 John Updike, "Introduction," *LL*, xxi.
14 See ch. 9 of Brian Boyd, *Vladimir Nabokov: The American Years* (Princeton University Press, 1991), 166–98.
15 In volume 2 of the two-volume revised edition of his translation-with-commentary of Alexander Pushkin's *Eugene Onegin* (Princeton University Press, 1981), Nabokov makes explicit reference to the writings of Mary Shelley, Percy Bysshe Shelley's "widow," when glossing a line (ch. 3, st. 9, l. 8) of Pushkin's poem: "according to his widow," Nabokov comments, "Shelley one summer evening heard the skylark and saw the 'glow-worm golden in a dell of dew' mentioned in his famous ode" ("Commentary to *Eugene Onegin*," vol. II, pt. 1, 344).
16 Mary Shelley, *Frankenstein, or the Modern Prometheus*, ed. Marilyn Butler (1818; New York: Oxford University Press, 1994). (Hereafter *F*.)
17 Ellen Moers, "Female Gothic," *Literary Women* (Garden City, NY: Doubleday, 1976); rpt. George Levine and U. C. Knoepflmacher (eds.), *The Endurance of Frankenstein: Essays on Mary Shelley's Novel* (Berkeley: University of California Press, 1979), 79.
18 Elisabeth Bronfen, *Over her Dead Body: Death, Femininity and the Aesthetic* (New York: Routledge, 1992), 130–31.

19 Anne K. Mellor, *Mary Shelley: Her Life, Her Fiction, Her Monsters* (New York: Routledge, 1988), 38, 137.
20 Mary Shelley, "Introduction," *Frankenstein: or, The Modern Prometheus*, rev. edn. (London: Henry Colburn and Richard Bentley, 1831); rpt. Butler (ed.), *Frankenstein*, app. A, 197.
21 Brink, *Obsession and Culture*, 123, 114.
22 See Ellen Pifer, "Innocence and Experience Replayed: From *Speak, Memory* to *Ada*," *Cycnos* 10.1 (1993): 19–25; and Pifer, "*Lolita*" in *The Garland Companion to Vladimir Nabokov*, ed. Vladimir E. Alexandrov (New York: Garland, 1995), 312–13, 316–18.
23 U. C. Knoepflmacher, "Thoughts on the Aggression of Daughters" in Levine and Knoepflmacher (eds.), *The Endurance of Frankenstein*, 90.
24 Patricia McKee, *Public and Private: Gender, Class, and the British Novel (1764–1878)* (Minneapolis: University of Minnesota Press, 1997), 68.
25 Knoepflmacher, "Thoughts on the Aggression of Daughters," 100–01, 112.
26 On the novel's "problematic comedy," see Philip Stevick, "*Frankenstein* and Comedy" in Levine and Knoepflmacher (eds.), *The Endurance of Frankenstein*, 222.
27 As Vladimir E. Alexandrov points out in *Nabokov's Otherworld* (Princeton University Press, 1991), Nabokov's Russian translation of *Lolita* (New York: Phaedra, 1967) "makes the point even more bluntly": the Russian version of the cited sentence reads, "Lolita's reality was successfully canceled ['otmenena']" (Alexandrov, *Nabokov's Otherworld*, 170–71; *LoR*, 49).
28 Bronfen, *Over her Dead Body*, 371.
29 In the Foreword to *Lolita*, ostensibly authored by John Ray, Jr., readers learn that both Humbert and Lolita die shortly after Humbert's "memoir" has been completed. On November 16, 1952, Humbert suffers a "coronary thrombosis" while awaiting trial for the murder of Clare Quilty; only weeks later, "on Christmas Day 1952," Mrs. Richard F. Schiller (Lolita's married name) dies in childbirth (5–6 ["Foreword"]).
30 Peter Brooks, "'Godlike Science/Unhallowd Arts': Language, Nature, and Monstrosity," in Levine and Knoepflmacher (eds.), *The Endurance of Frankenstein*, 220.
31 Nancy Fredricks, "On the Sublime and the Beautiful in Shelley's *Frankenstein*" (unpublished paper, 21 pp.), 19.
32 Linda Kauffman, "Framing *Lolita*: Is There a Woman in the Text?", *Special Delivery: Epistolary Modes in Modern Fiction* (University of Chicago Press, 1992); rpt. Bloom (ed.), *Lolita* 149.
33 *Frankenstein*, ed. Butler, app. A, 197; see also 192.
34 Brooks, "Godlike Science," 217.
35 Alfred Appel, Jr., "Nabokov: A Portrait," *Atlantic Monthly* 228 (September 1971): 88. See also *SM*, 65; and *SO*, 15, 94.

CHAPTER 9

Vladimir Nabokov and Rupert Brooke

D. Barton Johnson

Nabokov spent the better part of three years in England. The family arrived in London at the end of May, 1919. Although the parents and three younger children resettled in Berlin in the summer of the following year, Vladimir and Sergei remained at Cambridge University, graduating in 1922. Nabokov first recounts his Cambridge years in "Lodgings in Trinity Lane." All three versions of the memoirs and both of Nabokov's biographers show a young man immersed in the recreation of a lost Russian world and relatively indifferent to his English surroundings.[1] Most of his Cambridge friends were Russian émigrés.

The young Nabokov saw himself as a Russian poet, and poetry was to be his major project during his Cambridge years. Already the author of two collections published in Russia,[2] he had written many new poems during his sixteen-month Crimean exile. Nostalgic reconstructions of "his" Russia form the largest category of subject matter for the 1918–22 poems. So intent was Nabokov on this endeavor that little emotional energy was left over for England and Cambridge. Nabokov's first biographer, Andrew Field, quotes Nabokov as describing his Cambridge years as "a long series of awkwardness, mistakes, and every sort of failure and stupidity, including romantic."[3] In *Speak, Memory*, the author even insists that his Cambridge years "left such trifling impressions ... that it would be tedious to continue" (*SM*, 261 [ch. 13]). Although aware of its imposing history, the young poet "was quite sure that Cambridge was in no way affecting my soul." Nabokov later qualifies this, conceding that Cambridge supplied "not only the casual frame, but also the very colors and inner rhythms for my very special Russian thoughts" (*SM*, 269 [ch. 13]). Only near the end of his three years there, after completing his reconstruction of "Russia," did Nabokov find any affection for his idyllic setting. This takes the form of a

177

charming description of punting on the Cam which is somewhat offset by his account of an unpleasant return visit in 1939 when he was seeking academic employment (*SM*, 270–71 [ch. 13]).

Nabokov appears to have been more profoundly "Russian" at Cambridge than before or after. This was reflected not only in his poetry but in his essay "Kembridzh" (Cambridge) which he wrote after two years in England.[4] Gracefully done, it is nonetheless a recitation of the hackneyed stereotypes of the soulless English and the famous Russian "shirokaia dusha" (broad soul).

There is, I think, something lacking in Nabokov's account and in the information he shared with his biographers. No matter how immersed in recreating Russia, Nabokov could scarcely have insulated himself from British literary life while at Cambridge. G. B. Shaw, H. G. Wells, G. K. Chesterton, and Hilaire Belloc were all in their prime. Wells, whom the young Nabokov had met at the family table in St. Petersburg, was one of his favorite authors. Wells's son, George, who knew some Russian and had accompanied his father on a recent trip to Soviet Russia, was at Cambridge with Nabokov.[5]

Nabokov makes no mention of particular English college friends, but creates a single, synthetic figure whom he calls "Nesbit" in *Speak, Memory*, and "Bromston" in *Drugie berega*. Some of the people who went into this composite "Nesbit" were literary sophisticates. Nabokov mentions discussions with "Nesbit" about "the poets we both cherished." In the Russian version, *Drugie berega*, he writes of his exasperation at the political naivety of "Nesbit/Bromston" and his friends, who grasped the charming details in Joyce's *Ulysses* and could discuss John Donne and Hopkins with great subtlety, but imagined Lenin a cultivated aesthete (224). At least one of Nabokov's acquaintances, Robert Lutyens, was a poet.[6]

Nabokov, along with his Russian poems, was also writing English verse. Although only two of these English poems were published,[7] they, together with the references above, suffice to show that Nabokov moved in Cambridge literary circles. We also know he was reading contemporary English poetry and prose, in particular, the "Georgians." In retrospect, he writes how "horrified" he would have been "to discover what I see so clearly now, the direct influence upon my Russian structures of various contemporaneous ('Georgian') English verse patterns that were running about my room and all over me like tame mice" (*SM*, 266 [ch. 13]). The Russian version of this passage is at once both less and more informative, "Georgian" becomes "the stylistic dependence of Russian constructions on those English poets from Marvell to Houseman who had been infected by the very air of my present existence" (*DB*, 226).

Nabokov's belated realization of the unwelcome influence on his poetry is first voiced in a letter of April 20, 1942 to Edmund Wilson. Wilson had written to Nabokov that he had chanced upon a volume of Nabokov's poetry called *Gornii put'* (*The Empyrean Path*). Several letters and months passed before Nabokov responded, seemingly almost as an afterthought: "I am glad you bought the *Gorny Put* though it is a rather miserable little thing. The poems it contains were written while I was still in my teens and are strongly influenced by the Georgian poets, Rupert Brooke, De la Mare, etc., by whom I was much fascinated at the time" (*NWL*, 79).

Nabokov's exposure to the "Georgians," and specifically to Rupert Brooke's work, must have begun after his arrival in England in May 1919. Hence, the Georgian "influence" that Nabokov later lamented, would have commenced no earlier than 1919 and should have been evident in his collections *Gornii put'* and *Grozd'* (*The Cluster*). Although a few of the *Gornii put'* poems are from as late as June 1921, about half predate the Cambridge years. The imputed effect should be in the late poems of *Gornii put'*, and perhaps more clearly in *Grozd'*, which contains poems written between late June 1921 and late April 1922.[8] Although I do not feel very secure in my opinion, I do not find much difference in Nabokov's pre-Brooke and post-Brooke poems. Noticeable change in Nabokov's poetry becomes apparent only after 1925. If this judgment is accurate, why does Nabokov remark the malefic influence of the "Georgians" on his poetic development? To approach this question we must take a look at British literature, specifically the poetic scene in the period after 1910.

"Georgian poetry" has struck an indistinct note of "sentimental pastoralism" or "weekend ruralism" since the 1960s – if it has any resonance at all.[9] Its heyday was from 1912 until 1916, although the biennial anthology lingered on until 1922 when the new modernists such as Eliot and Pound carried the day. In its early stages Georgian poetry was, initially at least, seen as bold, daring, even revolutionary.[10] Although British fiction and drama had flourished in the early years of the century (Shaw, Wells), poetry had been in the doldrums. Then, as now, younger poets were mostly known to each other.

Rupert Brooke (1887–1915) was a brilliant figure at Cambridge, largely thanks to his great personal charm, blond good looks, and literary gifts. He was immediately tapped for "The Apostles," the famed secret society whose members would provide the male nucleus of the Bloomsbury circle. Actor, poet, scholar, president of the University Fabian Society, Brooke completed the Classical Tripos at Cambridge in 1909. Two years later, he published his first thin volume of verses to small acclaim. While still an undergraduate he had become acquainted with former Cantabrigian Edward Marsh (1872–1953), who was now Winston Churchill's private secretary and a man who moved in the highest circles of government and society. A Classicist by education, Marsh had recently become enamored of the new art and poetry and was soon to write an appreciation of Brooke's volume for Harold Munro's *Poetry Review*, a magnet for many young poets. Through Marsh, Brooke met many writers and poets both of the older generation (Shaw, Barrie, Masefield, Yeats), and the new – those who were to become fellow Georgians. As well, Marsh introduced the Apollo-like Brooke to his society friends, in particular, to Churchill, and to the family of the Liberal Prime Minister Herbert Asquith. Asquith's son Arthur was to become one of the Georgians, and, as Brooke's fellow officer, would help bury him on the Greek island of Skyros.

Half-jokingly, Brooke and Marsh hit upon the idea of putting out an anthology of recent poetry that might catch the public's taste. Marsh was to be the editor while Brooke was both major contributor and advocate. Apparently it was his idea to have the Prime Minister's car outside the print shop waiting to whisk the first copies of *Georgian Poetry 1911–1912* to 10 Downing Street.[11] Marsh, as might be expected of a Minister's secretary, was a first-rate organizer. He had many friends in the world of literary journalism and orchestrated reviews in all of the leading papers and magazines. Not the least of Marsh's contributions was the anthology's title, which he explained in a brief introduction: There is a renaissance of English poetry equalling the great ages of the past. It is a new poetry and deserves its own name. Since George V had ascended the throne in 1910, his name was chosen to represent the new poetic era.

Marsh and Brooke were shrewd in picking their contributors. Their prime intention was to promote the younger poets but they also included material from such figures as future Poet Laureate

John Masefield and G. K. Chesterton. The volume, as Marsh later said, "went up like a rocket." Its success was not undeserved and some of its contents are landmarks in twentieth-century poetry: Walter de la Mare's haunting poem, "The Listeners," well-known to British readers in the first half of the century, Brooke's "The Old Vicarage, Grantchester" and "Dining-Room Tea," D. H. Lawrence's "The Snapdragon," and so on. The volume's success led to four further *Georgian Poetry* collections: *1913–1915*, *1916–1917*, *1918–1919*, and *1920–1921*. Marsh both invented and ushered in the "Georgian Revolt" – for revolt it was. In his memoir, *A Number of People: A Book of Reminiscences*, Marsh set forth his guidelines. Poetry should be intelligible, musical, racy, and display some formal principle.[12] He goes on to qualify "racy": "I mean it to imply intensity of thought or feeling, and to rule out the vapidity which is too often to be found, alas, in verse that is written with due regard to sense, sound and 'correctness'."

Some (but not much) of the Georgian material was shocking, as in Brooke's famed "A Channel Passage" about a presumed romantic betrayal: "The damned ship lurched and slithered. Quiet and quick / My cold gorge rose; the long sea rolled; I knew / I must think hard of something or be sick; / And could think hard of only one thing – *you!*" The poem's last two lines read: "And still the sick ship rolls. 'Tis hard, I tell ye, / To choose 'twixt love and nausea, heart and belly." Even parts of the semi-serious, semi-humorous "The Old Vicarage," with its "spectral dance, before the dawn, / A hundred Vicars down the lawn" raised eyebrows. Many conservative reviewers found such poetry beyond the pale and its practitioners too racy for popular consumption. Nonetheless, the early *Georgian Poetry* volumes were immensely popular. Caught between the Victorian poetry of the past and the stirrings of the modernists, the reading public found the Georgians a happy compromise.

Brooke, who had published only one volume and a scattering of poems, came before a much wider public with the appearance of *Georgian Poetry*. National public fame came only after his April 23, 1915 death (blood poisoning from an infected mosquito bite) in Churchill's disastrous Gallipoli campaign. Brooke had, in the finest tradition of the English school man, greeted the news of war quipping "Well, if Armageddon is on, I suppose one should be there."[13] Brooke's exaltation to the status of a national monument rests on two 1914 sonnets that enthralled the nation – thanks in large part to shrewd, political manipulation by his powerful friends. The most famous is "The Soldier":

> If I should die, think only this of me:
> That there's some corner of a foreign field
> That is for ever England . . .
> And think, this heart, all evil shed away,
> A pulse in the eternal mind, no less
> Gives somewhere back the thoughts by England given . . .
> In hearts at peace, under an English heaven.

Just days before Brooke's death, William Inge, Dean of St. Paul's in London, had read and lauded "The Soldier" as part of his Easter sermon: "The enthusiasm of a pure and elevated patriotism had never found a nobler expression," although he expressed disquiet about the poet's view of the hereafter as "a pulse in the eternal mind."[14] A few days later, Winston Churchill wrote a letter to *The Times* expressing the nation's grief. Beginning "Rupert Brooke is dead," it concludes in Churchill's most orotund style:

The thoughts to which he gave expression in the very few incomparable war sonnets which he has left behind will be shared by many thousands of young men moving resolutely and blithely forward into this, the hardest, cruelest, and least rewarded of all the wars men have fought. They are a whole history of and revelation of Brooke himself. Joyous, fearless, versatile, deeply instructed, with classic symmetry of mind and body, ruled by a high undoubting purpose, he was all that one would wish England's noblest sons to be in days when no sacrifice but the most precious is acceptable, and the most precious is that which is mostly freely proffered.[15]

Brooke had departed for the Gallipoli campaign direct from 10 Downing Street where he had been staying with the Asquiths. His canonization was assured – perhaps most of all, at Cambridge, his *alma mater*.

Dead, Rupert Brooke had vastly more admirers than while alive. Images of the handsome young poet were idolized by thousands. Nor did his lionization end with the war. In 1918, Edward Marsh published Brooke's collected poems with a long biographical sketch based almost entirely on reminiscences from Brooke's friends and his correspondence: a joyous young man with an enormous gift for friendship; governed by the highest moral principles; poet, actor, and athlete; flower of the English public school system; a hero, dead at 27 in the service of his beloved country; his brilliant future as both poet and public figure cut tragically short. Marsh's biography presents an incredibly attractive human being.[16] The biography and collection of the poems, all prefaced by two Sherrill Schell 1913 photo-portraits of Brooke, first appeared in July of 1918. It had gone through ten impressions before Nabokov finished Cambridge.[17] In the month following Nabokov's matriculation, the fourth volume of *Georgian Poetry 1918–1919* appeared while the preceding volumes remained popular.[18] Interest in *Georgian Poetry* and particularly in Brooke was very great. In March 1919, Rugby had, with great fanfare, unveiled its memorial plaque with Brooke's profile sculpted from one of the Schell photo-portraits.[19] Brooke had also been an immensely popular figure at King's College and had remained near Cambridge to pursue an academic career. His fame spread even to America. F. Scott Fitzgerald was to take the title and epigraph of his first book, *This Side of Paradise* (1920), from Brooke's poem "Tiare Tahiti."

The Nabokovs' first lodgings in England were in Kensington not far from the British Library where the manuscript of "The Soldier" was on display. Whatever the circumstances of Nabokov's introduction to Brooke, the young Russian poet was much taken with his work. He translated all or parts of twenty poems in preparing an essay he sent to his parents in September, 1921.[20] "Rupert Bruk" appeared in the first issue of the Berlin émigré miscellany *Grani*. It was Nabokov's first published piece of literary criticism.[21]

Nabokov (who had taken an ichthyology class at Cambridge) stands gazing into an aquarium, admiring the subdued glitter of the moving fish. The scene reminds him of "the cool, radiant verses of an English poet who senses in these supple, rainbow-hued fish, a profound image of our existence."[22] The signature feature of Brooke's slender *oeuvre* is, Nabokov says, a sense of "radiant liquidity" ("siiaiushchaia vlazhnost'"), reflected both in his name and in his naval service. Brooke's world is a watery abyss in which the filtered light is refracted into many-colored hues of darkness just as death decomposes living flesh. Here Nabokov translates and paraphrases fragments from Brooke's "The Fish" in which the instinctual, dim world of the fish, at one with its environment, is contrasted with the richer but awkward, fragmented, often tormented existence of dwellers in the human world.[23] Brooke offers a more jocular treatment of piscine metaphysics in the poem "Heaven," in which the fish-philosopher reflects that "the reverent eye must see / A

Purpose in Liquidity. / We darkly know, by Faith we cry, / The future is not Wholly Dry" (21–22). The poem, for which Nabokov provides a full, rhymed translation, contains, he says, the "essence of all earthly religions." The final poem of Nabokov's introduction, "Tiare Tahiti," is Brooke's attempt to explain to his uncomprehending Tahitian mistress (not Hawaiian as Nabokov has it) the idea of an abstract, neo-Platonic heaven where dwell "the Eternals ... / whose earthly copies were / The foolish broken things we knew" (13–15). He realizes, however, that the world of perfect forms may be less than ideal for "there's an end, I think, of kissing, When our mouths are one with Mouth" (14). He then leads his lover down to the sensual pleasures of a tropical moonlight swim – pleasures to be enjoyed before lips, laughter, and "faces individual" fade. The poem, one of a series Brooke wrote during his South Seas sojourn, ends on the note "There's little comfort in the wise."

Nabokov is perceptive in noting Brooke's preoccupation with water, both as an alternative universe and as a moral cleansing agent.[24] Although Nabokov neglects to mention Brooke's contrast of worlds in the first poem, he rhetorically foregrounds Brooke's neo-Platonic series of antitheses in "Tiare Tahiti." Brooke contents himself with comparisons of the evanescent human and the immutable eternal: "There is the Face, whose ghosts we are; / The real, the never-setting Star; / And the Flower, of which we love / Faint and fading shadows here." Nabokov's prose paraphrase reframes this series of oppositions into the "there" vs. "here" (*tam/tut*) format so familiar in his later work. It is also noteworthy that Nabokov's translation of Brooke's *carpe diem* injunction in prospect of faded lips, laughter, and "faces individual" is much more sharply edged and personal: "poka u nas na litsakh ne sterlas' pechat' nashego 'ia'" (until the stamp of our 'I' has been erased from our faces).[25] Nabokov's Brooke translations are much freer and more personalized than in his later practice.[26]

The heart of Nabokov's essay focuses on Brooke's theme of death and the hereafter – even disproportionately so and, at times, inaccurately. In Nabokov's words, "Not a single poet has looked into the twilight of the hereafter ['potustoronnosti'] with such tormented and creative penetration.[27] Brooke feverishly offers one hypothetical hereafter after another "like a man searching for a match in a dark room while someone is knocking on the door." In "The Life Beyond," the protagonist, "who held the end was Death," awakens on a "long livid oozing plain / Closed down by the strange eyeless heavens." He sees himself as "a speck / Of moveless horror . . . / . . . a fly / Fast-stuck in grey sweat on a corpse's neck" (83). Although the quoted lines serve nicely as Nabokov's point of entry into his theme, it is in no small part a misrepresentation. The poem's unquoted final lines make clear that the death is the death of love, not that of the bereft lover who "almost strangely" lives on. In contrast to the ghastly fly image, Brooke presents a charming, if abstract, image of the hereafter in "Dust," where two motes from the bodies of deceased lovers dance and play in the sun. So strong is their aura that "the weak passionless hearts" of two mundane lovers will, for one moment, sense "what it is to love" (66–67). Brooke offers still other post-mortal images. An ancient Greek poet foresees how in Hades he shall wait and watch as his newly dead beloved crosses the Styx to join him ("Sonnet" ["Oh! Death will find me . . ."]) (63). In "The Hill," the merry poet-lover (Rupert, Nabokov says) counters the prospect of death by proclaiming that their souls will be resurrected in the kisses of future lovers (79). At first the pair are proudly, gaily defiant, but then the girl "suddenly cried, and turned away." By selective quoting Nabokov brushes away this note of doubt.

An intermediate prospect is offered by "Clouds" (31). The upward spiraling, massive columns of South Pacific clouds that ". . . turn with profound gesture vague and slow, / As who would pray good for the world, but know / Their benediction empty as they bless." Unlike those who suppose the dead hover near their loved ones, Brooke likens them to the clouds that look down impassively on the comings and goings of men. From this point, it is, Nabokov says, not far to a complete reconciliation with death, as expressed in Brooke's most famous 1914 poems. In "The Dead," the joys of existence are touched by death, a frost that leaves "a white / Unbroken glory, a gathered radiance, / A width, a shining peace, under the night"; while in "The Soldier," the hereafter is reduced to "a pulse in the eternal mind" (8, 9).

Nabokov seems ill at ease with Brooke's tentativeness about the hereafter. It is instructive that he does not mention "Choriambics – II" in which the poet abandons the wooded shrine he has kept: "God, immortal and dead! / Therefore I go; never to rest, or win / Peace, and worship of you more" (117–18). Nabokov asserts that Brooke "knows full well that death is only an astonishment, a surprise, for he is the bard of eternal life, tenderness, forest shadows, transparent streams, fragrances."[28] Nabokov is mistaken. Brooke's atheism is also avowed in his correspondence. To a despairing friend, Brooke writes "I still burn and torture Christians daily." He counsels a sort of Mysticism by which "I do not mean any religious thing, or any form of belief." It is a *"feeling . . .* only I refuse to be cheated by the feeling into any kind of belief."[29] He also viewed psychic phenomena with great suspicion. His "Sonnet (*Suggested by some of the Proceedings of the Society for Psychical Research*)" offers the whimsical thought that the dead have more edifying things to do than "beat on the substantial doors" of the living. Perhaps they might prefer to spend their time to "Learn all we lacked before; hear, know, and say / What this tumultuous body now denies; / And feel, who have layed our groping hands away; / And see, no longer blinded by our eyes" (30). Nabokov moves on from Brooke's views on death and the hereafter by observing that the poet seems less concerned with what he would find *there* than with what he would forsake *here*.

Brooke, who had a degree in Classics, casts much of his poetic speculation on post-mortality in terms of Platonic philosophy: "reality" is merely the transient reflection of a world of true, eternal essences. Nabokov, with his relatively modern, "secular" education, was probably not so prone to this particular frame of reference. Although he was later to speak harshly of Plato, his own philosophy of death and its aftermath (and also of art) rests upon a quite similar foundation. It was stated, however, not in classical, Platonic terms, but more abstractly and simply: here/there; this world/that world.

God and Home are the last themes examined by Nabokov. In "Failure," God is blamed for the separation of lovers. When the poet storms heaven to curse him, he finds only an empty throne and an overgrown courtyard. Nabokov, ever reluctant to see Brooke's atheism, asks "Has human love vanquished God or is He dead?" (140).

Nabokov's final thought is for the theme of the native land, not only in the larger sense but one special place. The theme had strong appeal for the young Russian exile who had made Russia and, especially his small corner of it, the major subject of his own poetry. For Brooke, that special place was "The Old Vicarage" in Grantchester where the poet lived during his last years at Cambridge.[30] A charming mixture of whimsy and nostalgia, Brooke wrote the anthology piece while living in Germany. Knowing the very personal nature of such locales, Nabokov concludes with a deflating account of his own bicycle trip through Grantchester and its wholly unremarkable setting.[31]

Nabokov's sketch closes with an account of Brooke's death on an Aegean island – a death that came before he had succeeded in "blending all the colors of the earth into a single shade, a shining whiteness." Nonetheless, it is clear that the goal of his art was "the passionate service of pure beauty" – an assertion that Brooke, with his Fabian social conscience, might have found problematic.

Nabokov's first use of the term *potustoronnost'*, the "hereafter," occurs as a preliminary to his discussion of Brooke's poem "The Life Beyond" (which Nabokov misread). Nabokov's first two volumes of poetry, *Stikhi* (*Poems*) and *Dva puti* (*Two Paths*), contain only love and/or nature themes.[32] Only with his Crimean period (November 1917–April 1919), do Nabokov's horizons widen: Russia, nostalgia, poetry and the Muse, death and the hereafter, etc. One suspects that it was the March 1919 death of his cousin and "best friend," Yuri Rausch von Traubenberg, that launched the "hereafter" theme, although there were doubtless other Civil War deaths among Nabokov's acquaintances. Nabokov, who admired his dashing kinsman and childhood playmate, had, at one point, decided to join his cousin's military unit. Yuri died in a heroic (and suicidal), lone cavalry charge on a Red machine-gun nest only days after a visit with the family. Death suddenly became real for Nabokov. Nabokov wrote at least three poems touching on Yuri's death. The first, written shortly after the funeral at which Nabokov was a pallbearer, sang their shared love of daring. The final stanzas are: "The future is nothing to us / And the past does not torment us. The black door to the final hour, / we fling open easily and boldly. I believe in the age-old tales / and naive revelations: / We shall meet in an aerial realm / and set the stars laughing with a quip."[33] Nabokov was to write two further poems about his friend who had been both a mentor and a rival poet in their adolescence. The second poem, "Pamiati druga" ("To the Memory of a Friend"), celebrates their childhood war games and recounts the news of Yuri's death, while a final poem, written during the Cambridge years, is addressed to his Muse, begging her benificence to one who has lost both home and closest friend (*GP*, 71 and 79). Nabokov was to write several novels in which the death of a loved one sets off the survivor's search for the hereafter. The death of his father only three years later would strongly reinforce the theme in his writing.

Yuri's death was still very fresh when Nabokov discovered the British poet. Yuri had been killed in March 1919 and only a few months later Nabokov was at Cambridge where Brooke had been a student and then faculty member only six years before. His collected verse with Edward Marsh's adulatory biography had appeared in July 1918 and was in its sixth printing by August 1919. Brooke was at the peak of his posthumous fame.

Brooke was closely associated with Cambridge from 1906 through 1913. Nabokov was there from 1919 until June 1922. For Brooke, it was a natural continuation of life from Rugby, where his father was a Master, to King's College, Cambridge, where his uncle was Dean. His Rugby friends accompanied him to Cambridge. Nabokov arrived newly uprooted from his homeland: in spite of his "English childhood" and his father's idealization of British "character" and institutions, he had neither roots in British society, nor a native country to return to. He found himself far more of an alien than he had anticipated. Nonetheless, the two poets must have had many common experiences.

Both wrote of punting on the Cam, but, doubtless, so have dozens of other Cambridge poets. One such coincidence was almost certainly a deliberate evocation of Brooke by Nabokov. On November 10, 1908, Brooke, waiting for the start of his Classical Tripos examination, had coolly filled in the time by writing a poem called "In Examination." As the poet waits, the golden sun suddenly floods the hall and the "Hunched figures and old, / Dull blear-eyed scribbling fools, grew fair." The light turns their eyes "young and wise," as "[a]rchangels and angels, adoring, bowing, / And a Face unshaded ... / Till the light faded." They are again dull fools. On April 28, 1921, Nabokov, awaiting the arrival of his examiners for the Medieval and Modern Languages Tripos, wrote a poem dedicated to "V. Sh.," Valentina Shulgina, *Speak, Memory*'s "Tamara."[34] The poem "If the wind of fate ..." envisions a chance reunion in Petrograd. The long-dreamed-of encounter proves to be unhappy as the lovers have changed, as has everything else (*GP,* 156). A month later, on May 23, Nabokov wrote another poem in the examination hall after finishing early.[35] The poem, "Belyi rai" ("A White Paradise"), finished at 11:42 a.m., is a memory of the snow-covered Russian countryside (*GP,* 161). Nabokov has emulated the circumstances of Brooke's "In Examination," but while the latter focuses on the moment, Nabokov looks back at his Russian past.

In spite of such quasi-biographical "overlays," and common bonds of theme and poetic stance, I do not think it possible to show that Brooke's poetry (or that of the other Georgians) had much, if any, impact on Nabokov's, notwithstanding his comment to Wilson.[36]

Brooke did have an impact on Nabokov but it was, I think, not on his poetry. Nabokov's fiction contains a number of references to Brooke, who is present in all three novels with scenes set in England. *Glory* was written in 1930. The title went through a series of transformations in both Russian and English. The successive working titles were *Voploshchenie* (*Embodiment*), *Zolotoi vek* (*The Golden Age*), and *Romanticheskii vek* (*Romantic Times*) before the final *Podvig*, meaning "gallant feat," "high deed."[37] The point of the title and the novel itself was, according to Nabokov, to assert that the high romance of human existence had not faded away into a drab, utilitarian, way of (post-war) life. Life still offers the "thrill and glamour that my young expatriate finds in the most ordinary pleasures as well as in the seemingly meaningless adventures of a lonely life" (*Glory*, xii–xiii ["Foreword"]). Martin Edelweiss, a rather ordinary young man of Russian and Swiss heritage, finds himself at Cambridge *circa* 1919. Raised on tales of knightly derring-do, he has vague longings for some feat of daring, a danger-fraught romantic geste. After testing himself in various ways, Martin, whimsically living out a picture hanging over his childhood bed, disappears while making his way along a wooded path across the perilous border into Bolshevik Russia. The act is undertaken to impress a fair, young damsel. Martin shares many of Nabokov's experiences at Cambridge. While I find no specific subtextual allusions to Brooke, the entire novel is a paean to the tradition of knightly chivalry, the "pure" hero in search of honor. Brooke was the national personification of this image in 1920s England.

In *The Real Life of Sebastian Knight*, Sebastian writes of "his" difficulties in adjusting to British life during his Cambridge years. Speaking of his loneliness, he says: "I had my Kipling moods and my Rupert Brooke moods, and my Housman moods" (*RLSK*, 66 [ch. 7]). Elsewhere in *Lost Property*, Sebastian's "most autobiographical novel," he writes "I always think that one of the purest emotions is that of the banished man pining after the land of his birth. I would have liked to show him straining his memory to the utmost in a continuous effort to keep alive and bright the image of his past: the blue remembered hills and the happy highways, the hedge with its unofficial rose and the field with its rabbits, the distant spire and the near bluebell" (*RLSK*, 24–25 [ch. 3]). As Brian Boyd notes, this passage is a mélange of fragments from poems of Thomas Gray, A. E. Housman, and Brooke's "The Old Vicarage, Grantchester."[38] The poem was written by Brooke as he sat in a Berlin cafe thinking of home: "*there* the dews / Are soft beneath a morn of gold. / Here tulips bloom as they are told; / Unkempt about those hedges blows / An English unofficial rose."

Sebastian Knight contains one other Georgian echo. When V. interviews Sebastian's only close friend at Cambridge, a literary scholar, he mentions that the don is the author of *The Laws of Literary Imagination* (*RLSK*, 45 [ch. 5]). In 1919, Walter de la Mare, a prominent Georgian author who was Brooke's friend and literary executor, published a small book, originally a memorial lecture at Rugby, called *Rupert Brooke and The Intellectual Imagination*. De la Mare was never connected with Cambridge but the similarity of title is striking.

Brooke's image was still with Nabokov in 1973 when he was writing *Look at the Harlequins!* The novel's narrator, the Russo-English writer Vadim, has attended Cambridge (1919–1922) where he meets Ivor Black, fellow student and amateur actor specializing in female roles.[39] In response to a drunken invitation, Vadim joins an unpleasantly surprised Ivor and his sister Iris at their Riviera villa. The narrator falls in love with Iris, who improbably returns his affections. As they lie on the *plage*, she fends off his attempt to kiss her knee, saying they are being watched by a pair of neighboring bathers, English schoolteachers, who have already remarked to her on his striking "resemblance to the naked-neck photo of Rupert Brooke." Boyd identifies the photo as the famous Sherrill Schell photo of Brooke that appeared as the second frontispiece to *The Collected Poems of Rupert Brooke* (1918). *Look at the Harlequins!* is also the novel in which Nabokov reintroduces the word *postustoronnost'*, used for the first time in the 1921 Brooke essay. The narrator of *Look at the Harlequins!* declares his love for Iris in his "philosophical love poem," "Vlyublyonnost'" ("The Condition of Being in Love"). Its last stanza reads: "Napominayu chto vlyublyonnost' / Ne yav', chto metiny ne te, / Chto mozhet-byt' potustoronnost' / priotvorilas' v temnote."

Vadim then provides an English paraphrase for Iris: "I remind you, that *vlyublyonnost'* is not wide-awake reality, that the markings are not the same ... and that, maybe, the hereafter stands slightly ajar in the dark" (*LATH*, 26 [pt. 1, ch. 5]). The comment about Vadim's resemblance to Brooke's photograph comes two pages later as Vadim and Iris discuss the poem on the beach (*LATH*, 28 [pt. 1, ch. 6]).

We have questioned Nabokov's statement that the Georgian poetry of his Cambridge years adversely affected his Russian verse by observing that the poetry in *Grozd'*, written just after the Brooke essay, does not seem greatly different from the Crimean poetry. The themes of the lost homeland and death and its aftermath become more prominent in Cambridge but they are already present in the Crimean material. The theme of death and the hereafter probably arises in connection with Yuri Rausch's death just a month before the Nabokovs fled the Crimea.

Nabokov brought from the Crimea yet another theme – that of knightly honor and valor. There are a surprising number of Nabokov poems from 1919 through the mid-twenties drawing on *La Morte d' Arthur* and its characters – especially Tristan. Further, Nabokov was studying Medieval French literature at Cambridge and, in particular, Chrétien de Troyes's tales, based on the Arthurian legend. Yuri probably was the immediate point of origin for the knightly valor theme, as well as that of the hereafter. The final stanza of Nabokov's first poem on Yuri's death seems to allude to both the knightly tradition and the hereafter: "Ia veriu skazkam vekovym / i otkroven'iam prostodushnym: / My vstretimsia v kraiu vozdushnom / i shutkoi zvezdy rassmeshim" ("I believe in the age-old tales / and naive revelations: / We shall meet in an aerial realm / and set the stars laughing with a quip") (*GP*, 52). Rupert Brooke's work and image certainly reinforced Nabokov's disposition for the themes.

Nabokov's theme of the hereafter received an even more powerful impetus when, in March, 1922, his father died in a heroic attempt to protect a colleague from an assassin's bullet. The third section of Nabokov's poetry collection *Grozd'* is devoted to the combined themes of the lost father and home. It opens with "Paskha" ("Easter"), dedicated to the death of his father, and speaks of the sights and sounds of spring, but "You are gone." If these signs of reviving nature are not "a blinding lie," but a summons to live again and flourish, then "you are in this song, you are in this radiance, you live!".[40] The third poem in the section, "Tristan," although not speaking openly of Nabokov's father, implies his image and spirit, as well as evoking the knightly valor theme. Nabokov's father, like Yuri, had an "absolute" sense of honor.

Nabokov's assertion that England served as a neutral backdrop for his development as a Russian writer is doubtful. England did leave its mark upon his work, not so much on his poetry as on his consciousness and the central theme of his future novels. Nabokov came from a culture that idolized its poets. Brooke personified an ideal – physically beautiful and personally charming, a public-school lad, athlete, actor, scholar, South Seas adventurer, social lion, war hero, and poet. He was the model for every Britisher, and for a younger Russian poet from an Anglophile home. Allowing for the age difference, their privileged lives had been rather similar: cultured homes, elite private schools, sports, much foreign travel, physical attractiveness, and poetry.[41] Nabokov, alienated in a culture he thought he knew well, found in Brooke a figure he could unreservedly admire.

Rupert Brooke was not the only British hero to capture Nabokov's imagination. Lying next to Brooke's manuscript of "The Soldier" in the British Library was the last diary of Naval Captain Robert Falcon Scott, the Antarctic explorer, who after having reached the South Pole in a 2,000 mile sledge journey, died on the return journey eleven miles from his base camp. His five-man party, immobilized by a storm and starving, all perished. Scott's journal, which he maintained to the end, was published in 1913. Scott had captured the British imagination much as Brooke was to do three years later.[42] He also caught Nabokov's. The year after his graduation from Cambridge and the death of his father, Nabokov wrote a one-act verse play *Polius* (*The Pole*), loosely based on the final pages of Scott's diary.[43] Death is also the theme and title of a second, longer verse play, *Smert'* (*Death*). Completed in 1923, the play, set at Cambridge University in 1806, is a speculative investigation of death.

Brooke was not the only Georgian to provide the young Nabokov with part of his master theme. Walter de la Mare, who appeared in almost all of the *Georgian Poetry* anthologies, may also have played a role. Nabokov makes reference to him in his 1924 short story "Revenge," which has plot affinities with Nabokov's Cambridge verse drama *Death*. In "Revenge," the wife feels sorry for her scientist husband, "because, as he studied the minutiae of life, he refused to enter her world where the poetry of de la Mare flowed and infinitely tender astral spirits hurtled" (*Stories*, 70). Much of de la Mare's quietly fantastic poetry and prose strongly hints that our world merely masks a deeper reality, and Gennady Barabtarlo has remarked certain parallels between the early Nabokov and the British poet and prose writer.[44] De la Mare applies the name "the otherworld" to this higher reality in at least one of his works.

We can sum up our conclusions very briefly. England and Cambridge were far from inconsequential for Nabokov's later career. Nor was his ambition to become a major Russian poet thrown off course by the influence of the regnant Georgian movement. He was drawn to it precisely because its poetry was similar in both form and content to what he had been writing for the preceding two or three years. What Nabokov did find in England – and particularly in Cambridge – was Rupert Brooke, or rather, the public image of Brooke. Nabokov came upon Brooke at a crucial time in his life. Nabokov's Cambridge years were framed by two deaths: that of his closest friend, Yuri, in March 1919, and that of his father in March 1922. He lost his homeland and experienced the death of his closest friend just eight months before going to Cambridge. The image of Brooke provided an Anglo-Saxon focal point for Nabokov's experience, as well as a powerfully appealing Platonic reformulation of what would become his "master theme" – death and the hereafter, or *potustoronnost'*, a term Nabokov first uses in his Brooke essay. Nabokov's adoption of this model was buttressed in March 1922 when his Anglophile father was killed. Rupert Brooke played a crucial role in the formulation of the *potustoronnost'* theme that was central to much of Nabokov's later art and life.

NOTES

1 Vladimir Nabokov, "Lodgings in Trinity Lane," *Harper's Magazine*, 202 (January 1951): 84–91; Vladimir Nabokov, *Conclusive Evidence. A Memoir*; repr. as *Speak, Memory* (hereafter *SM*); *Drugie berega* (New York: Izdatel'stvo imeni Chekhova, 1954) (Hereafter *DB*). Brian Boyd, *Vladimir Nabokov: The Russian Years* (Princeton University Press, 1990); Andrew Field, *Nabokov: His Life in Art* (Boston: Little, Brown, 1967).
2 Vladimir Nabokov, *Stikhi* (Petrograd: Union, 1916); and Andrei Balashov and Vladimir Nabokov, *Al'manakh: Dva puti* (Petrograd, 1918).
3 Field, *Nabokov: His Life in Art*, 63.

4 "Kembridzh," *Rul'*, October 28, 1921, 2.
5 Useful surveys of English writers read by Nabokov may be found in Jonathan Sisson, "Nabokov and Some Turn-of-the-Century English Writers," in *The Garland Companion to Vladimir Nabokov*, ed. Vladimir Alexandrov (New York: Garland, 1995), 228–35. A more speculative survey may be found in Nina Berberova's "Angliiskie predki Vladimira Nabokova," *Novyi zhurnal* 167 (1987): 191–205; an abbreviated English version appears in *Canadian-American Slavic Studies* 19 (1985): 262–67.
6 Boyd, *Vladimir Nabokov: The Russian Years*, 173.
7 The long poem, "Home," appeared in *Trinity Magazine* (November 1920): 26, and "Remembrance" in *The English Review* 144 (November 1920): 392. The latter is reproduced by Field in *Nabokov: His Life in Art*, 62.
8 Boyd, *Vladimir Nabokov: The Russian Years*, 201.
9 *Princeton Encyclopedia of Poetry and Poetics*, ed. Alex Preminger (Princeton University Press, 1965), 311.
10 A good historical account of the "Georgians" may be found in Robert H. Ross, *The Georgian Revolt 1910–1922: Rise and Fall of a Poetic Ideal* (Carbondale: Southern Illinois University Press, 1965).
11 *Ibid.*, 103.
12 Edward Marsh, *A Number of People: A Book of Reminiscences* (New York: Harpers, 1939), 322.
13 William E. Laskowski, *Rupert Brooke* (New York: Twayne, 1994), 27.
14 *Ibid.*, 29.
15 Ross, *Georgian Revolt*, 141.
16 More recent biographers who have access to a much wider range of materials have painted a more mixed figure – a man tormented by his sexual guilt, who treated women friends badly, and an anti-Semite. As well as the standard work, Christopher Hassall, *Rupert Brooke* (London: Faber and Faber, 1964), see John Lehmann, *Rupert Brooke: His Life and His Legend* (London: Weidenfeld and Nicolson, 1980); Paul Delany, *The Neo-Pagans: Rupert Brooke and the Ordeal of Youth* (New York: The Free Press, 1987); and Mike Read, *Forever England: The Life of Rupert Brooke* (Edinburgh: Mainstream, 1997).
17 *The Collected Poems of Rupert Brooke: With a Memoir*, ed. Edward Marsh (London: Sidgwick and Jackson, Ltd., 1924). All references to Brooke's poems and the *Memoir* are to this edition. Page numbers for subsequent references will be given in the text
18 *Georgian Poetry 1911–1922: The Critical Heritage*, ed. Timothy Rogers (London: Routledge and Kegan Paul, 1977).
19 Schell took a series of Brooke photos in 1913. For the last of the series, he proposed that Brooke strip to the waist. The shot, used by Marsh to preface the poems (a more sedate one was used for the book's frontispiece), shows Brooke's face in profile with bare neck and shoulders. It came to be known among the poet's friends as "your favorite actress"

(Read, *Forever England*, 173–74). The unveiling ceremony for the plaque is described by John Lehmann, *Rupert Brooke: His Life and his Legend*, 154–55.
20 Boyd, *Vladimir Nabokov: The Russian Years*, 182, and personal communication.
21 "Rupert Bruk," *Grani* (1922): 211–31. No English translation of this essay exists. It has been discussed both by Jonathan Sisson in his essay "Nabokov and Some Turn-of-the-Century English Writers" and in Galya Diment's essay "Uncollected Critical Writings" in Alexandrov, *The Garland Companion to Vladimir Nabokov*, 528–35 and 733–40.
22 "Rupert Bruk," 213.
23 *The Collected Poems of Rupert Brook*, 72–74.
24 Recent critics have linked Brooke's passion for bathing to something verging on a fetish. Mixed nude (but chaste) swimming had almost cult status among some of Brooke's friends (Laskowski, *Brooke*, 19).
25 "Rupert Bruk," 216.
26 Robin Kemball, "Nabokov and Rupert Brooke," in *Schweizerische Beiträge zum IX internationalen Slavistenkongress in Kiev, September 1983*, ed. Peter Brang et al. (Bern: Peter Lang, 1983), 35–73.
27 "Rupert Bruk," 216.
28 *Ibid.*, 224.
29 *The Collected Poems of Rupert Brooke*, lii–liii.
30 *Ibid.*, 53–57.
31 "Rupert Bruk," 230–31.
32 As exceptions, note *Dva puti*'s "Vechnyi uzhas. Chernye triasiny" ("Eternal terrors. Black quagmires") on original sin, and "U mudrykh i zlykh nichego ne proshu" ("I ask nothing of the wise or evil") about the creation of poetry (24–25).
33 Vladimir Nabokov, *Gornii put'* (Berlin: Grani, 1923), 52. (Hereafter *GP*). The poem is entitled "Yu. R.," i.e. Yuri Rausch (von Traubenberg).
34 Boyd, *Vladimir Nabokov: The Russian Years*, 182. Although Boyd here records the examination and the poem as being on April 28, he elsewhere dates the poem as April 29 ("Nabokov's Russian Poems: A Chronology," *The Nabokovian* 21 [Fall 1988]: 17).
35 Boyd, *Vladimir Nabokov: The Russian Years*, 183
36 Gerald S. Smith, "Nabokov and Russian Verse Form," *Russian Literature Triquarterly* 24 (1991): 271–305. Smith does note some change in metrical preferences between *Gornii put'* and *Grozd'*. The observation is, however, problematic since Smith considers *GP* the later work (as the publication date would imply), although most of its contents are in fact earlier than the poems in *Grozd'*.
37 Boyd, *Vladimir Nabokov: The Russian Years*, 353.
38 *Ibid.*, 476.
39 Brooke and his friend Justin Brooke (who specialized in playing female roles) established their own theater company at Cambridge (Marsh, *A Number of People*, xxxii–xxxv).

40 *Grozd'* (Berlin: Gamaiun, 1923), 41. Also in Vladimir Nabokov, *Stikhi* (Ann Arbor: Ardis, 1979), 66. (Hereafter *Stikhi* 1979).

41 The differences should not be ignored. Nabokov was far more aloof than Brooke and had not been exposed to the rigors and discipline of a school such as Rugby. Apart from his Canadian and South Seas venture, Brooke spent his entire life among a large circle of close friends. No less important is that while Brooke's sexual psychology was badly twisted by his Victorian upbringing, Nabokov had many affairs during his youth.

42 Scott assumed almost folkloric proportions among the British. In Rab Butler's memoirs, he recounts that his boarding school mistress always chastised those who left food on their plates with "Captain Scott would have given his eye for that egg"; see Richard Austin Butler, *The Art of the Possible: The Memoirs of Lord Butler* (London: Hamish Hamilton, 1971), 8. The young Nabokov was not immune to romantic hero worship. Among the few poets honored by Nabokov in verse was Nikolai Gumilev, a leading Acmeist, who was a traveler to exotic climes and a highly decorated army officer. He was shot as a counter-revolutionary conspirator by the Bolsheviks in August, 1921 while Nabokov was working on Brooke. See Nabokov's poem's "Pamiati Gumileva" ("In Memory of Gumilev") written March 19, 1923 and "Kak liubil ia stikhi Gumileva," ("How I loved Gumilev's poetry") written July 22, 1972 (see *Stikhi* 1979). Vladimir Alexandrov's "Nabokov and Gumilev" in *The Garland Companion to Vladimir Nabokov* (428–33) examines their relationship and remarks on several Nabokov poems that may have been influenced by Gumilev's work. Thus, in a sense, Gumilev, only a year older than Brooke, may have been for Nabokov a Russian Brooke.

43 For the texts of Nabokov's play and discussion of his use of Scott's material, see Vladimir Nabokov, *Krug*, ed. Natal'ia I. Tolstaia (Leningrad: Khudozhestvennaia literatura, 1990) and her article "'Polius' V. Nabokova i 'Posledniaia ekspeditsiia Skotta'," *Russkaia literatura*, 1 (1989): 133–36; and *The Man from the USSR and Other Plays*, trans. and introd. Dmitri Nabokov (San Diego: Harcourt Brace Jovanovich, 1984), 10–13, 266–83. (Hereafter *USSR*.)

44 Gennady Barabtarlo, "A Skeleton in Nabokov's Closet: '*Mest'*,'" in *A Small Alpine Form: Studies in Nabokov's Short Fiction*, ed. Charles Nicol and Gennady Barabtarlo (New York: Garland, 1993), 15–23.

CHAPTER 10

Clio laughs last: Nabokov's answer to historicism
Alexander Dolinin

Crossing a border between two worlds – whether physical or mental, spatial or temporal, literal or metaphorical – has always been one of Nabokov's major themes. A recurrent image in his work is that of a leap, a "knight's move" that transports a hero to a different reality, in some cases, even a realm beyond death. Thus it might seem surprising that he persistently underplays the turning point in the life of any expatriate – the moment when an exile crosses the state border and, like Byron's Childe Harold, says "Adieu, adieu!" to his native land. As Nabokov notes in his autobiography, at such a moment in his life he was concentrating on a game of chess with his father and "the sense of leaving Russia was totally eclipsed" by personal anxieties (*SM*, 251 [ch. 12]). When the hero of *Mary* is leaving the Russian shore, his memory registers some "trivia – and not nostalgia for his abandoned homeland ... as though only his eyes had been alive and his mind had gone into hiding" (*Mary*, 101 [ch. 5]). Likewise in *Glory*, Martin "followed the Russian shore with an almost indifferent gaze"[1] and only later, during his stay in Switzerland, "felt for the first time that he was, after all, an exile, doomed to live far from home" (*Glory*, 63 [ch. 15]). Another partial *alter ego* of the young Nabokov, Fyodor Godunov-Cherdyntsev does not ever mention his crossing of the Russian border.

An obvious reason for this "almost indifferent gaze" lies in the cultural identity of Nabokov and his autobiographical characters. By upbringing and education they belonged to the Westernized elite of Old Russia that considered itself an integral part of all-European culture. Polyglottal, cosmopolitan, refined, these "Russian Europeans" regarded the West as a legitimate "second home" rather than as a hostile alterity and so crossing the border for them was not a leap into the unknown but a sort of homecoming. To stress this point, Nabokov makes the hero of his *Glory*, Martin Edelweiss, one-quarter Swiss – a veiled retort to Dostoevsky whose Stavrogin in *The Devils*, a devil-like tempter, an arch-traitor to Russian spirituality, is branded as a citizen of the Swiss canton Uri. There is nothing demonic or non-Russian in Martin; on the contrary, in England he embraces "his unmistakably Russian essence" and understands that his earlier Europeanism has always been "filtered through his motherland's quiddity and suffused with peculiar Russian tints" (*Glory*, 54–55 [ch. 12]). Yet he remains a citizen of the world and assimilates Western culture in a natural, spontaneous manner, claiming it for his own.

However, as a result of their unmediated confrontation with the realities of Western life, the "Russian Europeans" suddenly found themselves not among their sympathetic kinsmen but among indifferent foreigners. In his memoirs Fedor Stepun, a prominent philosopher and Heidelberg alumnus, recalls the acute pain of his forced separation from beloved Germany and France during the Civil war in Moscow and describes his craving for "European smells" of flowers, cigars, libraries and express trains.[2] However, a year later the Bolshevik government deported him to Berlin, and after a quick reality check he had to admit that European life was at odds with his dreams. In his essay "Thoughts on Russia" he ruminated on the irony of exile:

Two years ago in Moscow I set out to compile a collection of short stories and asked some people who were close to my views for contributions. The result was really strange: not one of the stories had Russia as its setting. Côte d'Azur, Paris, Florence, Heidelberg, Munich, Egypt – that is what Russians, "good old Europeans," were writing about . . . in the years of the Revolution.

Yet here we are now, exiled from Russia to that very Europe for which we have lately been longing so passionately, and so what? Unclear as it might sound, it is true: by means of our exile to Europe we have been also exiled *from* Europe. We, "Russian Europeans," seem to have loved Europe only as a beautiful landscape, a view from the window cut by Peter the Great; a dear, native window sill supported our elbows – once it disappeared, the allure of the landscape vanished.[3]

Most of the Russian Westernizers who came to their proclaimed "second home" after the Revolution suffered a similar shock of disillusionment and disconnection. Describing his English impressions in his 1921 essay "Kembridzh" ("Cambridge"), young Nabokov vented a feeling of alienation that he would later learn to conceal or transmute:

Now and then I would sit in a corner looking around and seeing all these smooth faces, very nice faces, no doubt, – but for some reason always reminding me of shaving cream advertisements, and suddenly I would feel so bored and frustrated that I wished I could scream and break windows ...

Between them and us, the Russians, there is a kind of glass wall; they have their own world, round and hard, resembling a neatly colored globe ... and if you lose control and tell someone in heartfelt simplicity that you would give all your blood to see some little marsh near Petersburg – it's indecent to speak such thoughts; he would look at you in such a way as if you had whistled in church.[4]

The cold, scathing gaze of the autochthones pierced the veneer of the Russian émigrés' Europeanism and made them aware of their ineradicable otherness. This rejection was all the more painful since many of the newcomers thought they were entitled to a different type of treatment. In the Bolshevik Revolution they had witnessed, the Russian Europeans saw an integral part of European history, and they believed that their unique experience would be welcomed by their Western hosts. Yet almost no one in the West heeded their warnings and their message remained largely unnoticed. It turned out that from the Western perspective Russia had always been excluded from the European historical continuum and therefore Russian émigrés were denied the status of relatives or, at least, peers.

Driven away from the European house, Russian writers in exile often responded to the insult by taking the position of outside observers and critics who, thanks to their distance, are able to see what the insiders can not.[5] A typical description of Western life in émigré literature is, in fact, a denunciation, a diatribe against the suffocating boredom and vulgarity, the smug philistinism (*poshlost'*) of the bourgeois everyman. Very often the émigrés rationalized their disenchantment with their "second home" in historicist terms – as a reaction to the crisis or downfall of European civilization. In *The Gift* Yasha Chernyshevski, an epitome of émigré commonplaces, reads Spengler's *Decline of Europe* and, in his own words, "for a whole week ... was in a daze" (*Gift*, 38 [ch. 1]); this reflects the Russian exiles' infatuation with the German philosopher's idea that West European culture (he called it "Faustian") had reached the final stage of its natural life-cycle and was doomed to self-destruction. Spengler's critique of the modern epoch in the guise of a scientific historicist discourse and his eschatological predictions were congenial to the émigrés' apocalyptic vision of Europe and provided a convenient intellectual framework for their frustration. Thus in 1924 Nikolai Berdiaev, one of the most important philosophers of Russian emigration, following Spengler, came up with his own historicist concept of the modern epoch, comparing it to the collapse of the ancient world. "We are now taking part in the beginnings of the barbarization of Europe ... Now night is upon us. We are going into a period of senility and decay," he wrote in the book *Novoe Srednevekov'e* (*The New Middle Ages*), aptly renamed *The End of Our Time* in English translation.[6]

It is surprising to see how strongly these doctrines (combined, of course, with centuries-old Russian anti-Western stereotypes), influenced representations of the contemporary European scene in those émigré writings that made claims to reflecting some experienced realities. For example, Spengler's vision of Berlin as a "daemonic stone-desert" provided Russian outcasts who stayed in the German capital with a convenient philosophical model for castigating their unfriendly surroundings. Khodasevich's *European Night*, for instance, abounds in images of demonism, sterility, and decay: the houses of Berlin are like "rows of demons"; its constant attributes are dryness, darkness, and stench; the epitome of the city is an insane old man masturbating in an underground public toilet.[7] We can find similar motifs in the work of quite a number of Russian writers (for example, in Shklovsky's *Zoo* and Aleksei Tolstoy's stories) but it was Andrei Bely's book of essays *A Chamber in the Kingdom of Shadows* that finalized the myth of Berlin as a daemonic city. Bely's Berlin is "the bourgeois Sodom," Tartarus, Hades, the Egyptian Kingdom of Shadows; the surface of bourgeois boredom and order hardly conceals total madness, depravity, and perversity; old European culture has perished and in its place reign jazz bands, fox-trot frenzy, drugs, and Dadaism in which Bely, following Spengler, discerns signs of the final catastrophe, the onslaught of the "barbarous Dionysus" in the image of a pagan African deity – "the 'Negro' of new Europe but, in fact, the image of its death, its doom."[8]

In fact, this apocalyptic view of the Western world overlapped with the Marxist-Leninist concept of modern history according to which the epoch of capitalism was coming to an inexorable end, destined to give way to the new, Communist era. Any signs of degradation in the West, therefore, could be interpreted as symptoms of an unavoidable historical catastrophe, while the Soviet Russia that had already passed through the tortures of a necessary revolutionary transition moved to the enviable place of front-runner in the race to a radiant future. That is why Bely in the finale of his *A Chamber in the Kingdom of Shadows* contrasts the dying, suffocating, "brownish-gray" Berlin falling into the abyss with the lively, dynamic, colorful Moscow arising "after the avalanche" and associates the very chaos of Soviet life with the "creative laboratory of unprecedented future forms."[9] The logic of historicism allowed its proponents to uneasily perceive communism (or, as it were, fascism) as the lesser evil, and many of them – Bely, Shklovsky, Pasternak, Aleksei Tolstoy, Ehrenburg in the 1920s, Ladinsky in the 1940s – eventually returned to the Soviet Union.

Nothing could be further from Nabokov's position than such a surrender to historicist "general ideas." Even a cursory look at his descriptions of Weimar Berlin – the site of all his major Russian works except *Invitation to a Beheading* – is sufficient to show that Nabokov's vision is pointedly opposed to the image of the city as a "daemonic Sodom" on the verge of impending destruction. Where the émigré critics of the West see horrifying symbols of historical catastrophe, Nabokov discovers just the regenerated forms of eternal *poshlost'*. Disputing Andrei Bely's diatribes against "fox-trot frenzy," he writes in an early story "A Letter to Russia" ("Pis'mo v Rossiiu" [1925], translated as "A Letter that Never Reached Russia"):

Many fellow exiles of mine denounce indignantly (and in this indignation there is a pinch of pleasure) fashionable abominations, including current dances. But fashion is a creature of man's mediocrity, a certain level of life, the vulgarity of equality, and to denounce it means admitting that mediocrity can create something (whether it be a form of government or a new kind of hairdo) worth making a fuss about. (*Stories*, 139)

The narrator of this lyrical, plotless story, almost a poem in prose, strolls about Berlin at night, observing various insignificant incidents of urban life – the magic interplay of lights, colors and sounds, the "moist reflections" on the wet pavement, the amusing pantomime of people, vehicles and objects, and, to use the title of a famous documentary about Berlin in the 1920s, creates his personal "symphony of the big city" out of these trifles. In a sense, he is doing to the foreign environment what Humbert Humbert unsuccessfully tried to do with Lolita – he "safely solipsizes" it, transforming it into "another, fanciful" being with no life of its own, and he thereby transcends the pain of exile and isolation inflicted by history:

I am ideally happy. My happiness is a kind of challenge ... The centuries will roll by, and schoolboys will yawn over the history of our upheavals; everything will pass, but my happiness, dear, my happiness will remain, in the moist reflection of a street lamp, in the cautious bend of stone steps that descend into the canal's black waters, in the smiles of a dancing couple, in everything with which God so generously surrounds human loneliness. (*Stories*, 140)

The proud declaration of the narrator deftly defines Nabokov's authorial position with regard to his German surroundings as his object. The writer breaks the totality of Berlin into series of discrete "defamiliarized" particulars seen by an observant outsider from a safe distance of non-involvement – as it were, from a parallel reality, be it a construed view through "the kindly mirrors of future times" (*Stories*, 157), the creative consciousness of an artist in search of images and metaphors, or even, in "Details of a Sunset," the last gaze of a dying man at the city he is leaving forever. In order to "to find beauty in the alien," as Nabokov formulated his exilic agenda in "Cambridge," the viewer should distance oneself from his surroundings and behold the world around him from the "prospect high" of a happy outsider.

In a sense, Nabokov's position with respect to Berlin resembles that of a Baudelairean *flâneur* in Paris – a "passionate observer" of city life set upon "distilling the eternal from the transitory" and eager to "see the world, to be at the center of the world and to remain hidden from the world."[10] Like Baudelaire's heroic *flâneur*/dandy in Walter Benjamin's famous definitions, his exile goes "botanizing on the asphalt"[11] and treats the city in which he lives as a theater stage[12] or, in the case of Ganin in *Mary*, a "moving picture" (*Mary*, 52 [ch. 7]). Yet the curious parallels cannot but underscore the essential difference between the two types of urban spectatorship. Baudelaire's *flâneur*, to quote Benjamin once more, "is still on the threshold, of the city as of the bourgeois class. Neither has yet engulfed him; in neither he is at home. He seeks refuge in the crowd ... The crowd is the veil through which the familiar city lures the *flâneur* like a phantasmagoria."[13] Defying modernity, he seeks to define it by his very protest; he construes his role as the true hero of the new epoch[14] who distinguishes himself from the modern crowd and at the same time is bewitched by the pageant of constantly changing fashions – by "the transitory, the fugitive, the contingent" which, in Baudelaire's idiom, make up a half of modern art;[15] his outlook remains oriented towards the social and historical substratum.

Nabokov's exilic spectator, on the contrary, completely ignores the social intercourse of the foreign crowd. He sees himself not on the threshold but, so to say, in a different dimension, leading, as the writer remarked in *Speak, Memory,* "an odd but by no means unpleasant existence, in material indigence and intellectual luxury, among perfectly unimportant strangers, spectral Germans and Frenchmen" (*SM*, 276 [ch. 14]). Hence for him, in contrast to Baudelaire's *flâneur*, the theater of the "non-ego" he enjoys is devoid of any social and historical meaning; its message is entirely intimate and connected only to the spectator's personal fate and inner creative urge. It is the consciousness of the spectator that can transform the trivia of everyday things into "things of beauty" when it perceives them as parts of some extra-temporal reality at the moment of "cosmic synchronization."[16] While Baudelaire and his lyrical personas, the bewitched chroniclers and detractors of their age – so-called "modernity" – understood their alienation in historical terms, Nabokov and his "representatives" disdainfully rejected a self-indulgent way of looking at themselves as "victims of history." Moreover, unlike almost all the West European and Russian modernists from Baudelaire up to the writers of the "Lost Generation," Nabokov did not deem it possible to give an adequate definition of one's own epoch, or to predict its future from within. In an unpublished Russian essay of 1926 known under the English title "On Generalities" he wrote:

There is a very seductive and very harmful demon, the demon of generalities. He captivates human thought by labeling every phenomenon and carefully shelving it side by side with other thoroughly wrapped and numbered items. Thanks to him, such a turbid field of human knowledge as history turns into a tidy cubicle with so many wars and so many revolutions sleeping in the files where we can look over the previous centuries with comfort. This demon's favorite words are "idea," "movement," "influence," "period," "epoch." In the office of the historian this demon retroactively links and reduces phenomena, influences, and movements of centuries past. This demon brings with him a horrifying anguish – the consciousness (albeit entirely fallacious) that in spite of all its games and battles, mankind follows an unalterable course. This demon should be shunned. He is a cheat. He is a salesman in centuries who is pushing his price list.

And maybe worst comes to worst when we succumb to the temptation of comfortable generalities regarding not only times past and spent but also the time in which we live. Let the spirit of generalities in pursuit of intellectual comforts give the long row of guiltless years the name of "Middle Ages." That is still a pardonable sin, which might have saved modern students from more serious vices. Let them five hundred years from now find some intricate label, – say, "the Second Middle Ages" – to designate the twentieth century plus a couple of others ... But the question is: do we really need a name for our own century? Won't our attempts backfire when, preserved in thick books, they inflame the fantasies of future wizards?[17]

Though the immediate target of Nabokov's critique was obviously Berdiaev's recent *New Middle Ages*, he used it just as an illustration of the apocalyptic theories and prophesies prevalent in the socio-philosophical and journalistic discourse of the 1920s. In *The Gift* Fyodor makes fun not only of Yasha's "tasteless spiritual throes" over Spengler (*Gift*, 38 [ch. 1]) but, much more sweepingly, of the whole popular trend to blame the socio-historical situation for individual faults, failures, and stupidities. He easily imagines such trite interpretations of Yasha's suicide, only to disallow their adequacy:

Any corny man of ideas, any "serious" novelist in horn-rimmed glasses – the family doctor of Europe and the seismographer of its social tremors – would no doubt have found in this story something highly characteristic of the "frame of mind of young people in the postwar years" – a combination of words which in itself (even apart from the "general idea" it conveyed) made me speechless with scorn. I used to feel a cloying nausea when I heard or read the latest drivel, vulgar and humorless drivel, about the "symptoms of the age" and the "tragedy of youth." (*Gift*, 40–41 [ch. 1])[18]

In the essay "On Generalities" Nabokov questions the very notion of "our epoch," which, in his view, is too vague and abstract to relate to any individual experience. Even the major upheavals of the early twentieth century – the Great War, the Bolshevik Revolution, and their immediate political and economic consequences – should not be taken for universal determinants because *sub specie aeternitatis* (or, what for Nabokov is the same, *sub specie artis*) they are just a passing commotion that may affect surface conditions but not fundamental problems of human existence. He subverts, to quote *The Defense*, "the general opinion" that the Revolution "had influenced the course of every Russian's life" and "an author could not have his hero go through it without getting scorched, and to dodge it was impossible" (*Def*, 80 [ch. 5]). With the exception of Ganin in *Mary* (who has some dim military past), all the central characters of

Nabokov's Russian novels either are revolution- and war-dodgers or, like the characteristically non-Russian Dreyer (*King, Queen, Knave*), Krechmar/Albinus (*Camera obscura/Laughter in the Dark*), and Darwin (*Glory*), return from the trenches unscorched and unremembering. The main reason for the artistic failures of Soviet writers, according to Nabokov, was their common conviction that "the Revolution is an apocalyptic event destined to overturn the world and that the World War has changed some directions and some values." This point of view, he stated, cannot but destroy the artist – "a man operating in constants."[19]

Therefore, in defiance of the prevailing mind set, Nabokov refused to stigmatize the "decline of post-war Europe." The final part of his essay "On Generalities" recapitulates his dissident position:

One should not scorn our time. It is highly romantic, spiritually beautiful, and materially comfortable. The war, as any war, damaged many things but it is over, the wounds have healed, and we do not observe any particularly unpleasant consequences of it except for scores of bad French novels about *jeune gens d'après guerre*. The revolutionary fervor brought to life by chance will disappear by chance as has happened a thousand times in the history of mankind. Moronic communism in Russia will be replaced by something more intelligent, and in a hundred years from now, only historians will remember the extremely dull Mr. Ulianov. Let us then be like pagans or gods and enjoy our time, with its marvelous machines and gigantic hotels ... and, first and foremost, with its foretaste of eternity that every century of the past had and every century of the future will never lose.

This obstinate (and, from a historical perspective, somewhat short-sighted) apologia for the present echoes the ideas of Grigory Landau, the émigré philosopher and aphorist whom Nabokov personally knew and held in high regard.[20] Disputing popular deterministic theories about a dying European culture, Landau redefined modernity as a heroic epoch of intensive creativity and self-reliance. In his book *The Twilight of Europe* (*Sumerki Evropy*) he predicted that future generations would admire the chronicles of our age, which represented:

the spiritual drive of a generation that dared, in an environment without support, to rely upon itself both spiritually and materially. The heroic epoch of new self-assertion lies not in negation or a rebellion against God and nature, but in constructive activity where daring intentions create deeds and life rather than incorporeal images and thoughts.[21]

Landau sees the heroic essence of the modern age in its "passion for constructing, overcoming, and fulfilling" as embodied by discoveries in technology and science, setting records in sports, mountain climbing, polar expeditions, and other free acts of "pure will." Such modern exploits involving incredible effort and self-sacrifice are committed, in his view, not for the sake of gain or even glory but out of a spiritual urge to self-realization and creativity: "it is a pure desire to prevail, a heroism of categorical imperative, of freely set goals."[22]

This concept of modernity is reflected in Nabokov's *Glory* (*Podvig* [literally "exploit" or "high deed"]) – the novel for which the writer initially considered the titles *Embodiment* (*Voploshchenie*) and *Romantic Times* (*Romanticheskii vek*),[23] which would directly refer to Landau's argument. In order to discredit the "decline of the West" clichés, Nabokov puts them into the mouth of a laughable, discredited character, Martin's Uncle Henry. It is this shallow bourgeois who "spoke with horror and revulsion about the twilight of Europe,[24] about post-war fatigue, about our practical age, about the invasion of inanimate machines; in his imagination there existed some diabolical connection between the fox-trot and skyscrapers on one side and women's fashions and cocktails on the other" (*Glory*, 127 [ch. 29]).

In contrast to his uncle, the hero of the novel has no qualms concerning the century in which he lives:

No other epoch had such brilliance, such daring, such projects. Everything that had glimmered in previous ages – the passion for exploration of unknown lands, the audacious experiments, the glorious exploits of disinterested curiosity, the scientists who went blind or were blown to bits, the heroic conspiracies, the struggle of one against many – now emerged with unprecedented force. (*Glory*, 127 [ch. 29])

Following Landau, Nabokov regards the modern age not as a kingdom of materialism but as a well-set arena for displaying an individual's moral and spiritual energies. The protagonist of *Glory* – a sportsman, a mountain climber, a traveler – embodies that heroic "craving for the faraway" ("alkanie dalei") in which Landau saw the meaning of the epoch.[25] Martin's "high deed" ("podvig") is not just a "solitary and courageous expedition" across the Soviet border, a sacrificial journey to "the night of Zoorland" where "plump children are tortured in the dark, and a smell of burning and putrefaction permeates the air" (*Glory*, 150 [ch. 35]) but also his whole inner life, the pilgrimage of his soul towards ultimate self-realization. Through the plot of *Glory* Nabokov redefines the very notion of "exploit," resurrecting the original, antiquated meaning of the word *podvig* as "path," "way," "journey," "movement"[26] and playing upon the archaic expression "sovershit' podvig" (to live one's life). Throughout the novel he transforms the physical movements of his hero in its entire range of spatial imagery (linear path/winding path; border/ passage; forward/backward; ascent/descent; enclosures/openings; movement/stoppage; and so forth) into interconnected subtle metaphors for his spiritual emergence. The key words of the text – the Russian *tropa* and *tropinka*, i.e. a "path" (used more than fifteen times in the book) – thanks to their association with the Greek *tropos* (turn, direction, way), point at the device: the paths Martin takes are at the same time the tropes that reinterpret his short life. At a revelatory moment in chapter thirty-seven the hero himself redescribes his life in terms of a comfortable train voyage to a certain destination, a turning point, from which he has to move on his own: "He reflected what a strange, strange life had fallen to his lot, it seemed as if he had never left a fast train, had merely wandered from car to car ... 'And then I'll continue on foot, on foot,' muttered Martin excitedly – a forest, a winding path – what huge trees!" (*Glory*, 157 [ch. 37]).

Martin's final departure for Russia (and presumably for martyrdom) – the outwardly senseless act of "pure will" that is equivalent to an immortal poetic utterance – redeems his whole life, retrospectively investing it with order and meaning. Historically invisible and unrecognized, Martin's quest turns into a heroic *podvig* only on a meta-historical level when understood as an "artifice of eternity" semanticized through a complex system of intra-textual patterning on the one hand, and concealed inter-textual correspondences on the other. If the finale of the novel, for example, implies the hero's return from the dead and hence his immortality by repeating the cluster of important motives connected with the earlier episodes, the numerous allusions to Russian mythology, folklore, and literature reveal Martin's kinship with a carefully selected lineage of "eternal prototypes" – from the mythological Indrik the Beast, the fairy-tale Soldier Martin, and Egory the Brave, the son of Sofia the Wise (cf. the name of Martin's mother) who in religious folk verses sets out on an expedition to Russia in order to liberate the country from an evil ruler, up to Pushkin's Ruslan or the lyrical persona of

Lermontov's poetry.[27] According to Nabokov, the real "high deed" has nothing to do either with historical determinism or with the Romantic/Symbolist theatricalization of one's biography. Martin does not need admiring spectators nor does he seek any outside justification for his solitary acts; he, like Baudelaire's ideal voyager, "departs for the sake of departing" but, straining his will, moral spirit, and aesthetic consciousness to the utmost, he, without knowing it, in his own individual way "embodies" an eternal creative force and thereby earns the immortal glory of the hero.

It is obvious that Nabokov's treatment of the theme of "high deeds" in *Glory* was polemically directed against the bathos of contemporary Soviet literature which glorified the military and "socialist construction" exploits of its positive characters – staunch Party commissars or young Communist workers and soldiers. In his essay "The Triumph of Virtue" ("Torzhestvo dobrodeteli," 1930), written simultaneously with *Glory*, Nabokov derided these "Red Knights" and their hackneyed adventures "full of trials, high deeds ["podvigov"], and sufferings" that betray an affinity with cheap romances for children.[28] It is hardly a coincidence that he gave to his hero a relatively rare Russian name used several years before by the "proletarian" writer, Vladimir Bakhmet'ev, in his novel *The Crime of Martyn* (*Prestuplenie Martyna*), a work that was widely discussed by Soviet critics at the time.[29] Bakhmet'ev's Martyn is a failed "Red Knight," an ardent young Communist who believes that he "is destined for high deeds" ("podvig")[30] but at a crucial moment flees from danger. Later he tries to redeem his "crime" through the "high deed of repentance" ("podvig raskaianiia"),[31] and he eventually dies in a senseless battle, sacrificing not only his own life but also the lives of his comrades-in-arms when he disregards his duty to obey orders and make a retreat. The reason for Martyn's failure is his lingering individualism,[32] his unerased dream of personal glory and self-fulfillment that results in his inability to subordinate his will to the "iron necessity" of the class struggle. According to Communist doctrine, the real heroes are the masses "embodying" the law of history, and individual actions can acquire the status of a "high deed" only insofar as they have historical justification in the common cause.

Unlike his Soviet counterparts, Nabokov would claim that the very notion of historical laws is misleading, for it reduces the mysterious complexity of being to simplistic causality, leaving no space either for individual creativity or for the transcendence of the mundane. In *The Gift* a professor Anuchin lambasts Fyodor's *Life of Chernyshevski* for neglecting to discuss its hero from a historical perspective as a representative of a certain epoch and certain social ideas: "A certain epoch has been taken and one of its representatives chosen. But has the author assimilated the concept of 'epoch'? No. First of all one senses in him absolutely no consciousness of that *classification of time*, without which history turns into an arbitrary gyration of multicolored spots..." (*Gift*, 318 [ch. 5]). What Professor Anuchin does not understand is that this is exactly the point Fyodor (and, for that matter, Nabokov) is making: that history *is* a constant interplay of chance, "an arbitrary gyration of multicolored spots," which nowhere yields to classification. In his essay "On Generalities" Nabokov wrote:

> If every day in a man's life is a sequence of chance occurrences – and this is what invests it with divinity and power – all the more then the history of mankind is only chance. One may connect these chances and tie them up into tidy bouquets of periods and ideas, losing in the process the aroma of the past, and we see things not as they were but as we want them to have been ... Why should we imitate those paradoxical enemies of hazard who spend years over the green cloth at Monte Carlo, calculating the odds of red and black stakes in order to find some faultless system? There is no system. The roulette of history knows no laws. Clio laughs at our clichés ...[33]

If history is the realm of chance or, in Nabokov's parlance, "unreality"[34] or "dream and dust,"[35] the task of the artist is not to succumb to its pressures but to defy and transcend them – to escape into the private "oneiric house" of individual memory and imagination. Any surrender to historicism, even a minor concession, reveals the artist's vulnerability and leads to his destruction, as illustrated by Nabokov's short story "Cloud, Castle, Lake."

Vasiliy Ivanovich, the protagonist of the story – a Russian émigré in Berlin, a "representative" of the omnipotent author who endows him with the Nabokovian gifts of visual perceptiveness and poetic imagination – finds himself in a group of hideous Germans on "a pleasure trip" across the country. From his first minutes aboard a train (again an obvious metaphor of historical determinism), his relentless companions, exasperated by Vasiliy Ivanovich's otherness, set to humiliating and harassing him. However, on the third day a miracle happens: unnoticed by his tormentors, Vasiliy Ivanovich crosses some invisible border and enters a magical realm of poetic beauty in which time stands still: a pure blue lake with a large, motionless cloud always reflected in the water, and an ancient black castle, "arising from dactyl to dactyl" on the other side (*Stories*, 435). He decides to stay in this enchanted abode forever and to enjoy "a motionless and perfect correlation of happiness." But then he makes a fatal mistake – he goes back to his tormentors to say good-bye: "'My friends,' he cried, having run down again to the meadow by the shore, 'my friends, good-bye. I shall remain for good in this house over there. We can't travel together any longer. I shall go no farther. I am not going anywhere. Good-bye!'" (*Stories* 436). Alas, the henchmen of history are not the dreamer's friends, and they do not let him step aside. Once you join the herd, you are forced to march on together with "one collective, wobbly, many-handed being, from which one could not escape." The Germans drag Vasiliy Ivanovich away from the mirage, and, as soon as everyone gets aboard the train again, they torture and mutilate their victim. They crush Vasiliy Ivanovich's spirit, and, once back in Berlin, he begs his "master" to let him go, because he has not "the strength to belong to mankind any longer." "Of course, I let him go," remarks the omnipotent God of the story, bringing his parable to a poignant close (*Stories*, 437).

Paying undue respect to his enemies, Vasiliy Ivanovich misses a unique opportunity to slip out of historical reality into timelessness – an opportunity granted to him (as to Cincinnatus C. in *Invitation to a Beheading*, which is an obvious subtext for the story) as a reward for his heightened, quasi-artistic sensibilities. He belongs to a rare breed of seers in Nabokov's works who are able to discern a hidden pattern, an interrelation of several seemingly disparate things, and thereby to experience "cosmic synchronization." For Vasiliy Ivanovich, it is not only the alliterative triad of cloud-castle-lake but a configuration of three "insignificant objects – a smear on the platform, a cherry stone, a cigarette butt" that he sees through a window of the train-car "with such deathless precision" (*Stories*, 432).

The central element of the configuration – a cherry stone – seems to be an implanted marker referring to an important subtext for the story: the writings of Yury Olesha, a writer whose art of sensory metaphorism was congenial to Nabokov's aesthetics.[36] "The Cherry Stone" is the title of Olesha's well-known story (and book of 1931) in which the narrator tries to create his own "invisible country of

Attentiveness and Imagination" that would give him solace and refuge from the onslaught of victorious historical forces and to reconcile his timeless private world with the futuristic programs of the Communist regime. The allusion to the story (and the obvious thematic parallelism) allows us to interpret Nabokov's "Cloud, Castle, Lake" as a polemical response to Olesha's surrender of his "invisible country" to the adversary. In his speech at the first Congress of the Union of Soviet Writers (1934), Olesha declared his capitulation in the form of an allegory that bears a strong resemblance to Nabokov's story. He portrayed himself as a puny, pathetic beggar, a repulsive misfit ("nikomu ne nuzhnyj, poshlyi i nichtozhnyi") who wanders about the country passing by "the towers and lights of socialist construction sites." One day, though, when he is walking across a meadow, he notices a wall and its shadow on the grass and finds an arched entrance in the middle that reminds him of Renaissance paintings. He looks inside and sees a miraculous verdure. He makes a step over the threshold and suddenly, like Vasiliy Ivanovich, finds himself out of time: "I do not need anything. My doubts, my sufferings are over. I am young again." At this moment, however, Olesha cuts himself short and claims that he has made a decision to resist the temptation of the magical arch, and to accept his historical duty ("istoricheskaia zadacha") and to write useful, educational books for the heroic Soviet youth.[37]

Playing upon Olesha's symbolism of a journey, meadow, wall/castle, entrance into a magic space, verdure, mirror, Nabokov contradicted not his parable as such but rather its sudden cessation. In fact, he wrote a subversive ending to his counterpart's story, showing that the denial of a magic meta-historical retreat, a green paradise hidden from the eyes of the mob, is an "invitation to a beheading" for the artist; it can lead only to the loss of creativity and to self-destruction.

It is clear that Nabokov's militant anti-historicism was not the pose of a snob but a fundamental position shaped in the cultural context of the 1920s and 1930s. It originated as a response and challenge to the most influential philosophies of the day – Spenglerian eschatology and Marxist historical determinism – and formed the basis of Nabokov's world-view. Among Russian émigrés, the writer was not alone in his stand. Besides Grigory Landau and Mark Aldanov, we should name the prominent literary critic Petr Bitsilli who in his essay "The Crisis of History" called on Russian writers in exile to focus on ontology and metaphysics rather than on history or, in his terms, to reveal meta-historical patterns beneath the chaos and pain of historical changes. He defined meta-history as "a special a-temporal plane of being" on which our consciousness interacts with "immortal souls of the people whom we probably have never met and who could have lived thousands of years ago ... but who are more real for us than some of our contemporaries and compatriots, maybe more real than we ourselves."[38] It is this program of transcendence of history in culture that Nabokov fulfilled in his Russian writings and, paradoxically, it has proven quite viable from a historical perspective.

If we compare the fate of Nabokov with that of his Soviet counterpart Olesha, who reluctantly subordinated his creativity to historical necessity, we find out that Clio has been more benevolent to her arrogant detractor than to her novice. She silenced Olesha forever but allowed Nabokov to safely build up his enclosures of language, imagination, and memory amidst the "terribly cold world around." To paraphrase W. H. Auden, history in the long run pardons those who write well for rebelling against its authority.

NOTES

1 *Glory*, trans. Dmitri Nabokov in collaboration with the author (1971; New York: Vintage International, 1991), 25 (Ch. 7). (Hereafter *Glory*.)
2 See Fedor Stepun, *Byvshee i nesbyvsheesia* (New York: Izdatel'stvo imeni Chekhova, 1956), II:276.
3 Fedor Stepun, "Mysli o Rossii," *Sovremennye zapiski*, 17 (1923), 351–52.
4 Vladimir Nabokov, "Kembridzh," *Rul'*, October 28, 1921, 2; repr. in Vladimir Nabokov, *Rasskazy. Priglashenie na kazn'. Roman.: Esse, interv'iu, retsenzii* (Moscow: Kniga, 1989), 338.
5 Julia Kristeva asserts that such an outlook is characteristic of any foreigner. See her *Etrangers à nous-mêmes* (Paris: Fayard, 1988), 16. However, contrary to her paradigmatic outsider who is not surprised by the animosity he arouses and feels a certain inferiority in respect to the autochthones, Russian Europeans never regarded their exclusion as justified.
6 Nicholas Berdyaev, *The End of Our Time* (London: Sheed and Ward, 1935), 57–58.
7 On the imagery of *European Night*, see David M. Bethea, *Khodasevich: His Life and Art* (Princeton University Press, 1983), 287–94
8 Andrei Belyi, *"Odna iz obitelei tsarstva tenei"* (Leningrad: Gosudarstvennoe izdatel'stvo, 1924), 48–50.

9 *Ibid.*, 73.
10 I quote Baudelaire's essay "Le peintre de la vie moderne," from *Oeuvres complètes de Baudelaire* (Paris: Gallimard, 1961), 1160–63.
11 Walter Benjamin, *Charles Baudelaire: A Lyric Poet in the Era of High Capitalism* (London: Verso, 1983), 36.
12 Walter Benjamin, *Gesammelte Schriften* (Frankfurt am Main: Suhrlamp Verlag, 1974), 5:437.
13 Walter Benjamin, *Reflections: Essays, Aphorisms, Autobiographical Writings* (New York and London: Harcourt Brace Jovanovich, 1978), 156.
14 On the heroic stance of the *flâneur*, see Graeme Gilloch, *Myth and Metropolis: Walter Benjamin and the City* (Cambridge, MA: Polity Press, 1996), 152–55.
15 Baudelaire, *Oeuvres complètes*, 1163.
16 On Nabokov's concept of "cosmic synchronization," see Vladimir Alexandrov's seminal book *Nabokov's Otherworld* (Princeton University Press, 1991).
17 New York Public Library, Berg Collection, Vladimir Nabokov Archive. I am indebted and grateful to Dmitri Nabokov for his kind permission to study the archive materials and to use them in this work.
18 In her excellent article "Suicide as Literary Fact in the 1920s" Anne Nesbet pointed out that the story of Yasha was based on a real-life double suicide in the Grunewald forest in April 1928 when a Russian student, Aleksei Frenkel', shot and killed his girlfriend and himself; see her "Suicide as Literary Fact in the 1920s," *Slavic Review* 50 (1991): 827–35. She also cites a newspaper column by Semen Frank, the prominent Russian philosopher, who, much like Nabokov's "corny men of ideas," interpreted this drama as a symptomatic "tragedy of Russian youth" caused by the loss of spiritual values (S. Frank, "Tragediia russkoi molodezhi," *Rul'*, April 28, 1928). The younger generation of Russian émigrés, concludes Frank, had become an innocent victim of the Russian revolution without having taken part in it.
19 Vladimir Nabokov, "Neskol'ko slov ob ubozhestve sovetskoi belletristiki i popytka ustanovit' prichinu onogo," New York Public Library, Berg Collection, Vladimir Nabokov Archives.
20 In the early 1920s, Grigory Landau (1877–1941) worked together with Nabokov's father Vladimir Dmitrievich Nabokov on the editorial board of the Berlin newspaper *Rul'*. After the assassination of his friend and colleague, Landau published a moving obituary essay in which he stated that the integrity and candor of V. D. Nabokov were akin to Pushkin's "simplicity" ("prostota") defined as "the merging of culture and nature into a second nature." In Russian culture, argued Landau, Pushkin's legacy had been overshadowed by the "underground problematics" of Dostoevsky and Rozanov, the "subtle deformities of modernism," Tolstoy's anarchic return to "simple life," and the hollow simplism of Chernyshevsky and his disciples: "caught amidst these oversimplifications and simplism, amidst these problematics and defor-

mities, Pushkin's light is dimming; and Nabokov's simplicity – personal and social, political and spiritual – might have been one of its rare last gleams" (Grigorii Landau, "Pokhoronnoe," *Rul'*, April 6, 1922). This characterization might have prompted Nabokov to identify Pushkin with Fyodor's father as two interrelated parental figures who may be contrasted to Chernyshevsky in *The Gift*. Landau's tribute to Nabokov's father as a source for *The Gift* gives additional support to Gavriel Shapiro's recent suggestion that he could be the prototype for two fictitious sages with similar names mentioned in the novel: Hermann Lande and Delalande (see Gavriel Shapiro, "Hermann Lande's Possible Prototypes in *The Gift*," *The Nabokovian* 37 [Fall 1996]: 53–55). As late as 1957 Nabokov quoted an aphorism from Landau, calling him a "subtle philosopher" ("tonkii filosof") and mentioning his tragic death in a Soviet prison (Vladimir Nabokov-Sirin, "Zametki perevodchika," *Opyty* 8 [1957]: 45).

21 Grigorii Landau, *Sumerki Evropy* (Berlin: Izdatel'stvo "Slovo," 1923), 56.
22 *Ibid.*, 334–35, 354–61.
23 See Brian Boyd, *Vladimir Nabokov: The Russian Years* (Princeton University Press, 1990), 353.
24 In the original, Nabokov used here the Russian title of Spengler's book, *Zakat Evropy* (literally, *The Sunset of Europe*).
25 Landau, *Sumerki Evropy*, 336. Cf. Fyodor's declaration in *The Gift*: "I keep straining for the faraway" (*Gift*, 329 [ch. 5]).
26 See: Vladimir Dal', *Tolkovyi slovar' zhivogo velikorusskogo iazyka* 3 (St. Petersburg and Moscow: Izdani ... M. O. Vol'fa, 1882), 164. Nabokov hints at the etymological and semantic connection between "podvig" and the verb "dvigat'sia" (move) in the scene of Martin's heroic rock climbing when he uses four verbs of motion that have the same root: "PODVIGaias'," "naDVIGalas'," "PrODVIGat'sia," "zaDVIGalsia" (*Podvig* in *Sobranie sochinenii v chetyrekh tomakh* [Moscow: "Pravda," 1990] II.213). It is worth noting that the very word "podvig" is used twice in the novel in proximity to the verbs "PODVIGalas'" (was moving [about a horse], *Podvig* 241–42) and "DVInulsia" (walked on [about Darwin in the final phrase of the novel], 295–96).
27 Some of the Russian fairy tales and religious folk verses that serve as important subtexts for *Glory* were indicated and discussed in Edythe C. Haber's insightful article "Nabokov's *Glory* and the Fairy Tale," *Slavic and East European Journal* 21 (1977): 214–24. Yet many intertextual parallels significant for an understanding of the novel have never been identified.
28 *Rul'*, March 5, 1930, 2–3; repr. in Vladimir Nabokov, *Romany, rasskazy, esse* (St. Petersburg: Entar, 1993), 216–21.
29 I am indebted to Omri Ronen who mentions *The Crime of Martyn* as a possible source for *Glory* in his forthcoming article on Nabokov's "A Guide to Berlin," which I had the privilege to read in advance of

publication. He suggests that Nabokov could have known of Victor Shklovsky's negative review of Bakhmet′ev's novel in *LEF* (reprinted in Nikolai Chuzhak's famous anthology *Literatura fakta* [Moscow: Federatsiia, 1929], 130–35), since the critic emphasized the theme of the "high deed" ("podvig") in *The Crime of Martyn* and compared it to Conrad's *Lord Jim*.

30 Vl. Bakhmet′ev, *Prestuplenie Martyna* (Moscow: Khudozhestvennaia literatura, 1936), 211.
31 *Ibid.*, 192.
32 It is explained in the novel as the consequence of his mixed "class origins," for Martyn is the son of a fisherman and a gentry woman. The mixed Russian/Western ethnic and cultural origins of Nabokov's Martin can be regarded as a response to Bakhmet′ev's vulgar class determinism.
33 Nabokov's anti-historicist views are similar to the ideas of Mark Aldanov and were most probably formed with some influence from the latter.
34 *Eugene Onegin. A Novel in Verse by Aleksandr Pushkin*, trans. with commentary by Vladimir Nabokov, 4 vols. (1964; rev. edn. Princeton Unviversity Press, 1975), 3:177. (Hereafter *EO*.)
35 Vladimir Nabokov, "Mr. Masefield and Clio," *New Republic*, December 9, 1940, 808.
36 On Nabokov and Olesha, see Edward J. Brown, "Nabokov, Chernyshevsky, Olesha, and the Gift of Sight," in *Literature, Culture and Society in the Modern Age. In Honor of Joseph Frank*, ed. Edward J. Brown *et al.*, Stanford Slavic Studies 4 (1992), 2:280–94; Jane Grayson, "Double Bill: Nabokov and Olesha," in *From Pushkin to Palisandria: Essays on the Russian Novel in Honor of Richard Freeborn*, ed. Arnold McMillin (New York: St. Martin's Press, 1990), 181–200.
37 Iurii Olesha, *Povesti i rasskazy* (Moscow: Khudozhestvennaia literatura, 1965), 425–30.
38 Petr Bitsilli, "Krizis istorii," *Sovremennye zapiski* 58 (1935): 335.

CHAPTER 11

Poshlust, culture criticism, Adorno, and Malraux
John Burt Foster, Jr.

I

In January 1937, with Hitler's Germany ever more dangerous for his Jewish wife and half-Jewish son, Vladimir Nabokov left Berlin, ostensibly on a reading tour but also to explore his options elsewhere; in July, he and his family moved to France for a brief second exile. There, as he wrote *The Real Life of Sebastian Knight*, he began the difficult process of becoming an English-language novelist. By that time the German-born sociologist of music and aesthetician Theodor Adorno, just four years his junior and himself partly Jewish, had lost his academic job in Frankfurt due to the Nazi racial laws. After a period in England, Adorno would move to the United States in 1938, two years before Nabokov, who departed in May 1940 on one of the last American steamers before France fell to Germany.

Though Nabokov and Adorno already enjoyed some recognition, neither of them became well-known internationally until after World War II. By contrast, their French contemporary André Malraux was a precocious celebrity, first in the Paris art world, then as a novelist, finally as an opponent of the Nazis. Two years younger than Nabokov, he had toured the United States for the Spanish Republic in 1937, only to witness Franco's victory early in 1939. With the coming of World War II he enlisted in a tank corps and was taken prisoner, but he soon escaped to the Vichy zone. Though his books were banned in occupied France, he managed to live for a time on smuggled advances from his American publisher.

Beyond the turmoil of persecution, flight, and exile, all three men would have strong personal reasons to know how lucky they were to survive Hitler's triumphs. Nabokov's brother Sergei, who stayed in Europe, perished in a concentration camp near the end of the war.

Adorno's friend Walter Benjamin, who later became famous as a theorist and literary critic, committed suicide on the French–Spanish border to avoid capture by the Gestapo. After Malraux joined the French Resistance, he would again be taken prisoner; but he lived to tell the tale, unlike his two half-brothers who died in the hands of the Nazis.

In the course of juxtaposing Nabokov's life during the period of Hitler's victories with Adorno's and Malraux's, this three-way biographical sketch has suggested important parallels and contrasts in their lives. One notes their distinctively Russian, German, and French points of departure; their shared situation as Western intellectuals growing up with the twentieth century; their varied involvements in the fall of France; and their ties to the United States as a resource or place of refuge. Looking past how their lives intertwine, however, this comparative essay will focus on some related confrontations in their writings: on the web of intersections and divergences to be found in their engagement with culture criticism during these years. Having matured under the powerful influence of modernist innovators like Proust, Kafka, or Gide in literature, Schoenberg in music, or Picasso in the visual arts,[1] how did these authors react to the harsh challenge posed by Hitlerism to their deepest assumptions about the value of the arts and their role in Western culture?

Here we see a striking parallel between Nabokov and his two counterparts. Between 1941 and 1943, when Hitlerism was at its peak, and Nabokov was living in Cambridge, Massachusetts, Adorno in Los Angeles, and Malraux in Vichy France, all three writers chose to reflect on cultural degradation and its expression in bad art. In Nabokov's case, the result was his best-known piece of explicit culture criticism: the self-contained twelve-page digression in his Gogol book of 1944 on the Russian word *poshlost'* (the prime after the "t" transcribes a so-called "soft sign" in the original Russian). Nabokov tentatively rewrites this word, which roughly means "self-satisfied mediocrity," to coin a new English word "poshlust" which becomes the focus of his discussion.[2] The corresponding work by Adorno, also published in 1944, was the fourth chapter in *Dialectic of Enlightenment*, a still-controversial critique of "the culture industry" that he co-authored with Max Horkheimer.[3] Malraux, meanwhile, had already addressed similar issues in the title episode of his last novel, *The Walnut Trees of Altenburg*, published in

1943. Much later, he would rework this "walnut trees" episode as a keynote passage in his unconventional memoirs, which started to come out just before he retired as France's first Minister of Culture under de Gaulle.[4]

Culture criticism is, of course, a minor strand in Nabokov's prose. Though his comments on "poshlust" appear in an analysis of Gogol's fiction, and though they reflect back on situations in his own fiction, they depend much more directly on expository techniques like definition, argument, and evidence than the novels, short stories, and autobiographical writings treated elsewhere in this collection of essays. It cannot be denied, moreover, that both Adorno and Malraux are better known as cultural commentators and activists. Adorno's contributions to the Frankfurt School of cultural theorists and critics remain a benchmark for recent work in cultural studies, even if his findings have often been contested; and Malraux is now memorialized both at the French Ministry of Culture, near the Louvre Museum which was once one of his charges, and in the Pantheon, the shrine of the now restored French Republic. Still, a triangulation of Nabokov's most-discussed venture in culture criticism with similar work by two more famous contemporaries in that field does make sense, if taken in a surveyor-like spirit of working to improve our bearings on "poshlust." By opening up Western European and American vistas on a term whose Russian meanings have been well researched,[5] comparison with Adorno and Malraux should yield a more nuanced sense of Nabokov's place and stature as a culture critic.

II

As is well known, Adorno and Horkheimer use an economic model to explain the degradation and bad art that they associate with mass culture, their main target in the "culture industry" chapter. Their discourse grows out of the German philosophical tradition, and is rigorously theoretical; despite its emphasis on economic factors, it is not narrowly Marxist, for it draws as well on Freud and Nietzsche and above all on Hegel's dialectic. Still, the economic model marks Adorno and Horkheimer's very choice of "culture industry" as a key term, which suggests the expansion of mass-production methods from the early twentieth-century factory to advertising, radio, the recording business, and the movies. Nabokov had little interest in this kind of economic argument; "bourgeois," he can remark (without noting the irony that Marx's daughter translated *Madame Bovary* into English), is a word he uses "in the Flaubertian, *not* in the Marxist sense" (*NG*, 67). He is thinking of Flaubert's unfinished dictionary of received ideas,[6] as well as the passive, even stupefied acquiescence in stale formulas and conventions that sometimes afflicts the characters in Flaubert's novels of everyday life, *Madame Bovary* and *Sentimental Education*. Moreover, when Nabokov insists that poshlust is "beautifully timeless" (*NG*, 64) or calls it an "immortal spirit" (*NG*, 65), he rejects the historicist along with the economic claims of Marxism. As a result, he can detect poshlust among the ads, best sellers, and comics of 1944 America just as much as in Gogol's very different nineteenth-century Russia of landowners, serfs, and tsarist officials.

I will return to this "timelessness" later; but when *Pale Fire* evokes the televised image of a movie star "dissolving in the prism / Of corporate desire" (*PF*, 49 [ll.456–57]), the economic meaning of "corporate" is slight. More immediate meanings include "bodily" – "corporate" as allied to "corporeal" – but especially "like-minded groups." In context, Nabokov stresses the broadcasting of feminine stereotypes which in effect "dissolve" the possibility of uniqueness and individuality. Here again he resonates with Horkheimer and Adorno, for whom mass culture and the media posed an even more serious threat to the individual. But their theoretical mode of discourse was utterly alien to Nabokov, who arguably despised Freud even more than he did Marx. It should be noted, however, that he did respect the Hegelian dialectic, though not as a type of logic or method of thought. For Nabokov, recalling with some warmth the popularity of "Hegel's triadic series … in old Russia," the dialectic offered a rationale for one of his leading master-images, the temporal spiral in which "twirl follows twirl, and every synthesis is the thesis of the next series" (*SM*, 275 [ch. 14]).

Nabokov's rejection of theory and his just-noted recourse to imagery, word-play, or Flaubert's spirit of impassive narrative probably make him seem literary alongside the rigorously philosophical persona projected by Adorno.[7] But this impression is only partly correct, and a discussion of Malraux will reveal how much Nabokov relies on traditional methods of exposition. Inadvertently falling into a Russian tradition of social commentary that he usually detested, Nabokov's cultural critique takes the form of freely digressive reflections on a literary work, with a strong topical charge. Malraux, by contrast, embeds his critique in a work of fiction, so that his ideas become fully "novelized." That is to say, though no reader would fail to see that the walnut trees episode belongs to a drama of ideas, the development of both character and action and especially the use of imagery make essential contributions to Malraux's theme.

Victor Berger, the hero of *Walnut Trees*, is an Alsatian with ties to both French and German culture; his name fittingly makes sense in either language. Returning home in early 1914 after years in the Muslim world, he happens to attend a colloquium on the "Permanence and Metamorphosis of Man" organized by his uncle, a retired historian who runs the former Altenburg priory as a conference center. After a discussion whose rapid give-and-take generates a wide range of ideas about culture, followed by a harangue on the impossibility of cross-cultural communication by a German anthropologist named Möllberg, Berger walks into the surrounding countryside. When he sees a pair of walnut trees, their simple visual appearance seems to give an answer to the dilemma posed at the colloquium, on whether culture possesses some inherently universal quality or whether it is irremediably multiple, compartmentalized, and divisive. Thus as Berger gazes at the trees, "the strength with which the twisted branches sprang from their enormous trunks, the bursting into dark leaves of this wood which was so heavy and so old that it seemed to be digging into the earth and not sprouting from it, created at the same time the impression of one will and an unending metamorphosis."[8] Trunk and branches, wood and leaves seem to intertwine at this moment of special insight, which seeks to reconfigure the colloquium's heated contrast between unity and multiplicity as a single, unified process of organic unfolding into multifariousness. Metamorphosis, of course, was also a key word for Nabokov, but he usually saw it as a biological process at work among moths and butterflies, not as a general cultural transformation.[9]

Malraux's more purely novelistic treatment of his ideas leads, in contrast to Nabokov's or Adorno's concerns with cultural pathology, to an affirmative, even utopian vision of positive value. To give this vision to a hero with ties to both French and German culture at a time when France was under German occupation is remarkable. As both its basic focus on cultural matters and the statue-like appearance of the walnut trees suggest, the scene continues the meditations on creativity and the visual arts which, interrupted by Malraux's involvement in the Spanish Civil War, would be resumed in *The Voices of Silence* (1951), his most ambitious book on painting and sculpture. Of special bearing on the Altenburg colloquium is Malraux's key idea of an "imaginary museum," which undercuts traditional barriers of time and place in the arrangement of collections by deliberately juxtaposing works from different cultures. The equivalent project for Nabokov would be his translation of *Eugene Onegin* (1964), also dedicated to crossing cultural boundaries but in the medium of poetry, which is notoriously less amenable to such movement than visual images. The roots of this project can be traced back through the Gogol book to Nabokov's 1937 centennial essay on Pushkin,[10] which appeared in French in the *Nouvelle revue française*, the influential journal which also published Malraux. Both *Walnut Trees* and *Gogol* are thus intermediate wartime expressions of their authors' longer commitments to cross-cultural communication.

In 1943, however, the depiction of Berger's generous vision of cultural interplay and mutual enhancement does not blind Malraux to cultural degradation, shown most forcefully in the character of Möllberg. An ultra-nationalist modeled on Frobenius, a pioneering German interpreter of African culture, and more remotely on the cultural historian Spengler, the best-selling author of *The Decline of the West*, this Hegelian anthropologist has just destroyed his life's work in a sudden fit of revulsion at the perceived otherness of Africa. He now argues for extreme cultural compartmentalization, asserting that the boundaries of a culture are as ineluctable to its members as "the aquarium is to the fish swimming inside it" (*WT*, 105). He also seems to advocate a nihilistic brand of patriotism: "if the human adventure had any meaning," he can declare, "then Germany would be chosen to give it meaning" (*WT*, 113). In sharp contrast to Berger's exalted vision of the walnut trees, he enjoys creating melancholy figurines, "as though sculpted in half melted fat" which, like certain images of Goya's, seem "to remember they were once human" (*WT*, 78).[11]

This portrait of Möllberg in 1914 points a warning. For Malraux, looking back from the French defeat in 1940 with which his novel both begins and ends, this character seems to suggest a first fissure in the basic sense of common humanity that, greatly widened, would produce Hitlerism. Möllberg also prepares for a more disquieting German nationalist in the next unit, a research chemist who supervises a horrifying experiment in gas warfare on the Eastern front in 1915. Malraux only learned later, however, that an even more ghastly form of "gas warfare" in the East was being planned in Berlin even as he wrote these pages.[12] Still, given both Adorno's and Nabokov's interest in Hegel, it is striking that Malraux should link Möllberg's ultranationalism with his Hegelianism, making it seem in context more ominous than his Alsatian hero's equally explicit admiration for Nietzsche. In fact, given Berger's multiple cultural identity, the Nietzsche of *Walnut Trees* is probably meant as an opposite to both Möllberg and Hitler. Far from the proto-Nazi of popular stereotype, he is a German transnationalist whose love of French culture suggests a more productive vision of relations between the two countries.

If we turn from ideology to imagery, the relapsed humanity of Möllberg's figurines seems even more dangerous than his devotion to Hegel. Their reduction of living tissue to melted and molded fat uncannily resembles one of Nabokov's early attempts to express the moral disaster of the Hitler years, the miniature dog of congealed grease in *Despair* (*Des*, 96–97 [ch. 5]). Hermann's triple dream of this loathsome creature is followed by his impulsive decision to end a meeting with his supposed double and intended victim. This warning, of course, is not repeated, and Hermann soon resumes his murderous scheme. As an explicitly *Russian* German, however, Hermann suggests a broader critique of mounting dehumanization than Malraux attempts with Möllberg: Nabokov wants to push beyond the Hitlerian frame of reference implied by the 1930s German setting of *Despair* and made explicit in Fassbinder's movie adaptation. Thus Hermann's repeated and perhaps somewhat forced admiration for "Soviet" methods anticipates the more convincing attack on "Communazism" that underlies the picture, in *Bend Sinister*, of an imagined Germano-Slavic dictatorship.

Beyond these sociopolitical overtones, Hermann's revolting vision of congealed grease shaped like a living creature has some affinities with poshlust itself. Thus Nabokov senses a bloated rotundity in Chichikov, the swindler protagonist in Gogol's *Dead Souls*. There is, he affirms, "something sleek and plump about *poshlust*"; and he feels that "this gloss, these smooth curves" (*NG*, 71) or again the basic "'roundness' of *poshlust*" (*NG*, 74) must have attracted Gogol. For an even more graphic instance of swollen humanoid vacuity, however, Nabokov turns to "a certain poster in old Europe," a tire advertisement featuring "a human being entirely made of concentric rings of rubber" (*NG*, 74). That the innocuous Michelin man could acquire such sinister implications bears witness to the level of Nabokov's desperation and sense of looming disaster in France, between his first and second flights from Hitler.

III

Nabokov's discussion of "poshlust" is thus less novelistic than Malraux's visionary walnut trees, despite a striking parallel in the way they imagine dehumanization. Still, even though his methods are mainly expository, this section seems to be designed, like the Gogol book as whole, to frustrate some of our standard expectations for literary criticism, leaving a gap for creative collaboration from readers. For example, Nabokov begins by announcing the crucial importance of a Russian word, for which there are no English, French, or German equivalents; yet he never discusses how Russians actually define that word. Then, after an overly long, even dizzying list of English synonyms, he undercuts its authority by remarking that his source also "lists 'rats, mice' under 'Insects'" (*NG*, 64). He ends with a refusal to sum things up: instead of an overarching concept, he asks readers to think in terms of a quasi-musical pattern, with a "main theme" or "leitmotiv" in Gogol's novel and "different aspects ... noted at random" in the critic's text that ideally combine "in such a way to form an artistic phenomenon" (*NG*, 74). The interpretation of these random aspects and even the sense of how to combine them are left to his readers, who by definition will be capable of understanding Nabokov only once they have succeeded in becoming "artistic."

The best illustration of this willingness to rely on the reader's creativity, or perhaps on a strategy for coaxing that creativity into existence, would be the linguistic texture of Nabokov's key term, through which more of his assumptions and thought processes can be glimpsed. In straddling two languages and cultures, "poshlust" resembles Malraux's choice of "Berger" as his hero's name. But in Nabokov's case the bilingual term evokes the author's personal situation between two languages, not a political rivalry like the one dividing Germany and France, with the Alsace as the bone of contention. More narrowly, as an invented English word, "poshlust" recalls the telescoped portmanteau words in Lewis Carroll's "Jabberwocky" or Joyce's *Finnegans Wake*; in its reliance on a Russian root, however, it comes closer to the Anglo-Russian coinages in Anthony Burgess's *A Clockwork Orange* (1962), like "horrorshow" for *khorosho*, from the Russian word for "good." When put into English on these terms, the Russian "poshlost'" loses some of its original sense, though not – as in Burgess – to the point of reversal. More important, it also gains crucial English implications: for when read as "posh-lust," it suggests an overwhelming, even sexualized desire for the posh, which in turn refers to upscale consumer goods that confer a certain prestige on their owners.

True to the studied quirkiness of his argument, Nabokov does not make this definition explicit. But it is strongly implied by one detailed example from current American advertising: "Open the first magazine at hand," he urges his readers, and you will see a smiling family gathered around a car, a radio set, or some other consumer item. Such an advertisement implies, he continues, that "the acme of human happiness is purchasable," indeed – and here the posh begins to separate itself from mere consumerism – that "its purchase somehow ennobles the purchaser" (*NG*, 67). Lust remains discreetly hidden in this vignette, except perhaps for the "dazed delight" or "ecstatic smiles" of the customers; but later in the section Nabokov mentions a truly grotesque item: the gift to "lonely soldiers" of "silk hosed dummy legs modeled on those of Hollywood lovelies and stuffed with candies and safety razor blades." In general, however, the lust in poshlust is tepid, for it belongs to a world where, to follow the metaphysical cue of Gogol's suggestive title, "nothing spiritual remains"; it is also a world where "the game of the senses is played according to bourgeois rules," rules which (as already noted) come from Flaubert.

When Nabokov revisited this topic in an interview with Herbert Gold in 1966, he replaced "poshlust" with "poshlost," which sounds closer to the original Russian. But the force of this "lost" is phonetic, not semantic, since – after another eclectic flood of items – one of his two definitive examples is an illustrated airline advertisement which, far from evoking "posh-lost" as a dead-soul state of spiritual torpor or as bitter resentment for vanished luxury, still revolves around "posh-lust" as the libidinal pull of upscale consumerism.[13] Taken from a more exclusive era of air travel, the advertisement shows "the snack served by an obsequious wench to a young couple – she eyeing ecstatically the cucumber canapé, he admiring wistfully the hostess"

(*SO*, 101). The snobbishly English-sounding and by now improbable cucumber canapé may hark back to an unreliable Anglo-Indian etymology for "posh" – as the acronym for the cooler northern cabins on steamers east of Suez, "port outbound, starboard home." Lust, whether in the stewardess's becoming a "wench" or in the gazes of the couple, is more obvious than in 1944, due both to a declining puritan consensus in the United States, which allows the author of *Lolita* to be more explicit, and to the more ardent consumerism implicit in the wife's ecstasy. We shall return to the other defining example of poshlust in this passage, from what Nabokov calls an entirely different "range" of experience: "And, of course, *Death in Venice*," he adds, naming the novella by Thomas Mann (*SO*, 101).

Nabokov's advertisement-induced vision of a fully commercialized world, where nothing spiritual remains, at least gestures toward Adorno and Horkheimer's "administered world," with its baleful sense of quasi-totalitarian control in all modern societies, not just the Europe of the dictators. Thus they suggest that "[t]he blind and rapidly spreading repetition of words with special designations links advertising with the totalitarian watchword" (CI, 165). In a similar spirit the Germano-Slavic dictatorship in *Bend Sinister* will gather strength, at a crucial point in its rise, from a misguided cult for a Dagwood-like comic strip (*BS*, 77–80 [ch. 5]). But in the Gogol book, no sooner does Nabokov glimpse this possibility than he abruptly changes direction. The real point, he optimistically concludes, is that such advertisements form "a kind of satellite shadow world" that Americans do not take seriously (*NG*, 66–67). In 1944, however, when most factories had been converted to war production, one wonders whether a newcomer could get perspective on American consumer society. Would Nabokov have shown the same equanimity if faced with our torrents of junk mail or with that brazen bumper sticker of the nineties, "Born To Shop"? And of course he was living among academics in New England, who were hardly likely to take Madison Avenue at face value; whereas Adorno, in close proximity to Hollywood, could darkly remark that "Real life is becoming indistinguishable from the movies" (CI, 126).

Still, as a recent inhabitant of Germany, Nabokov did have to qualify his optimism about the United States in one major way. In an intricate set of maneuvers, the Gogol book acknowledges the racial bias of advertisements which seem to assume that "If a commercial artist wishes to depict a nice little boy he will grace him with freckles" (*NG*, 67). After trying to combat the stereotype with humor – these freckles "assume a horrible rash-like aspect in the humbler funnies" – Nabokov faces matters head-on: "Here poshlust is directly connected with a forgotten convention of a faintly racial type." This comment seems many-sided to the point of incoherence: "faintly" concedes that American racism is less virulent than the Nordic-Aryan brand he had recently fled, but "forgotten convention" implies that a similar blond-haired, blue-eyed stereotype might be a potentially decisive subconscious presence. The opening comment, "poshlust is directly connected," is forceful, even accusatory. Perhaps Nabokov chose to soften his point as the only way to address a divisive issue in wartime.

Adorno and Horkheimer would be much less tactful, in part because they were not writing in English for an American audience. Thus they find similar stereotypes even in a well-intentioned anti-Fascist movie: "The ears of corn blowing in the wind at the end of Chaplin's *The Great Dictator* give the lie to the anti-Fascist plea for freedom. They are like the blond hair of the German girl whose camp life is photographed by the Nazi film company" (CI, 149). With Nabokov, in the more intimate forum of a letter to Edmund Wilson, we can sense that he also felt a refugee's shock of recognition at something all-too-familiar in American racial mores. When he describes his meeting with W. E. B. Du Bois in November 1942, during a lecture tour in the South, the famous black leader's Marxism seems so unimportant alongside his work for racial justice that Nabokov can say, in a startling flight of fancy, that Du Bois reminded him of a White Russian general (*NWL*, 88).

By the late 1950s, in any case, Nabokov would be much more forthright in his widely circulated afterword to *Lolita*. For when he offers a list of subjects that might shock the American mainstream as much as Humbert Humbert's treatment of Lolita, he sardonically mentions "a Negro-White marriage which is a complete and glorious success" (*Lo*, 314). In the same spirit several years later, he could attach a long essay to his *Onegin* translation on the subject of Pushkin's African ancestry. However, though media images of freckled children will still bother Nabokov in "Philistines and Philistinism," an essay in *Lectures on Russian Literature* which recycles several passages on poshlust from *Nikolai Gogol*, they no longer take him so uncomfortably close to Hitlerian racism. If the boys in the ads "are blond or redheaded, with freckles," he jocosely observes, "the handsome young men ... are generally dark haired ... The evolution is from Scotch to Celtic" (*LRL*, 313). In abandoning an all-too-real Continent for a more fanciful British Isles, Nabokov has turned from Hitler's Nordic fantasies to the idiosyncratic classification system that also colors the Beardsley School persona of "dark-and-handsome, not un-Celtic ... Dr. Humbert" (*Lo*, 188 [pt. 2, ch. 8]).

IV

Although Nabokov's vignettes of American advertising do cast light on his conception of poshlust, it is important to realize that his discussion originates elsewhere, with a weird Gogolian anecdote that is apparently intended as a critique of German romanticism. According to Gogol, a young German spurned in love finally won the reluctant maiden's hand by swimming in front of her lakeside home with two trained swans, which he would keep embracing. Presumably the tactic worked, Gogol goes on, due to "something poetically antique and mythological in these frolics" (*NG*, 66). In other words, once we realize that this story replaces the opening definition in a more formal argument, Nabokov has revealed yet another assumption about poshlust – that it can include a grotesquely misplaced striving for the mythic. His reason for insisting that poshlust is timeless then becomes clearer: Nabokov is not necessarily rejecting Adorno's aim of understanding bad art in historical terms, but registering an awareness that the cultural defect which he calls poshlust mirrors the grandiose superhistorical ambitions of myth. To the extent that both attitudes seek to reawaken the "poetically antique," they each try to subordinate the individual experience of time to a larger, all-encompassing structure.

Indeed, we might even say that this aspect of Nabokovian poshlust critically revalues myth. Unlike those literary modernists who sought a revitalizing mythic contact with the remote past, Nabokov's culture criticism highlights the dark side of such a quest: the blind glorification of the collective, the submergence of originality and individual difference, and the omnipotence of stereotypes. Adorno and Horkheimer, who had also observed the Hitlerian politics of myth from close up, were equally critical of modernism's fascination with archaic survivals. But unlike Nabokov they looked past romanticism and interpreted modern myth as a dialectical by-product of enlightenment rationalism. The more unrelenting the efforts of reason to flatten and simplify its procedures so that it becomes mere "instrumental reason," the more powerful the reaction of the mythic outlook in what amounts to a return of the repressed. Thus, despite the grotesque brilliance of Gogol's German swimmer and his swans, Adorno and Horkheimer have a more nuanced sense of intellectual history and a fuller awareness of reason's limits and its current predicament than Nabokov. Where the Gogol book brings German romanticism and American advertising together to form an "artistic" combination, *Dialectic of Enlightenment* tries to explain their historical connection.

Twenty years later, when Nabokov again addressed poshlust in the interview with Herbert Gold, this polemic with German romanticism helps make sense of his attack on Mann's *Death in Venice* (*SO*, 101) which he had described as "asinine" in an earlier interview (*SO*, 57). He might have been thinking, for example, of the hero Aschenbach's euphoric mood of mythical transfiguration in chapter 4. When the ageing writer imagines his ignoble pursuit of the Polish boy Tadzio as a dignified Platonic dialogue,[14] he does indeed resemble Gogol's German swimmer with the swans. But such a reading would ignore Mann's many ironies about Aschenbach, such as the cholera epidemic and social demoralization that accompany his mythical awakening. Adorno, in sharp contrast, actually became Mann's musical adviser in the early forties for *Doctor Faustus*, a novel about a Schoenberg-like composer that has many affinities with *Death in Venice* and that launches its own critique of Hitlerism. Thus, though *Dialectic of Enlightenment* is just as suspicious of myth as Nabokov, Adorno recognized that Mann was not simply a mythmaker but a critic of myth.

Despite this possible problem with Nabokov's attack on *Death in Venice*, the reference to Mann in 1966 is revealing in another respect. For by proposing two "ranges" of poshlust, along a continuum from a "high" variant of myth to a "low" variant of mass culture, it provides a retrospective explanation for the glide from German definition (the swimmer with the swans) to American application (the advertisements and comics) in the 1944 Gogol book. Moreover, this acknowledgment of different levels of poshlust points up another, more explicit distinction in 1944. For later in the passage, when Nabokov's survey of the American scene turns to best-sellers, he enters the realm of what might be called mid-level poshlust. Here it is significant that when he calls literature one of the best breeding grounds for poshlust, he makes an exception for pulp writing which, "curiously enough, contains sometimes a wholesome ingredient" (*NG*, 68). As a result, even Superman comic books can represent nothing more for him than "a mild, unpretentious form" of poshlust; they are probably a mass-culture variant of traditional fairy tales. Best-sellers, however, are real culprits; and in pursuing this point, Nabokov's diagnosis of cultural degradation and bad art seems to move beyond mass culture. For he attacks the best-seller not because it commercializes literature or turns it into an article for mass consumption, but because it exploits the upscale aspirations of its audience – in plain English, the readers' urge to be posh.

In fact, Nabokov reserves his harshest rhetoric for artifacts that teeter on the uncertain border between the readily available and the elite. He stresses that poshlust "is especially vigorous and vicious when the sham is *not* obvious," that it achieves its strongest effects by simulating what is "considered, rightly or wrongly, to belong to the very highest level of art, thought or emotion." Though this diagnosis no longer seems typical of best-sellers in our era of Stephen King and Danielle Steele, it still has an edge: it is easy to imagine Nabokov's distaste for certain New Age enthusiasms and preoccupations. In effect, the best-seller as bearer of poshlust becomes a sinister counterpart to the insect look-alikes that delighted Nabokov the scientist: it deceives by its elaborate cultural mimicry.

From this viewpoint the leading example of poshlust in *Lolita* would not be its heroine's immersion in mass culture of the late forties – the teen magazines, the popular music, or even the glamorous Drome advertisement depicting Quilty. Nor, despite the praise that Nabokov's depiction of her mother drew from many of the novel's original critics in the fifties, would it be Charlotte with her weakness for Humbert's "European" cultivation. Instead it is Beardsley School with its much loftier pretensions to culture. After all, by sponsoring a student production of that fashionably arty play *The Enchanted Hunters*, Beardsley was the agent that in delivering Lolita from Humbert drew her into Quilty's orbit.

So poshlust for Nabokov, though widespread in American mass culture as he first met it in the 1940s, did not culminate there but in various higher realms, in the idealistic enthusiasms of German romantics, in the modernist writer's quest for myth, and in pretentious best-sellers. Only the last item has some bearing on his experiences after arriving in the United States, but since the Gogol book names no names, we must turn to *Bend Sinister* to learn of Nabokov's loathing for Franz Werfel's *The Song of Bernadette* (1941), which he pillories as "that remarkable cross between a certain kind of wafer and a lollipop" (*BS*, 29). Through the colorful vituperation, we again notice the characteristic drift in Nabokov's core sense of poshlust, away from mass culture in itself and toward the transitional space between a serious, even spiritual effort to gain access to a valued peak experience and the varied consumer products which travesty that effort.

Adorno and Horkheimer also disliked Werfel's novel, but with their sharper focus on mass culture they singled out the equally popular movie version to illustrate how the culture industry worked to convert everything it touched to smooth cultural currency. Werfel was merely a forerunner in this larger process of finding and disseminating a suitably eclectic mix of stereotypes: "Even before Zanuck acquired her, Saint Bernadette was regarded by her latter-day hagiographer as brilliant propaganda for all interested parties" (CI, 129). Adorno and Horkheimer are thus less hopeful about the possibility of genuine spiritual meaning than Nabokov. Indeed, when they maintain that "to speak of culture was always contrary to culture" since "culture as a common denominator already contains in embryo that schematization and process of cataloging and classification which bring culture within the sphere of administration" (CI, 131), they put cultural critique itself into a position of paradoxical instability. It has to exist in a world where, to return to Nabokov's metaphor, even the lollipops that are all we can hope for, have been adulterated.

In objecting to *The Song of Bernadette*, however, neither Adorno nor Nabokov mentions that Werfel, like themselves, was a refugee from Hitler's Europe. Not only had he written this novel about the miraculous apparition of the Virgin Mary in the mid-nineteenth century and the healing spring at Lourdes in gratitude for his own lucky escape from occupied France in 1940, but, as a youthful friend of Kafka's and the husband of Gustav Mahler's widow, he had lived in the same international world of modern art that they did. Behind Nabokov's and Adorno's invectives against this particular American best-seller and Hollywood hit, accordingly, there seems to lurk something deeper and more unruly. Did they feel that Werfel's sudden though brief American, even global popularity at the peak of

Hitlerism somehow glossed over and trivialized the enormity of the Nazis' radical threat to basic values? Their own experiences, and then their thoughts and writings, told a different story – one of cultural degradation, manipulation, and hideous dehumanization.

v

The comparative historian Robert Wohl, who has written a fine book on the "the generation of 1914" in Spain, Italy, England, France, and Germany, once suggested that Nabokov was the last member of that generation.[15] For Wohl this group of intellectuals, writers, and artists, in addition to coming of age in circumstances that made World War I and the Russian Revolution into formative experiences, was also the first generation that "grew up *within* modernism."[16] It is the fourth of five modernist generations that appeared at fifteen-year intervals. Preceded by a precursor generation of 1875 (for example, Nietzsche and Mallarmé), a founding generation of 1890 (Freud and Conrad), and a 1905 generation of "realizers" (Proust, Picasso, Kafka, Woolf), the generation of 1914 was followed by a 1930s generation that had absorbed modernism and then went on to question it. In Wohl's scheme, both Malraux and Adorno would probably be senior members of this fifth generation.

Such a sharp distinction between the three major figures in this essay would make sense if we contrasted Nabokov's approach to fiction with Malraux's, or noted the sharp difference between Nabokov's aestheticism and Adorno's sociology of art. But in their shared role as culture critics during the ascendancy of Hitlerism, this triad is much more compatible. Not only had all three of them grown up within modernism, in Wohl's happy phrase; but whatever the formative role of war and revolution during their teenage years, they all had to pass through an inferno shortly after the Dantean age of thirty-five. In a situation of such extremity, Nabokov, Adorno, and Malraux come together on the question of what the German catastrophe had to say about the general health of Western culture and the future of the arts.

When Nabokovian poshlust is examined on this common ground, it clearly involves more than the catalogue of personal prejudices that might strike the casual reader, more even than its quite precise and important Russian meaning. Thus, though Nabokov likes to cast himself as an anti-theoretical writer, as a creator of pointed images rather than general ideas, here his mode of presentation is in fact more complicated. Occupying a position between Adorno and Horkheimer's conceptual/theoretical method and Malraux's novelistic one, at times showing affinities with either side and at times bringing out the conceptual force of novelistic texts, his writing cannot avoid a certain generality of implication as well as real intellectual provocation. But conceptualization in Nabokov is itself a tricky issue, for despite some deference to definition and exposition his most important points do not depend on those methods but on a brilliant combination of word play and sardonic anecdote. Notable as well in this regard is the way that the Russian-Gogolian point of departure is supplemented by various Western European and American materials: Flaubert's received ideas, the German swimmer with the swans, the French Michelin man, the American advertisements and comic strips, Mann's *Death in Venice*, Werfel's *Song of Bernadette*. Most notable of all is the bilingualism which turns the Russian "poshlost'" into the English "poshlust," meshing sound with meaning to create a tool for exploring and criticizing a new cultural environment. Once we factor in the verbal precision of Nabokov's coinage and the intellectual fruitfulness of his most detailed, "defining" anecdotes, he emerges as a more subtle, penetrating, and varied culture critic than is usually assumed, even in this era of cultural studies.

The synthetic term poshlust is also the key to distinguishing the main focus of Nabokov's culture criticism from Malraux's and Adorno's. If, as Malraux holds, the basic challenge posed by Hitlerism was its belief in extreme cultural compartmentalization, and if, as Adorno adds, its success in exploiting the mass media was crucial in enforcing that belief, then Nabokov ultimately takes a somewhat different tack. To be sure, he does agree with Malraux on the actual permeability of cultural boundaries, no matter how strongly policed. The Anglo-Russian word "poshlust" chimes with the Franco-German name "Berger," and cultural metamorphosis is a plus for both Malraux and Nabokov. Alerted by Hitlerism, moreover, Nabokov can be just as relentless as Adorno and Horkheimer in exposing the dark side of myth or in ferreting out potentially sinister stereotypes in the American mass media.

But in the end, when he emphasizes the different "ranges" of poshlust, the upscale implications of the word take hold, and Nabokov parts company with Adorno. He swerves from mass culture in itself to condemn second-rate literature, especially when it mimics and usurps the first-rate. Here his condemnation passes beyond the middle-brow region inhabited by Charlotte Haze. Without any attempt to avoid controversy and at times perhaps criticizing too hastily, it comes to focus on items traditionally classified as high culture, from German romanticism and Thomas Mann to the widespread interest of modernist writers in "the mythical method."[17] Just beyond this dangerously pretentious realm are the truly great literary works, which for Nabokov were written mainly in Russian, French, and English. This is a broad array of languages for a modern writer; nonetheless, and here Nabokov parts with Malraux, it is narrower than the horizons implicit in the walnut trees episode. As indicated by Möllberg's and Berger's past experiences, the vision of creativity in this scene moves outward from the multiplicity of its Alsatian setting, beyond the mainly Western reference frame assumed by both Nabokov and Adorno, to take in Africa and the Muslim world, Europe's neighbors to the south and east.

However, if Nabokov in 1944 put more emphasis on first-rate work in the European modernist tradition than either Malraux or Adorno, he surely had good cause. For even as he wrote the Gogol book, unlike his two counterparts whose work right after the war would be exclusively critical, Nabokov's own creativity was about to turn back to fiction and autobiography, where it would enter a major new phase of accomplishment. Despite Hitlerism and the difficult transition from Russian to English, *Speak, Memory* and *Lolita* would soon rise on his horizon.

NOTES

Acknowledgments: Parts of this essay were first presented at a meeting of the International Nabokov Society, organized by Zoran Kuzmanovich at the 1992 convention of the Modern Language Assocation. I am grateful to him as well as to Leona Toker, Gennady Alexis Barabtarlo, and Julian W. Connolly, all of whom gave helpful suggestions and encouragement.

1 These names do not include Nabokov's important affiliations with Russian and English high culture, but they do suggest what he shared with Adorno and Malraux as an heir to the literary and artistic achievements of the preceding generation. Important distinctions remain, however. Thus Nabokov greatly admired Proust and Kafka, and Gide somewhat less; but music left him cold, and he apparently

detested Picasso, who was perhaps Malraux's greatest hero in modern art. Malraux was also close to Gide, but he kept some distance from Proust, who along with Kafka was important for Adorno (and even more for his friend Benjamin). Given Adorno's interest in music, however, Schoenberg was his top favorite in this group.

2 See chapter 3, section 2 of *Nikolai Gogol* (1944; New York: New Directions, 1961) (on *Dead Souls*), 63–74.

3 Max Horkheimer and Theodor W. Adorno, *Dialectic of Enlightenment*, trans. John Cumming (New York: Continuum, 1972), originally published in 1944 as *Dialektik der Aufklärung*. The full title of chapter 4 is "The Culture Industry: Enlightenment as Mass Deception," cited parenthetically in the text as CI.

4 The walnut trees episode has had a complicated publication history. It first appeared in *Les Noyers de l'Altenburg*, published in Lausanne (1943), then Paris (1948). Planned as the first part of a project which Malraux never finished, it thereafter circulated only in limited editions, if at all. In 1967, however, a shortened version of the walnut trees episode became the first narrative segment of Malraux's autobiography.

The novel has recently been reprinted, with a full scholarly apparatus, in the Pléiade edition of Malraux's complete works. For the English translation, see *The Walnut Trees of Altenburg*, introd. Conor Cruise O'Brien, trans. A. W. Fielding (University of Chicago Press, 1992). (Hereafter *WT*.)

5 For an overview of Russian perspectives, see Sergej Davydov, "Poshlost'," *The Garland Companion to Vladimir Nabokov*, ed. Vladimir Alexandrov (New York: Garland, 1995), 628–33. For a more detailed literary and cultural analysis, which gives valuable insights into the evolution of the word *poshlost'* and which also makes some shrewd comments about Nabokov's place in this tradition, see Svetlana Boym, *Common Places: Mythologies of Everyday Life in Russia* (Cambridge, MA: Harvard University Press, 1994), 41–66.

6 Nabokov mentions an "Encyclopédie des Idées Reçues," but Flaubert had planned a "Dictionnaire." In 1954 New Directions, which had published the Gogol book, brought out a translation called *The Dictionary of Accepted Ideas*.

7 From this literary point of view, Adorno might seem too abstract and abstruse, the ultimate German mandarin; yet philosophers might equally fault Nabokov for avoiding conceptual clarity and being pointlessly playful. Except among those who know Russian, after all, his references to poshlust will mean less at first glance than Adorno and Horkheimer's incisive "culture industry." As I will show, however, Nabokov's treatment of this word occupies an intermediate position that cannot be placed solely on the literary side of a literature – theory dichotomy.

8 *WT*, 115. I have altered the translation somewhat for greater clarity.

9 Nabokov does use this metaphor to speak of his own cultural trans-

formation, from writing in Russian to writing in English: "such multiple metamorphosis, familiar to butterflies, had not been tried by any human before" (*SM*, 13 ["Foreword"]).

10 "Pouchkine ou le vrai et le vraisemblable," *La Nouvelle revue française* 25 (March 1937): 362–78.

11 Malraux had returned from the Spanish Civil War haunted by Goya's pictures of the Napoleonic army's acts of reprisal in occupied Spain.

12 In his autobiography Malraux interprets the writing of the gas warfare scene as an intuitive but historically informed premonition of the ultimate Hitlerian degradation: "after this attack on the Russian front came Verdun, the mustard gas in Flanders, Hitler, the extermination camps" (*André Malraux: Oeuvres Complètes*, ed. and introd. Marius-François Guyard [Paris: Pléiade, 1996], 3:787; translation mine). However, Möllberg's affinity with the chauvinistic chemist and especially his aquarium metaphor for cultural compartmentalization are even more uncanny, since here Malraux's novelized cultural critique anticipates one of Primo Levi's major points in *Survival in Auschwitz*. When Levi is interviewed by Doctor Pannwitz, a chemist with the I. G. Farben laboratory that recruited prisoners from the death camp, he is struck by the look in his eyes, "which came as if across the glass window of an aquarium between two beings who live in different worlds." In Pannwitz's sense of absolute separation between people from different cultures, Levi finds "the essence of the great insanity of the third Germany." See Primo Levi, *Survival in Auschwitz: The Nazi Assault on Humanity*, trans. Stuart Woolf (New York: Collier, 1961), 96.

13 My wife Andrea Dimino has suggested the first neglected possibility, building on the concern with spiritual vacancy in the Gogol book; I would add the second, based on Nabokov's careful denial of such resentment when discussing his family's losses in the Russian revolution (*SM*, 73 [ch. 3]).

14 *Death in Venice: A Case Study in Contemporary Criticism*, ed. Naomi Ritter, trans. David Luke (Boston: Bedford, 1998), 61–62. For Mann's story as cultural critique, see my essay in that volume, "Why is Tadzio Polish? *Kultur* and Cultural Multiplicity in *Death in Venice*," 192–209.

15 Robert Wohl, *The Generation of 1914* (Cambridge, MA: Harvard University Press, 1979). Wohl mentions Nabokov in "The Generation of 1914 and Modernism" in *Modernism: Challenges and Perspectives*, ed. Monique Chefdor, Ricardo Quinones, and Albert Wachtel (Urbana and Chicago: University of Illinois Press, 1986), 71.

16 Wohl, *Modernism*, 73.

17 T. S. Eliot used this famous phrase to describe Joyce; see "*Ulysses*, Order, and Myth," *Selected Prose of T. S. Eliot*, ed. and introd. Frank Kermode (London: Faber and Faber, 1975), 178.

Selected bibliography

WORKS BY VLADIMIR NABOKOV

Ada, or Ardor: A Family Chronicle, 1969; New York: Vintage International, 1990; Harmondsworth: Penguin, 1990.
The Annotated Lolita, ed. with preface, introduction, and notes by Alfred Appel, Jr., 1970; rev. ed.: New York: Vintage International, 1991; Harmondsworth: Penguin, 1995.
Bend Sinister, 1947; New York: Vintage International, 1990; Harmondsworth: Penguin, 1989.
Collected Stories, 1995; Harmondsworth: Penguin, 1997.
Conclusive Evidence: A Memoir, New York: Harper, 1951.
The Defense, trans. Michael Scammell in collaboration with the author, 1964; New York: Vintage International, 1990. See also *The Luzhin Defence*.
Despair, 1966; New York: Vintage International, 1989; Harmondsworth: Penguin, 1990.
Drugie berega, New York: Izdatel'stvo imeni Chekhova, 1954; repr., Ann Arbor: Ardis, 1978.
The Enchanter, trans. Dmitri Nabokov, 1986; New York: Vintage International, 1991.
Eugene Onegin. A Novel in Verse by Aleksandr Pushkin, translation with commentary by Vladimir Nabokov, Bollingen Series 72, 4 vols., 1964; rev. ed.: Princeton: Princeton University Press, 1975.
The Eye, trans. Dmitri Nabokov in collaboration with the author, 1965; New York: Vintage International, 1990; Harmondsworth: Penguin, 1992.
Gornii put', Berlin: Grani, 1923.
The Gift, trans. Michael Scammell with the collaboration of the author, 1963; New York: Vintage International, 1991; Harmondsworth: Penguin, 1992.
Glory, trans. Dmitri Nabokov in collaboration with the author, 1971; New York: Vintage International, 1991; Harmondsworth: Penguin, 1990.
"Home," *Trinity Magazine* 5.2 (November 1920): 26.
Invitation to a Beheading, trans. Dmitri Nabokov in collaboration with the

author, 1959; New York: Vintage International, 1989; Harmondsworth: Penguin, 1990.
"Kembridzh," *Rul'*, October 28, 1921, 2; repr. in Vladimir Nabokov, *Rasskazy. Priglashenie na kazn'. Roman. Esse, interv'iu, retsenzii*, Moscow: Kniga, 1989, 337–40.
King, Queen, Knave, trans. Dmitri Nabokov in collaboration with the author, 1968; New York: Vintage International, 1989; Harmondsworth: Penguin, 1993.
Laughter in the Dark, 1938; New York: Vintage International, 1989; Harmondsworth: Penguin, 1998.
Lectures on Don Quixote, ed. Fredson Bowers, New York: Harcourt Brace Jovanovich / Bruccoli Clark, 1983.
Lectures on Literature, ed. Fredson Bowers, New York: Harcourt Brace Jovanovich / Bruccoli Clark, 1980.
Lectures on Russian Literature, ed. Fredson Bowers, New York: Harcourt Brace Jovanovich / Bruccoli Clark, 1981.
"Lodgings in Trinity Lane," *Harper's Magazine* 202 (January 1951): 84–91.
Lolita, 1955; New York: Vintage International, 1989; Harmondsworth: Penguin, 1995.
Lolita: A Screenplay, 1974; New York: Vintage International, 1997.
Look at the Harlequins! 1974; New York: Vintage International, 1990; Harmondsworth: Penguin, 1991.
The Luzhin Defence, Harmondsworth: Penguin, 1994.
Mary, trans. Michael Glenny in collaboration with the author, 1970; New York: Vintage International, 1989; Harmondsworth: Penguin, 1990.
The Man fom the USSR and Other Plays, introductions and translations by Dmitri Nabokov, New York: Harcourt Brace Jovanovich / Bruccoli Clark, 1984.
"Mr. Masefield and Clio," *The New Republic*, December 9, 1940, 808–09.
The Nabokov-Wilson Letters, 1940–1971, ed., annotated, and with an introductory essay by Simon Karlinsky, New York: Harper Colophon, 1980.
Nikolai Gogol, 1944; New York: New Directions, 1961.
Pale Fire, 1962; New York: Vintage International, 1989; Harmondsworth: Penguin, 1991.
Pnin, 1957; New York: Vintage International, 1989; Harmondsworth: Penguin, 1997.
Poems and Problems, New York: McGraw-Hill, 1970.
"Pouchkine ou le vrai et le vraisemblable," *La nouvelle revue française* 25 (March 1937): 362–78.
The Real Life of Sebastian Knight, 1941; New York: Vintage International, 1992; Harmondsworth: Penguin, 1995.
"Remembrance," *The English Review* 144 (November 1920): 392.
"Rupert Bruk," *Grani* 1 (1922): 211–31.
Selected Letters, 1940–1977, ed. Dmitri Nabokov and Matthew J. Bruccoli, New York: Harcourt Brace Jovanovich / Bruccoli Clark Layman, 1989.

Sobranie sochinenii v chetyrekh tomakh, Moscow: Pravda, 1990.
The Song of Igor's Campaign, trans. Vladimir Nabokov, New York: McGraw-Hill, 1975.
Speak, Memory: An Autobiography Revisited, 1967; New York: Vintage International, 1989; Harmondsworth: Penguin, 1991.
Stikhi, Petrograd: Union, 1916.
Stikhi, Ann Arbor: Ardis, 1979.
The Stories of Vladimir Nabokov, 1995; New York: Vintage International, 1997.
"Torzhestvo dobrodeteli," *Rul'*, March 5, 1930, 2–3; repr. in Vladimir Nabokov, *Romany, rasskazy, esse*, St. Petersburg: Entar, 1993, 216–21.
Tragediia Gospodina Morna, *Zvezda* 4 (1997): 10–98.
Transparent Things, New York: Vintage International, 1989; Harmondsworth: Penguin, 1990.
"Zametki perevodchika," *Opyty* 8 (1957): 36–49.

Also Balashov, Andrei, and Vladimir Nabokov, *Al'manakh: Dva puti*, Petrograd, 1918.

WORK ON VLADIMIR NABOKOV

Alexandrov, Vladimir E., ed., *The Garland Companion to Vladimir Nabokov*, Garland Reference Library of the Humanities 1474, New York: Garland, 1995.
Alexandrov, Vladimir E., "Nabokov and Gumilev," in Alexandrov, *The Garland Companion to Vladimir Nabokov*, 428–33.
  Nabokov's Otherworld, Princeton University Press, 1991.
Alter, Robert, "*Invitation to a Beheading*: Nabokov and the Art of Politics," *TriQuarterly*, 17 (1970): 41–59; repr. in Appel, Jr., and Newman (eds.), *Nabokov*, 41–59; and in Connolly (ed.), *Nabokov's* Invitation to a Beheading, 47–65.
  "Nabokov and Memory," *Partisan Review* 58 (1991): 620–29.
  Partial Magic: The Novel as a Self-Conscious Genre, Berkeley: University of California Press, 1975.
Amis, Martin, *The Sublime and the Ridiculous. Nabokov's Black Farces*, London: Weidenfeld and Nicolson, 1979.
Appel, Alfred, Jr., "Conversations with Nabokov," *Novel* 4 (1971): 209–22.
  "Introduction," in Vladimir Nabokov, *The Annotated Lolita*, ed. with preface, introduction, and notes by Alfred Appel, Jr., New York: Vintage International, 1991.
  "Nabokov: A Portrait," *Atlantic Monthly*, September 1971, 77–92.
  Nabokov's Dark Cinema, New York: Oxford University Press, 1974.
Appel, Alfred, Jr., and Charles Newman (eds.), *Nabokov: Criticism, Reminiscences, Translations and Tributes*, Evanston: Northwestern University Press, 1971.

Averin, B., N. Malikova, and A. Dolinin (eds.), *V. V. Nabokov: Pro et contra*, St. Petersburg: Izdatel'stvo Russkogo Khristianskogo gumanitarnogo instituta, 1997.
Bader, Julia, *Crystal Land: Artifice in Nabokov's English Novels*, Berkeley: University of California Press, 1972.
Barabtarlo, Gennady, *Aerial View: Essays on Nabokov's Art and Metaphysics*, New York: Peter Lang, 1993.
  "A Skeleton in Nabokov's Closet: 'Mest'," in Nicol and Barabtarlo (eds.), *A Small Alpine Form*, 15–24.
  Phantom of Fact: A Guide to Nabokov's Pnin, Ann Arbor: Ardis, 1989.
  "Those Who Favor Fire (On *The Enchanter*)," *Russian Literature Triquarterly* 24 (1991): 89–112.
Berberova, Nina, "Angliiskie predki Vladimira Nabokova," *Novyi zhurnal* 167 (1987): 191–205; repr. in a shortened form in *Canadian-American Slavic Studies* 19 (1985): 262–67.
Berman, Jeffrey, "Nabokov and the Viennese Witch Doctor," *The Talking Cure: Literary Representations of Psychoanalysis*, New York University Press, 1985, 222–38; repr. in Bloom (ed.), *Lolita*, 105–19.
Bloom, Harold (ed.), *Lolita, Modern Literary Characters*, New York: Chelsea House, 1993.
  Vladimir Nabokov, Modern Critical Views, New York: Chelsea House, 1987.
Boyd, Brian, *Nabokov's Ada: The Place of Consciousness*, Ann Arbor: Ardis, 1985.
  "Nabokov's Russian Poems: A Chronology," *The Nabokovian* 21 (Fall 1988): 13–28.
  Vladimir Nabokov: The American Years, Princeton University Press, 1991.
  Vladimir Nabokov: The Russian Years, Princeton University Press, 1990.
Brink, Andrew, *Obsession and Culture: A Study of Sexual Obsession in Modern Fiction*, Madison: Fairleigh Dickinson University Press, 1996.
Bronfen, Elisabeth, *Over Her Dead Body: Death, Femininity and the Aesthetic*, New York: Routledge, 1992.
Brown, Edward J., "Nabokov, Chernyshevsky, Olesha, and the Gift of Sight," *Literature, Culture and Society in the Modern Age: In Honor of Joseph Frank*, part 2, ed. Edward J. Brown et al., *Stanford Slavic Studies* 4, part 2 (1992): 280–94.
Bruss, Elizabeth W., *Autobiographical Acts: The Changing Situation of a Literary Genre*, Baltimore: The Johns Hopkins University Press, 1976.
Buhks, Nora, "Nabokov and Dostoevskii: Aesthetic Demystification," *Russian Writers on Russian Writers*, ed. Faith Wigzell, Oxford: Berg Publishers, 1994, 131–37.
Centerwall, Brandon S., "Hiding in Plain Sight: Nabokov and Pedophilia," *Texas Studies in Literature and Language* 32 (1990): 468–84.
Connolly, Julian W., "The Function of Literary Allusion in Nabokov's *Despair*," *Slavic and East European Journal* 26 (1982): 302–13.
  "Madness and Doubling: From Dostoevsky's *The Double* to Nabokov's *The Eye*," *Russian Literature Triquarterly* 24 (1990): 129–39.

"Nabokov's Dialogue with Dostoevsky: *Lolita* and 'The Gentle Creature'," *Nabokov Studies* 4 (1997): 15–36.

Nabokov's Early Fiction: Patterns of Self and Other, Cambridge University Press, 1992.

Connolly, Julian W. (ed.), *Nabokov's* Invitation to a Beheading*: A Critical Companion*, Evanston: Northwestern University Press, 1997.

Couturier, Maurice, "Nabokov's *Pale Fire*, or the Purloined Poem," *Revue Française d'Etudes Américaines* 1 (1976): 55–69.

Nabokov ou la tyrannie de l'auteur, Paris: Ed. du Seuil, "Coll. Poétique," 1993.

"The Subject on Trial in Nabokov's Novels," in *Proceedings of a Symposium on American Literature*, ed. Marta Sienecka, Poznan University Press, 1980.

Davydov, Sergej, "Dostoevsky and Nabokov: The Mortality of Structure in *Crime and Punishment* and *Despair*," *Dostoevsky Studies* 3 (1982): 157–70.

"Teksty-Matreshki" Vladimira Nabokova, Munich: Otto Sagner, 1982.

Dembo, L. S. (ed.), *Nabokov: The Man and His Work*, Madison: University of Wisconsin Press, 1967.

Diment, Galya, *Pniniad: Vladimir Nabokov and Marc Szeftel*, Seattle: University of Washington Press, 1997.

"Uncollected Critical Writings," in Alexandrov (ed.), *The Garland Companion to Vladimir Nabokov*, 733–40.

Dolinin, Alexander, "Caning of Modernist Profaners: Parody in *Despair*," *Cycnos* 12.2 (1995): 43–54

"Caning of Modernist Profaners: Parody in *Despair*," 7 p., online at http://www.libraries.psu.edu/iasweb/nabokov/doli1.htm.

"Plata za proezd (Beglye zametki o genezise nekotorykh literaturnykh otsenok Nabokova)," *Nabokovskii vestnik* 1 (St. Petersburg: Dorn, 1998): 5–15.

"Tri zametki o romane Vladimira Nabokova 'Dar'," in Averin et al. (eds.), *V. V. Nabokov*, 697–740.

Engel-Braunschmidt, Annelore, and Dieter E. Zimmer, "Ammerkungen," in Vladimir Nabokov, *Die Gabe, Gesammelte Werke* 5, ed. Dieter Zimmer, Reinbek bei Hamburg: Rowohlt, 1993.

Ermath, Elizabeth Deeds, "Conspicuous Construction; or, Kristeva, Nabokov, and The Anti-Realist Critique," *Novel* 21 (1988): 330–39.

Feldman, Jessica R., *Gender on the Divide: The Dandy in Modernist Literature*, Ithaca: Cornell University Press, 1993.

Field, Andrew, *Nabokov: His Life in Art*, Boston: Little, Brown and Co., 1967.

Nabokov: His Life in Part, New York: Viking, 1977.

Fomin, A., "Sirin: dvadtsat' dva plius odin," *Novoe literaturnoe obozrenie* 23 (1997): 302–04.

Foster, John Burt, Jr., *Nabokov's Art of Memory and European Modernism*, Princeton University Press, 1993.

Foster, Ludmila A., "Nabokov in Russian Emigré Criticism," in Proffer, *A Book of Things About Vladimir Nabokov*, 42–53.
Grabes, Herbert, "A Prize for the (Post-)Modernist Nabokov," *Cycnos* 12.2 (1995): 117–24.
Grayson, Jane, "Double Bill: Nabokov and Olesha," in *From Pushkin to Palisandria: Essays on the Russian Novel in Honor of Richard Freeborn*, ed. Arnold McMillin, New York: St. Martin's Press, 1990, 181–200.
Green, Geoffrey, *Freud and Nabokov*, Lincoln: University of Nebraska Press, 1988.
Green, Hannah, "Mister Nabokov," in Quennell (ed.), *Vladimir Nabokov*, 34–41.
Guy, Laurence, "Les anagrammes cosmopolites de l'auteur dans son oeuvre, ou l'identité renversée de Vladimir Nabokov," *Cahiers du Monde russe* 37 (1996): 337–48.
Haber, Edythe C., "Nabokov's *Glory* and the Fairy Tale," *Slavic and East European Journal* 21 (1977): 214–24.
Hyde, G. M., *Vladimir Nabokov: America's Russian Novelist*, Critical Appraisals Series, London: Marion Boyars, 1977.
Johnson, D. Barton, "'Terror': Pre-texts and Post-texts," in Nicol and Barabtarlo (eds.), *A Small Alpine Form*, 39–64.
  Worlds in Regression: Some Novels of Vladimir Nabokov, Ann Arbor: Ardis, 1985.
  with Wayne C. Wilson, "Alphabetic and Chronological Lists of Nabokov's Poetry," *Russian Literature Triquarterly* 24 (1991): 355–415.
Juliar, Michael, *Vladimir Nabokov: A Descriptive Bibliography*, Garland Reference Library of the Humanities 656, New York: Garland, 1986.
Karlinsky, Simon, "Nabokov and Chekhov: The Lesser Russian Tradition," in Appel, Jr., and Newman (eds.), *Nabokov*, 7–16.
Karlinsky, Simon (ed.), *The Nabokov–Wilson Letters. Correspondence Between Vladimir Nabokov and Edmund Wilson, 1940–1971*, New York: Harper Colophon Books, 1980.
Kauffman, Linda, "Framing *Lolita*: Is There a Woman in the Text?" *Special Delivery: Epistolary Modes in Modern Fiction*, University of Chicago Press, 53–79; repr. in Bloom (ed.), *Lolita*, 149–68.
Kemball, Robin, "Nabokov and Rupert Brooke," in *Schweizerische Beiträge zum IX internationalen Slavistenkongress in Kiev, September 1983*, ed. Peter Brang et al., Bern: Peter Lang, 1983, 35–73.
Khodasevich, Vladislav, "On Sirin," trans. Michael H. Walker, ed. Simon Karlinsky and Robert P. Hughes, *TriQuarterly* 17 (1970): 96–101; repr. in Appel, Jr., and Newman (eds.), *Nabokov*, 96–101.
Kosman, L., "Vladimir Nabokov i evreistvo," *New American* 1.12 (1988): 47–48.
Lehrman, Alexander, "An Etymological Footnote to Chapter Three of *Speak, Memory*," *The Nabokovian* 24 (1990): 32–33.
Lodge, David, "What Kind of Fiction did Nabokov Write? A Practitioner's

View," *Cycnos* 12.2 (1995): 135–47; repr. in *The Practice of Writing*, London: Secker and Warburg, 1996.

Long, Michael, *Marvell, Nabokov: Childhood and Arcadia*, Oxford University Press, 1984.

Liuksemburg, A. M. and G. F. Rakhimkulova, *Magistr igry Vivian Van Bok (Igra slov v proze Vladimira Nabokova v svete teorii kalambura)*, Rostov-on-Don: Rostovskii gosudarstvennyi universitet, 1996.

McCarthy, Mary, "A Bolt from the Blue," *New Republic*, June 4, 1962, 21–27; repr. in Page (ed.), *Nabokov*, 124–36.

McNeely, Trevor, "'Lo' and Behold: Solving the *Lolita* Riddle," *Studies in the Novel* 21 (1989): 182–99; repr. in Bloom (ed.), *Lolita*, 134–48.

Meyer, Priscilla, *Find What the Sailor Has Hidden: Vladimir Nabokov's Pale Fire*, Middletown: Wesleyan University Press, 1988.

Moynahan, Julian, "A Russian Preface for Nabokov's *Beheading*," *Novel* 1 (1967): 12–18.

Vladimir Nabokov, Minneapolis: University of Minnesota Press, 1971.

Nabokov, Dmitri, "The *Lolita* Legacy: Life with Nabokov's Art," *The Nabokovian* 37 (Fall 1996): 8–29.

Naumann, Marina T., "Nabokov as Viewed by Fellow Emigrés," *Russian Language Journal* 28, no. 99 (1974): 18–26.

Nesbit, Anne, "Suicide as Literary Fact in the 1920s," *Slavic Review* 50 (1991): 827–35.

Nicol, Charles and Gennady Barabtarlo (eds.), *A Small Alpine Form: Studies in Nabokov's Short Fiction*, New York: Garland, 1993.

Nivat, Georges, "*Speak, Memory*," in Alexandrov (ed.), *The Garland Companion to Vladimir Nabokov*, 672–85.

O'Connor, Katherine Tiernan, "Rereading *Lolita*, Reconsidering Nabokov's Relationship with Dostoevskij," *Slavic and East European Journal* 33 (1989): 64–77.

Ostanin, B., "Ravenstvo, zigzag, trilistnik, ili o trekh rodakh poezii," *Novoe literaturnoe obozrenie* 23 (1997): 298–302.

"Sirin: 22 + 2," *Novoe literaturnoe obozrenie* 23 (1997): 305.

Page, Norman (ed.), *Nabokov: The Critical Heritage*, The Critical Heritage Series, London: Routledge and Kegan Paul, Ltd, 1982.

Pifer, Ellen, "Innocence and Experience Replayed: From *Speak, Memory* to *Ada*," *Cycnos*, 10.1 (1993): 19–25.

"*Lolita*," in Alexandrov (ed.), *The Garland Companion to Vladimir Nabokov*, 305–21.

Nabokov and the Novel, Cambridge, MA: Harvard University Press, 1980.

Proffer, Carl R. (ed.), *A Book of Things About Vladimir Nabokov*, Ann Arbor: Ardis, 1974.

Keys to Lolita, Bloomington: Indiana University Press, 1968.

Quennell, Peter, *Vladimir Nabokov: A Tribute*, New York: William Morrow, 1980.

Raguet-Bouvart, Christine, *Lolita: un royaume au-delà des mers*, Bordeaux: Presses Universitaires de Bordeaux, 1996.

Rimmon, Shlomith, "Problems of Voice in Vladimir Nabokov's *The Real Life of Sebastian Knight*," *PTL* 1 (1976): 506–11.

Rivers, J. E., and Charles Nicol (ed.), *Nabokov's Fifth Arc: Nabokov and Others on His Life's Work*, Austin: University of Texas Press, 1982.

Rorty, Richard, introduction to Vladimir Nabokov, *Pale Fire*, New York: Everyman's Library / Knopf, 1992, v–xvii.

Roth, Phyllis A. (ed.), *Critical Essays on Vladimir Nabokov*, Critical Essays on American Literature, Boston: G. K. Hall, 1984.

Rowe, W[illiam] W[oodin], *Nabokov's Spectral Dimension*, Ann Arbor: Ardis, 1981.

Saraskina, Liudmila, "Nabokov, kotoryi branitsia..." in Averin et al. (eds.), *V. V. Nabokov*, 542–70.

Schuman, Samuel, *Vladimir Nabokov: A Reference Guide*, Boston: G. K. Hall, 1979.

Shakhovskaia [Shakhovskoy], Zinaida, *V poiskakh Nabokova*, Paris: La presse libre, 1979.

Shapiro, Gavriel, "Hermann Lande's Possible Prototypes in *The Gift*," *The Nabokovian* 37 (Fall 1996): 53–55.

"*Lolita* Class List," *Cahiers du Monde russe* 37 (1996): 317–36.

"Nabokov's Allusions: Dividedness and Polysemy," *Russian Literature* 43 (1998): 329–38.

"Two Notes on *Pnin*," *The Nabokovian* 29 (1992): 36–37.

Shrayer, Maxim, "After Rapture and Recapture: Transformations in the Drafts of Nabokov's Stories," *Russian Review* 58 (1999).

The World of Nabokov's Stories, Austin: University of Texas Press, 1999.

Sisson, Jonathan Borden, "Cosmic Synchronization and Other Worlds in the Work of Vladimir Nabokov," Ph.D. diss., University of Minnesota, 1979.

"Nabokov and Some Turn-of-the-Century Writers," in Alexandrov (ed.), *The Garland Companion to Vladimir Nabokov*, 228–35.

Smith, Gerald S., "Nabokov and Russian Verse Form," *Russian Literature Triquarterly* 24 (1991): 271–305.

Stegner, Page, *Escape into Aesthetics: The Art of Vladimir Nabokov*, New York: The Dial Press, 1966.

Stuart, Dabney, *Nabokov: The Dimensions of Parody*, Baton Rouge: Louisiana State University Press, 1978.

Sweeney, Susan Elizabeth, "The V-Shaped Paradigm: Nabokov and Pynchon," *Cycnos* 12.2 (1995): 173–80.

Tammi, Pekka, *Problems of Nabokov's Poetics: A Narratological Analysis*, Suomalainen Tiedeakatemian Toimituksia Annales Academiae Scientiarum Fennicae B 231. Helsinki: Suomalainen Tiedeakatemia, 1985.

Toker, Leona, *Nabokov: The Mystery of Literary Structures*, Ithaca: Cornell University Press, 1989.

Updike, John. Introduction to Vladimir Nabokov, *Lectures on Literature*, ed. Fredson Bowers, New York: Harcourt Brace Jovanovich / Bruccoli Clark, 1980.

Weidle, Vladimir, "Vladimir Weidle on Sirin," in *The Complection of Russian Literature*, compiled by Andrew Field, New York: Atheneum, 1971, 238–40.
Wood, Michael, *The Magician's Doubts: Nabokov and the Risks of Fiction*, Princeton University Press, 1995.
Zavyalov-Leving, Yuri, "Phantom in Jerusalem, or the History of an Unrealized Visit," *The Nabokovian* 37 (Fall 1996): 30–44.
  "Samuel Izrailevich: *Pnin*'s Character, Nabokov's Friend," *The Nabokovian* 39 (Fall 1997): 13–17.
Zverev, Aleksei, "Literary Return to Russia," in Alexandrov (ed.), *The Garland Companion to Vladimir Nabokov*, 295–305.

Index

Abrams, Meyer 74
Adorno, Theodor W. 9, 216–20, 222, 225–26, 227–28, 230–33, 233–34 n. 1, 234 n. 7
   Dialectic of Enlightenment (with Max Horkheimer) 217, 218, 225–26, 226–28, 230, 234 n. 3
Aksenov, Vasily 1
Aikhenval'd, Yuly 74
Albee, Edward 1
Aldanov, Mark 74, 211, 215 n. 33
Alexandrov, Vladimir 9, 52 n. 8, 176 n. 27
Alter, Robert 3, 41, 55
Amis, Martin 109
Andreev, Leonid 153
Appel, Alfred, Jr. 20, 41, 159
Asquith, Arthur 180
Asquith, Herbert 180
Auden, W. H. 212
Austen, Jane 94, 160–61
   Mansfield Park 160, 163

Bader, Julia 55
Bakhtin, Mikhail 94, 105
Bakhmet'ev, Vladimir 208
Banfield, Ann 69
Barabtarlo, Gennady 8, 29
Barrie, James M. 180
Barth, John 1
Barthes, Roland 66, 69
   The Pleasure of the Text 66
Bateson, Gregory 66
Baudelaire, Charles 170, 202–03, 208
Beckett, Samuel 61, 65
Belloc, Hilaire 178
Bely, Andrei 4, 200–01
   A Chamber in the Kingdom of Shadows 200–01
   Petersburg 4
Benjamin, Walter 202, 217, 234 n. 1
Benois, Alexandre 5
Berdiaev, Nikolai 200, 204

Bernstein, Michael André 106 n. 16
Bitov, Andrei 1
Bitsilli, Petr 211–12
Blok, Alexander 3, 5
Bloom, Harold 141
Blum, Virginia 159
Booth, Wayne C. 67, 69
Boyd, Brian 1, 36, 48, 55, 110, 112, 117, 123, 134–35
Boym, Svetlana 234 n. 5
Brink, Andrew 158–59, 163
Bronfen, Elizabeth 162, 172
Brooke, Rupert 5, 9, 177–96 *passim*
Brooks, Peter 173–74
Bruss, Elizabeth 37, 40
Buckley, Jerome H. 44, 45
Bulgakov, Mikhail 2, 3
Bunin, Ivan 3, 5, 9
Burgess, Anthony 224
   A Clockwork Orange 224
Byron, George Gordon, Lord 197

Calderon, Don Pedro 130
Canetti, Elias 97, 106
Carroll, Lewis 223
Céline, Louis Ferdinand 6
Centerwall, Brandon 160
Chagall, Marc 5
Chaplin, Charles 226
   The Great Dictator 226
Chekhov, Anton 9, 18, 123, 137
Cherny, Sasha 74
Chernyshevsky, Nikolai 17, 19, 77
Chesterton, Gilbert Keith 178, 181
Churchill, Winston 180, 181, 182
Christus, Petrus 34 n. 47
Cicero, Marcus Tullius 30 n. 1
Cockshut, O. J. 43, 44
Coe, Richard N. 46
Collins, Joseph 51 n. 12
Connolly, Julian W. 9

Conrad, Joseph 231
Couturier, Maurice 8, 71 ns. 4 and 5
Cuddon, J. A. 52 n. 15

Dagwood 225
Dante Alighieri 136, 138, 168
   Inferno 168
Davydov, Sergej 152
de la Mare, Walter 181, 190, 193
Dickens, Charles 137, 160
   Bleak House 61, 163
Diment, Galya 8
Dobuzhinsky, Mstislav 5, 23
Dolinin, Alexander 9, 147, 152–53
Dombrovsky, Yury 107 n. 26
Donne, John 178
Dostoevsky, Fedor 9, 36, 94, 96, 101, 121, 123, 141–57, 198
   Crime and Punishment 101, 147, 150–51, 153–54
   The Devils 96, 106 n. 15, 147, 152, 198
   The Double 36, 144–46, 147, 148, 149
   "Dream of a Ridiculous Man" 156 n. 11
   "The Gentle Creature" 157 n. 26
Du Bois, W. E. B. 226

Ehrenburg, Il'ia 153, 201
Eliot, T. S. 5, 6, 179, 235 n. 16
Ermath, Elizabeth 159
Esenin, Sergei 4
Eyck, Jan van 29, 34 n. 47

Fassbinder, Rainer Maria 222
Faulkner, William
   The Sound and the Fury 61
Feldman, Jessica 7
Field, Andrew 43, 55, 70
Fitzgerald, F. Scott 183
Flaubert, Gustave 160, 219, 224, 232
   The Dictionary of Accepted Ideas 234 n. 6
   Madame Bovary 219
   Sentimental Education 219
Fleishman, Avrom 40
Florensky, Pavel 108 n. 33
Fludernik, Monika 69, 72 n. 12
Fondaminsky, Il'ia 74
Forster, E. M. 6, 69
Foster, John Burt, Jr. 9, 152
Frank, Semen, 213 n. 18
Fredricks, Nancy 173
Freud, Sigmund 49, 58, 67–68, 106 n. 10, 218, 219, 231
Frobenius, Leo 221
Frye, Northrop 105 n. 3

Gaulle, Charles de 218

Genette, Gérard 69, 141
Georgian Poetry 180, 181, 183
Gessen, Iosif 74
Gide, André 217, 233
Gogol, Nikolai 21, 33 n. 32, 36, 219, 222, 227
   Dead Souls 36, 222, 223, 224
Gold, Herbert 224, 228
Goya, Francisco de 221
Gray, Thomas 190
Grayson, Jane 2
Greco, El 20
Grinberg, Roman 74
Grinberg, Savely 74
Gumilev, Nikolai 23, 33 n. 34, 196 n. 42

Haber, Edythe 214 n. 27
Harington, Donald 1
Hart, Francis R. 40
Hegel, Georg Wilhelm Friedrich 218, 219, 222
Henderson, Timothy 113
Hitchcock, Alfred 31 n. 1
Hitler, Adolf, and Hitlerism 216–17, 221–22, 223, 226–28, 230–32, 233
Hoffmann, E. T. A. 156 n. 14
Hopkins, Gerard Manley 178
Horace 101, 105
Housman, A. E. 179, 189, 190
Hyde, G. M. 9, 36

Inge, William 182
Iser, Wolfgang 66, 69

James, Henry 94
Johnson, D. Barton 9, 27
Joyce, James 4, 5, 15, 178, 224, 235 n. 16
   Finnegans Wake 224
   Ulysses 4, 5, 54, 131, 178

Kafka, Franz 4, 160, 217, 230, 231, 233–34 n. 1
   Metamorphosis 4
Kagan, Abram 74
Kaminka, Avgust 74
Kandinsky, Wassily 5
Karlinsky, Simon 9
Kauffman, Linda 173
Käsebier, Gertrude 18–19
Kazin, Alfred, 36
Kerensky, Alexander 45
Khlebnikov, Velimir 32 n. 9
Khodasevich, Vladislav 2, 5, 200
Kipling, Rudyard, 189
Knoepflmacher, U. C. 164–66
Koestler, Arthur 106 n. 10

Korff, Christina von 45
Kovalevsky, Sof'ia 19
Kristeva, Julia 159, 212 n. 5
Krook, Dorothea 105 n. 1
Kruger, Paul 19
Krym, Solomon 74

Lacan, Jacques 65
Ladinsky, Antonin 201
Landau, Grigory 74, 205–06, 211, 213 n. 20
    The Twilight of Europe 205
Lawrence, D. H. 181
Lenin, Vladimir 178
Lermontov, Mikhail 123, 125, 208
Levi, Primo 235 n. 12
    Survival in Auschwitz 235 n. 12
Levin, Harry 74
Levin, Richard 110, 111
Lewis, Wyndham 6
Long, Michael 63–64
Lubbock, Percy 69

Mahler, Gustav 230
Malevich, Kazimir 5
Mallarmé, Stéphane 231
Malraux, André 6, 9, 216–18, 219–23, 231–33, 233–34 n. 1, 234 n. 4, 235 n. 12
    The Voices of Silence 221
    The Walnut Trees of Altenburg 217–18, 220–22, 233, 234 n. 4
Mandelshtam, Osip 2, 74
Mann, Thomas 225, 228, 232, 233
    Death in Venice 225, 228, 232
    Doctor Faustus 228
Marsh, Edward 180, 181, 182
Marvell, Andrew 179
Masefield, John 180, 181
Marx, Karl 218–19, 226
Mayakovsky, Vladimir 2, 3
McCarthy, Mary 54, 55
McKee, Patricia 165
McLuhan, Marshall 65
McNeely, Trevor 159
Mellor, Anne 162
Memling, Hans 34 n. 47
Moers, Ellen 161–62
Morris, John N. 43
Morte d'Arthur, La 191
Munro, Harold 180

Nabokov, Dmitri Vladimirovich (son) 20, 112, 119
Nabokov, Elena Ivanovna (mother) 112, 118
Nabokov, Sergei Vladimirovich (brother) 42, 86, 216

Nabokov, Véra Evseevna (*neé* Slonim) (wife) 23, 75, 76, 112, 119
Nabokov, Vladimir Dmitrievich (father) 52 n. 32, 112
Nabokov, Vladimir Vladimirovich
  Works:
    Ada 22, 57, 68, 69, 102, 103, 110, 117, 125, 128, 149
    "The Admiralty Spire" ("Admiralteiskaia igla") 102
    "A Bad Day" ("Obida") 20
    "An Affair of Honor" ("Podlets") 129
    "Beatitude" ("Blagost'") 117
    "Belyi rai," *see* "A White Paradise"
    Bend Sinister 30, 76, 93, 95, 96, 99, 101, 113, 121, 135, 222, 225, 230
    "Cambridge" ("Kembridzh") 178, 198–99, 202
    Camera Obscura, *see Laughter in the Dark*
    "Cloud, Castle, Lake" ("Oblako, ozero, bashnia") 22, 95–96, 209–10, 211
    The Cluster (*Grozd'*) 179, 191, 192, 195 n. 36
    Conclusive Evidence 36–51 *passim*
    "Conversation Piece, 1945" 87–89
    Dar (*see also The Gift*) 35 n. 50
    Death (*Smert'*) 192
    The Defense (*Zashchita Luzhina*) 89 n. 1, 95, 96, 97, 98, 99, 105, 120, 121, 122, 204
    Despair (*Otchaianie*) 58, 92, 97–98, 135, 144, 146–47, 150, 152–54, 222
    "Details of a Sunset" ("Katastrofa") 100, 202
    "The Doorbell" ("Zvonok") 89 n. 1
    "Double Talk" (*see* "Conversation Piece, 1945")
    Drugie berega 16, 49
    Dva puti, *see Two Paths*
    "Easter" ("Paskha") 191
    The Empyrean Path (*Gornii put'*) 179, 195 n. 36
    The Enchanter 17–18, 22, 116, 125, 136
    Eugene Onegin (translation and commentaries) 17, 175 n. 15, 221, 226
    "An Evening of Russian Poetry" 28–29
    The Event (*Sobytie*) 113, 122, 129
    The Eye (*Sogliadatai*) 97, 111, 115, 144–46, 147, 150
    The Gift (*Dar*) 16, 17, 18, 19, 21, 22, 26, 35 n. 50, 40, 77–83, 92, 93, 100, 101–02, 104, 113, 121, 127, 147, 154, 156 n. 17, 197, 199, 204, 209
    Glory (*Podvig*) 89 n. 1, 92, 93, 97, 100, 101, 105, 115, 129, 189, 197–98, 205, 206–08
    Gornii put', *see The Empyrean Path*
    Grozd', *see The Cluster*
    "Here is what we call the moon" ("Vot eto my zovem lunoi") 17

Nabokov, Vladimir Vladimirovich (*cont.*)
　"How I loved Gumilev's poetry" ("Kak liubil ia stikhi Gumileva") 196 n. 42
　"In Memory of Gumilev" ("Pamiati Gumileva") 23, 196 n. 42
　Invitation to a Beheading (*Priglashenie na kazn'*) 16, 18, 19–20, 24, 25, 26, 27, 89 n. 1, 93, 96, 99, 100, 147, 149, 201, 210
　"Iu. R.," *see* "Yu. R."
　"Kak liubil ia stikhi Gumileva," *see* "How I loved Gumilev's poetry"
　"Kembridzh," *see* "Cambridge"
　King, Queen, Knave (*Korol', dama, valet*) 21, 22, 24, 26, 92, 97, 99, 131, 204
　Korol', dama, valet, see also King, Queen, Knave 21, 23–24, 25, 26
　"Kon'kobezhets," *see* "The Skater"
　"Lance" 113
　Laughter in the Dark (*Kamera obskura*) 113, 205
　Lectures on Literature 15, 22, 30, 100, 134
　"A Letter that Never Reached Russia" ("Pis'mo v Rossiiu") 201–02
　Lolita 1, 2, 9, 16, 21, 22, 57, 58, 67, 68, 89 n. 1, 92, 96, 98, 100, 102, 104, 105, 113, 125, 135, 136, 151–52, 153–54, 158–74, 201, 225, 226–27, 229, 233
　Lolita (Russian) 24
　Lolita: A Screenplay 37 n. 1
　Look at the Harlequins! 22, 71, 99, 103, 104, 154, 136
　Mary (*Mashen'ka*) 89 n. 1, 92, 142–44, 197, 202, 204
　"Music" ("Muzyka") 102
　Nikolai Gogol 98, 217–18, 221, 222, 223–28, 230, 233, 235 n. 13
　"On Generalities" 203–04, 205, 209
　Pale Fire 8, 54–72, 92, 93, 96, 97, 99, 105, 113, 116, 117, 121, 126, 135, 136, 148–49, 150, 219
　"Pamiati Gumileva," *see* "In Memory of Gumilev")
　"The Paris Poem" ("Parizhskaia poema") 127, 132
　"Paskha," *see* "Easter"
　"Perfection" ("Sovershenstvo") 21, 97
　"Philistines and Philistinism" 226
　Pnin 29–30, 58, 73, 83–87, 92, 93, 94–95, 96, 97, 98, 99, 101, 105, 106 n. 17, 107 n. 20, 121, 125
　Poems (*Stikhi*) 187
　The Pole (*Polius*) 192
　Polius, see The Pole
　"The Potato Elf" ("Kartofel'nyi el'f")
　"Pouchkine ou le vrai et le vraisemblable" 221
　Priglashenie na kazn', see also Invitation to a Beheading 25, 27
　The Real Life of Sebastian Knight 21, 26–27, 27–28, 58, 89 n. 1, 101, 105, 147–48, 149, 189, 190, 216
　"Recruiting" ("Nabor") 89 n. 1, 100
　"The Return of Chorb" ("Vozvrashchenie Chorba") 19, 117
　"Revenge" ("Mest'") 122, 123, 124, 192–93
　"Rupert Brooke" ("Rupert Bruk") 183
　"Rupert Bruk," *see* "Rupert Brooke"
　"The Skater" ("Kon'kobezhets") 23
　"Signs and Symbols" 96, 99, 113
　Smert', see Death
　"Solus Rex" 126
　The Song of Igor's Campaign (translation and commentaries) 17
　Speak, Memory 9, 16, 17, 21, 22, 36–51 *passim*, 74, 99, 103–05, 112, 117–19, 127, 129, 134, 149–50, 197, 203, 219, 233, 235 n. 9, 235 n. 13
　Stikhi, see Poems
　Strong Opinions 16, 18, 20, 22, 30, 99, 104
　"Spring in Fialta" ("Vesna v Fial'te") 112–17, 123
　"Terra Incognita" 99
　"Terror" ("Uzhas") 117
　"That in Aleppo Once " 125, 137
　"Torzhestvo dobrodeteli," *see* "The Triumph of Virtue"
　Tragediia Gospodina Morna, see The Tragedy of Mr. Morn
　The Tragedy of Mr. Morn (*Tragediia Gospodina Morna*) 8, 121–38 *passim*
　Transparent Things 22, 95, 96–97, 98, 99, 100, 103–04, 107 n. 20, 115
　"Tristan" 192
　"The Triumph of Virtue" ("Torzhestvo dobrodeteli") 208
　Two Paths (*Dva Puti*) 187, 195 n. 32
　"Ultima Thule" 100–01, 117
　"Ut pictura poesis" 23
　"The Vane Sisters" 97, 98, 100, 105, 115, 128
　"Vasiliy Shishkov" 131
　"Vot eto my zovem lunoi," *see* "Here is what we call the moon"
　"A White Paradise" ("Belyi rai") 188
　"Yu. R." ("Iu. R.") 187, 191
Nesbet, Anne 213 n. 18
New Yorker 87
Nietzsche, Friedrich 218, 222, 231
Nivat, Georges 45
Nouvelle revue française 221
Novoe slovo 76

O'Connor, Katherine 151
Olesha, Yury 2, 3, 48–50, 210–11, 212
   "The Cherry Stone" 49, 210–11
   Envy 48
   No Day Without a Line 49–50
Ong, Walter 65
Orpheus 96

Pascal, Roy 52 n. 19
Pasternak, Boris 2, 3, 201
Paustovsky, Konstantin 46
Pertzoff, Peter 114
Picasso, Pablo 217, 231, 234 n. 1
Pifer, Ellen 5, 9, 174 n. 1, 176 n. 22
Pilling, John 47
Plato 184, 186
Poe, Edgar Allan 156 n. 14
Pound, Ezra 6, 179
Pregel', Sofiia 74
Prismanova, Anna 74
Protocols of the Elders of Zion 75, 81, 87
Proust, Marcel 4, 8, 49, 160, 217, 231, 233–34 n. 1
   À la recherche du temps perdu 4
Pushkin, Alexander 1, 17, 33 ns. 32 and 34, 36, 70, 207, 221, 226
   Eugene Onegin 36, 175 n. 15

Rausch von Traubenberg, Yuri 187, 191, 193
Richardson, Samuel 62
   Pamela 61, 62
Ricoeur, Paul 61
Ronen, Omry 214 n. 29
Rosoff, Samuil 74
Rosengrant, Judson 50
Rostand, Edmond 123
Rousseau, Jean Jacques 108 n. 29, 164

Schell, Sherrill 183, 190, 194 n. 19
Scott, Robert Falcon 192, 195 n. 42
Schoenberg, Arnold 217, 228, 234 n. 1
Sebald, W. G. 1
Shakespeare, William 15, 17, 123
Shakhmatov, Aleksei 16
Shakhovskoi, Alexander 17
Shakhovskoy (Shakhovskaia), Zinaida 75
Shalamov, Varlam 107
Shapiro, Gavriel 8, 214
Shaw, George Bernard 178, 179, 180
Schreber, Daniel Paul 58
Shelley, Mary 9, 161–74
   Frankenstein 9, 161–74
Shelley, Percy Bysshe 175 n. 15
Sherman, Savely (A. A. Savel'ev) 74

Shirinsky-Shikhmatov, Sergei 17
Shishkov, Alexander 17
Shklovsky, Victor 37, 48, 200, 201, 215 n. 29
Shrayer, Maxim 8
Sirin 2, 9
Slavitt, David 1
Slonim, Evsei 75
Spender, Stephen 38–39, 42–46
   World Within World 38–39, 42–46
Spengemann, William 40
Spengler, Oswald 199–200, 204, 211, 221
   The Decline of the West 199, 221
Sokolov, Sasha 1
Somov, Konstantin 5
Stalin, Joseph 96
Stanzel, Franz Karl 69
Stegner, Page 3, 53
Stepun, Fedor 198
Sterne, Laurence 37, 48, 64
   Tristram Shandy 37, 48, 64–65, 67
Stevenson, Robert Louis 156 n. 14
Stevick, Philip 176 n. 26
Strannoliubsky, Alexander 19
Stuart, Dabney 36
Superman 229
Swift, Jonathan 70
Szeftel, Marc 74

Tammi, Pekka 31
Toker, Leona 8
Tolstoy, Aleksei 200, 201
Tolstoy, Leo 9, 42, 150
Trifonov, Yury 1
Tsetlin, Mark (Amari) 74
Tsvetaeva, Marina 2, 3, 32 n.9
Tynianov, Yury 141

Updike, John 1, 160

Verdi, Giuseppe 81
   Aida 81
Vinaver, Maksim 74
Vishniak, Mark 74
Vrubel, Mikhail 5, 18

Weidle, Vladimir 2
Wells, George 178
Wells, H. G. 178, 179
Werfel, Franz 230, 232
   The Song of Bernadette 230–31, 232
White, Edmund 1
White, Katharine 128
Wilson, Edmund 3, 150, 160, 162–63, 189, 226
Wohl, Robert 3, 6, 231

Wolf, Naomi 158
Wood, Michael 107 n. 20
Woolf, Virginia 4, 6, 231
Wordsworth, William 47–48, 50, 165

Yeats, William Butler 180

Zenuck, Darryl 230
Zelensky, Filipp 74

CAMBRIDGE STUDIES IN RUSSIAN LITERATURE

General editor CATRIONA KELLY

Editorial board: ANTHONY CROSS, CARYL EMERSON,
BARBARA HELDT, MALCOLM JONES, DONALD RAYFIELD,
G. S. SMITH, VICTOR TERRAS

In the same series

Novy Mir
EDITH ROGOVIN FRANKEL

The Enigma of Gogol
RICHARD PEACE

Three Russian Writers and the Irrational
T. R. N. EDWARDS

Words and Music in the Novels of Andrey Bely
ADA STEINBERG

The Russian Revolutionary Novel
RICHARD FREEBORN

Poets of Modern Russia
PETER FRANCE

Andrey Bely
J. D. ELSWORTH

Nikolay Novikov
W. GARETH JONES

Vladimir Nabokov
DAVID RAMPTON

Portraits of Early Russian Liberals
DEREK OFFORD

Marina Tsvetaeva
SIMON KARLINSKY

Bulgakov's Last Decade
J. A. E. CURTIS

Velimir Khlebikov
RAYMOND COOKE

Dostoyevsky and the Process of Literary Creation
JACQUES CATTEAU

The Poetic Imagination of Vyacheslav Ivanov
PAMELA DAVIDSON

Joseph Brodsky
VALENTINA POLUKHINA

Petrushka – The Russian Carnival Puppet Theatre
CATRIONA KELLY

Turgenev
FRANK FRIEDEBERG SEELEY

From the Idyll to the Novel: Karamzin's Sentimentalist Prose
GITTA HAMMARBERG

The *Brothers Karamazov* and the Poetics of Memory
DIANE OENNING THOMPSON

Andrei Platonov
THOMAS SEIFRID

Nabokov's Early Fiction
JULIAN W. CONNOLLY

Iurii Trifonov
DAVID GILLESPIE

Mikhail Zoshchenko
LINDA HART SCATTON

Andrei Bitov
ELLEN CHANCES

Nikolai Zabolotsky
DARRA GOLDSTEIN

Nietzsche and Soviet Culture
edited by BERNICE GLATZER ROSENTHAL

Wagner and Russia
ROSAMUND BARTLETT

*Russian Literature and Empire
Conquest of the Caucasus from Pushkin to Tolstoy*
SUSAN LAYTON

*Jews in Russian Literature after the October Revolution
Writers and Artists Between Hope and Apostasy*
EFRAIM SICHER

Contemporary Russian Satire: A Genre Study
KAREN L. RYAN-HAYES

Gender and Russian Literature: New Perspectives
edited by ROSALIND MARSH

The Last Soviet Avant-Garde: OBERIU – Fact, Fiction, Metafiction
GRAHAM ROBERTS

Literary Journals in Imperial Russia
edited by DEBORAH A. MARTINSEN

Russian Modernism: The Transfiguration of the Everyday
STEPHEN C. HUTCHINGS

Reading Russian Fortunes
Print Culture, Gender and Divination in Russia from 1765
FAITH WIGZELL

English Literature and the Russian Aesthetic Renaissance
RACHEL POLONSKY

Christianity in Bakhtin: God and the Exiled Author
RUTH COATES

The Development of Russian Verse
MICHAEL WACHTEL

Nabokov and his Fiction: New Perspectives
edited by JULIAN W. CONNOLLY